SOCIAL RESPONSIBILITY IN AN AGE OF REVOLUTION

Edited by LOUIS FINKELSTEIN

A volume in the Ethics of Today Series
The Herbert H. Lehman Institute of Talmudic Ethics
The Jewish Theological Seminary of America

NEW YORK / 1971

Copyright © 1971 by The Jewish Theological
Seminary of America.

Library of Congress Catalogue Card Number: 76–126202
Printed in the United States.

ISBN 0-87334-105-8

Contents

Foreword

THE present volume is a modest effort to analyze some of the moral dilemmas of our time, and to indicate elements of hope for the future. The essays refer to a variety of complex situations, each of which seems to threaten our generation, but which, approached creatively, may turn out to be a stage in the improvement of the human condition. The volume is based on the premise that consideration of man's ethical life should be given the same attention now directed to scientific and technological achievement, and indeed that this achievement be utilized, when possible, for the better understanding of the meaning and goals of life.

Each essay contributes toward this purpose. Dr. Nathan W. Ackerman is concerned with ethical issues created in the development of psychotherapy. Most significant is his analysis of "the ambiguity of [Freud's] value of 'no-values' for the practice of psychoanalytic healing." Dr. Ackerman discusses problems resulting from strict adherence to the code of "no-values," and shows how the need for therapy often arises precisely because of the deterioration of moral values in the community.

Professor Reinhold Niebuhr recognizes that ecumenism, the child of modern advances in communication and transportation, holds pitfalls for contemporary civilization even as it marks a great forward step in man's development. With mellow wisdom, he suggests that "The main goal of all religious communities in a pluralistic but increasingly secular culture which subjects all historical and natural events to empirical scrutiny, is to bear witness to the necessity of the realm of the transcendent, even if it must be interpreted symbolically." In succinct analysis, he indicates how various American religious traditions have contributed uniquely to the betterment of mankind, and how much would be lost if any one of them disappeared in a conglomerate of faceless "religiosity."

In an essay honoring the late Edmond Cahn, Professor Daniel Day Williams seeks to demonstrate the former's thesis that the search for justice goes on in the context of the human search for a viable way of life. He investigates the bearing of Cahn's studies in ethics on a burning contemporary issue: the strike of public employees for redress of grievances. Professor Williams writes: "The most critical problem of law and disorder in our democracy . . . is how, in a highly technical, vulnerable community, every group can have freedom to assert its demands against the government and against other groups, while enough public order is preserved to enable the community to survive." He suggests that basic to the solution of this problem is the development of a "sense of injustice," and an unwillingness on the part of individual members of the community to participate in injustice, directly or indirectly. This leads Professor Williams to a discussion of the roles of Judaism and Christianity in the development of such a sensitivity.

Professor Walter Kaufmann, on the other hand, begins with the assumption that our age is one in which religion, and even law, have lost their influence over moral behavior. His analysis of the complexities involved in the attempt to discover what is "justice," particularly in our time, leads him to posit four cardinal "virtues," new concepts and attitudes that would more effectively minimize injustice in our increasingly complex age.

Professor Milton Konvitz explores, with vast erudition, the light shed by the Hebraic Prophetic tradition, and by the philosophic insights of Plato and Aristotle, on the relationship between ethics, considered as right behavior to be expected of man, and law, which must deal with the realities of life. The extent to which inequities can be overcome through legislation or the judicial process, and how much must always be left to the education of the mind and heart of the individual, involves a paradox. For justice cannot be achieved without law; but neither can just laws be achieved without men seeking deep moral insights and commitments.

As an educator, Dr. Charles Merrill is primarily concerned with the problems of youth, particularly as they will develop in an over-populated society. He reminds us of the moral issues involved, analyzes the serious drawbacks of "family planning," and stresses the imperative need to prevent the emergence of an "anodyne society" that is already, in his opinion, in the making. Dr. Merrill offers no solution to the problem of overpopulation, which may turn out to be the most difficult in all of human history, both in practical terms and as a challenge to ethical thought. But the presentation of the issue with courage, directness, and clarity is itself an important contribution to the search for a solution.

Mr. Philip Sporn discusses the need for ethical sensitivity in the vast range of activities covered by the term "business," whether governmental or private. Does corporate responsibility involve only the assurance of profits for the stockholder, or does it extend beyond that? The issue has been argued elsewhere, but Mr. Sporn presents it with new force, and from a fresh approach.

Professor Esther Jackson analyzes the human problem of our time as perceived by some of our most sensitive spirits, the creative artists, and particularly the dramatists. She offers a serious and profound challenge to the intellectual leaders of our age, particularly the philosophers and theologians, leaders of "those institutions traditionally charged with the preservation of the culture," to formulate "objective interpretations of the common destiny of all members of the body politic."

Like other critics before her, Professor Jackson demonstrates how artists, and more particularly dramatists, frequently become aware of new trends in popular thought and action before they are sufficiently widespread to be remarked even by trained observers of society. "If the drama today," she writes, "mirrors the 'broken world' of our making, perhaps it is yet the potential instrument of reconciliation not only between man and man, but also between man and his environment, and ultimately between man and himself. It would seem that the contemporary world challenges both drama and theology to seek the evolution of a symbolism capable of reconciling profound and divisive conflicts . . . to test alternatives which might tend toward the achievement of . . . universal goals in a climate of justice, peace and liberty."

Mr. Chief Justice Warren, whose essay closes this volume, brings to bear on the problems of our time his acumen and wealth of experience as Governor of California and as Chief Justice of the United States. His call is for a "new federalism," which might play that pioneering role in the emerging world civilization which the Constitutional Convention of 1787 played in the emerging American political structure. Violence among the American states was averted (except for the tragic Civil War) through the invention of a system of government which, had the ancient Greeks been capable of it, might have averted the Peloponnesian War, and preserved Greek democracy. Is it really beyond the ability of modern America to envisage the necessary accommodations which would bring into existence such a Parliament of the Mind, capable of dealing with the tensions between blacks and whites, between poor and affluent, between country and city, between young and old, between students and teachers, among religious groupings, and ultimately among peoples of the world?

Having in mind the varied problems raised by the contributors to this volume, which include men and women of different religious attitudes, races, callings, and backgrounds, I agreed to my colleagues' urging and appended an essay which may serve as an example of the application of relatively delimited historical research to the general human condition. The significance that the sectarian conflicts in ancient Judea may have for the incomparably more complex conflicts of our time has been my concern for much of my mature life. The more I have studied that partly forgotten conflict between Pharisees and Sadducees, the more clearly have I come to appreciate the wisdom and sagacity of the ancient scholars which prevented inter-group divergences and challenges from bursting into bitter and destructive conflict. These leaders of an oppressed group sought justice not simply for their constituents, but for all; they rejected the hunger for power in favor of a hunger for achievement. It was the crowning and unforgettable achievement of the Pharisaic sages to create, in Professor Jackson's language, a "symbolism capable of reconciling profound and divisive conflicts." Perhaps the reader will agree that the exploration of their symbolism may prove useful in our vastly more difficult society.

IT IS A PLEASURE to acknowledge the help given in the preparation of this volume which has emerged out of original plans for a Quarterly devoted to "Ethics for Today." The notion of such a Quarterly and its possible contents were discussed in a series of seminars in which a number of friends, colleagues and associates participated. The discussions proved very useful and stimulating to me, and perhaps to the other participants. However, it soon became clear that it would not be possible for the group to issue a Quarterly of the type projected. It was therefore decided that the material available be published in the present volume which, hopefully, might be the first in a series. The members of the seminar would, I believe, prefer to remain anonymous. However, I wish to thank Mrs. William Ash and Mrs. Carl Gutman who coordinated the seminar meetings.

The articles here published were read in manuscript by Mrs. Hertzel Fishman who was entrusted with the task of preparing the manuscript for publication. The proofs were read and corrected by her and Mrs. William Catlin.

Finally, it is a pleasure to express publicly my own indebtedness, and that of the community, to my beloved and honored friend, Simon H. Scheuer, who generously provided the entire cost of publication of this volume. Mr. Scheuer is a rare example of human sympathy and understanding, and it is appropriate that a book dealing with issues of ethics for today should appear under his sponsorship.

LOUIS FINKELSTEIN

Acknowledgments

"Some Ethical Issues in Psychotherapy, Past and Present" by Nathan W. Ackerman, M.D. appeared in slightly revised form in *Conservative Judaism*, Vol. XXIII, No. 3, © 1969, The Rabbinical Assembly.

"Drama: A Mirror of Conflict; A Prophecy for the Future" by Esther M. Jackson was originally presented as a lecture at The Institute for Religious and Social Studies of The Jewish Theological Seminary of America, © 1970, The Institute for Religious and Social Studies. The material is adapted from a larger work-in-progress on "Ideas in American Drama."

"Doubts About Justice" by Walter Kaufmann was presented in somewhat different versions at The University of Pennsylvania, on Law Day, May 1, 1965, and as the Dr. Joseph and Rosemary Shuchart Backlar Memorial Lecture, sponsored by the University of Judaism in Los Angeles, May 16, 1966. It was also read at the International Philosophy Year at Brockport, New York, and at the Conference on Jewish Philosophy at Columbia University, both in November 1967. It has been included in *Ethics and Social Justice*, volume 4 of *Contemporary Philosophic Thought*, edited by Howard E. Kiefer and Milton K. Munitz, from which it is reprinted by permission of the State University of New York Press. © 1970, Walter Kaufmann.

"Law and Morals in the Hebrew Scriptures, Plato and Aristotle" by Milton R. Konvitz appeared in *Conservative Judaism*, Vol. XXIII, No. 2, © 1969, The Rabbinical Assembly.

"Reflections on Over-Population" by Charles Merrill appeared in the *Harvard Divinity School Bulletin*, Winter 1969, with permission of The Jewish Theological Seminary of America.

"Toward a New Cultural Federalism" by Earl Warren was originally presented as an address at the Louis Marshall Award Dinner of The Jewish Theological Seminary of America, November 10, 1968.

"Law and Disorder: Some Reflections on the Political Philosophy of Edmond Cahn" by Daniel Day Williams was presented as a lecture before the joint faculties of Union Theological Seminary and The Jewish Theological Seminary of America in February, 1969. It has appeared in the *Union Seminary Quarterly Review,* Vol. XXV, No. 1, © 1969, Union Theological Seminary.

Editor's Introduction

———————————

By this time it must be evident to everyone that we are living in an age of world-wide revolution. This revolution should not surprise religious men and women, for it is the culmination of the teachings of the Prophets of Israel and their great disciples. At long last Man is claiming his proper heritage as bearer of the Divine Image, no matter what his personal background, no matter what the pigmentation of his skin, no matter what his physical or intellectual disadvantages.

As in the first stages of all earlier and more limited revolutions, a crucial decision has to be made now by those whose special prerogatives are threatened. Will they live up to their own ideals, and arrange an easy, quiet, civilized sharing of power, authority, and responsibility? Or, resisting the claims which they themselves have urged on the oppressed, will they invite violence, whose ultimate results no one can foresee?

The world-wide revolution of the underprivileged against those enjoying many privileges takes special form in the United States where the poor are not an overwhelming majority, as elsewhere, but a minority. A weak minority, they despair of winning their rights against the will of the majority, and in their disillusionment they court injury to themselves as well as to the community as a whole.

This may seem utter folly to those privileged to have an

education. But why should we expect the ignorant and the untutored to be wiser than others? Resisting the claims of the poor to a place in the sun, to good education, to satisfactory housing, to creative life, we are jeopardizing our nation and, indeed, much of civilization.

If man were a wholly rational animal, we could all swiftly calculate the perils of resistance to the demands of the poor and would no more take the risk involved than deliberately expose ourselves to cholera. But we are not altogether rational in our decisions. We find parting with status very difficult, and rationalize our objection to sharing goods and position with those denied them. But precisely these rationalizations were used by feudal barons to deny tradesmen and artisans the advantages all of us now enjoy.

In a curious aberration we make every conceivable preparation against attack by rival empires, except the most important. At great cost to ourselves, we engage in rivalry at arms. We maintain military conscription in times of peace. We support an elaborate and expensive spy-system. We struggle to maintain alliances with potentially hostile nations, some of whose leaders we can scarcely respect. Yet we neglect the indispensable preparation for defense—uniting our people so that each individual will feel that the interests of our country are his own.

But how can our country be united, when each day we repeat the folly committed by the Patriarch Jacob who gave his son Joseph an especially beautiful coat, certain to arouse the envy and therefore the hostility of his brothers? It is preposterous and indefensible that our nation's vital statistics are given in two columns, one for white Americans, the other for black Americans. A future generation will be scandalized that in 1969 the life expectancy of a black baby was seven years less than that of a white baby born on the same day in the same city.

America is a land of many minorities, theoretically equal under the law, but hardly so in daily life. The existence of injustice, prejudice, and of grinding poverty in the midst of a society of wealth and luxury, is unendurable in a free America—and may be forgotten only at our peril.

The problem of the unification of America cannot be escaped nor its solution too long delayed. Yet no effort at solution commensurate with the difficulties and complexities has been proposed. This is not seen to be *the* danger to America, but one problem among many. To those who inflict and tolerate discrimination, it is merely a *facet* of our culture. To those who suffer from discrimination, it is the *basic fact* of American life.

It should be within the power of our nation's leaders to help reduce and eventually eradicate prejudice. Toward this end we should seek to develop new forms of ethical behavior or, to use the modern term, new expressions of social responsibility. This is particularly significant in our age, when the traditional sense of individual responsibility for the welfare of others is under considerable attack.

The natural impulse of good people, when they see others in distress, is to come to their aid. This impulse, however, is not altogether altruistic. Often, by helping a person in need, we proclaim our superiority to him, a superiority which we have no desire to lose.

To understand the nature of altruism, we might consider the ideal set before teachers, for example. Teachers are supposed to educate people who will not only carry on their work, but do better than they, as indeed they frequently do. Thus, Aristotle was Plato's disciple. But he proclaimed that while he loved Plato, he loved truth more, and proceeded to demolish much of Plato's philosophic structure. In the Jewish tradition, the most famous commentator on the Talmud was a scholar named Rashi who lived in France in the eleventh century. His grandchildren were the pupils of his disciples, and their criticism of their illustrious grandfather's commentary left virtually no point unattacked. But their work is as much a glory of Talmudic literature as that of Rashi himself.

The medieval Jewish philosopher-physician, Maimonides, outlined eight degrees of philanthropy, of which the highest is to enable a person to assume responsibility for himself. This form of philanthropy is judged the highest because it recognizes man's preeminent need for self-respect. It is much harder to help a man help himself than it is to help him directly. It requires the extension of faith in the recipient as a person, as well as the expenditure of large sums of money and great amounts of patience. Assistance given condescendingly denies the needy person the respect due a human being and robs him of the personal conviction that he deserves such respect.

As a nation, the United States applied the principle of helping others to help themselves through the Marshall Plan, which staved off chaos in post-war Western Europe and undoubtedly saved thousands of people from starvation and the perils of civil war. Secretary George Marshall "sold" the plan to our hard-headed Congressmen and to many American citizens, as good politics. It happened to be very good politics. We fought a war on the grounds that the American frontier was on the Rhine; we had to wage peace on the same basis. But it must be admitted that so generous and wise a plan would not have occurred to an ungenerous person or nation. It was the combination of the moral and the practical that produced one of the greatest ideas of the post-war period, and helped make that period one of comparative peace and prosperity.

We do not ordinarily regard the Marshall Plan or the work of a teacher essentially as deeds of moral idealism. We tend to regard the Marshall Plan as American politics, and the work of a teacher as a profession. This is as it should be. But we must not lose sight of the deeper meaning implied in both. They are examples of human altruism at its best.

WHAT ARE THE APPLICATIONS of ethical concern within the complex world of modern technology and business? How can business and science serve the disadvantaged of the earth? Most of them are hungry for bread; many will die before their time. Yet their pain and suffering would not disappear if we could supply their food and prolong their lives, for their most serious disadvantage is lack of self-respect and self-confidence.

This lack of self-confidence may lie at the root of the fierce nationalisms and antagonisms of the world. We tend to be most aggressive and belligerent when we feel most threatened and least secure. Conversely, the most wretched and deprived conditions can be sublimated by a positive self-image.

In the Middle Ages, Jews, persecuted as few peoples have been persecuted in history, banished from their home towns and countries, their lives always precarious, humiliated, insulted, poor beyond any concept of poverty in our time, managed to survive, both as individuals and Jews, because of their immense self-respect and self-confidence.

They were sustained in their sorrows and deprivations by their self-image as the People of the Book. The words of the Psalmist, "If Thy law had not been my delight, I should have perished in my desolation," foreshadowed the actual history of the Jewish people.

If the main problem of the disadvantaged is lack of self-respect, how can it be solved?

Our generation requires the development of a new type of ethics in business and in public life, not simply the old ethics of avoiding wrong, but a positive, creative philosophy of deeds. It is only when we have turned the naturally generous impulses within our nation into an action-philosophy of social responsibility toward all those who are lacking essential needs and a sense of self-worth, that this country will be able to bind the wounds that once again threaten to tear it asunder.

It is frequently said that the future peace of the world can only be ensured through world government. That may be true. But world government itself will have to be based on a still widely rejected view of Man—namely, that no matter how lowly, different, uneducated, backward, awkward, or primitive a person may be, his essential humanity clothes him with supreme value and makes his suffering the suffering of all of us.

The responsibility of the privileged of this generation is, therefore, far greater than is usually recognized. Our task is to convince ourselves, rationally and emotionally, to look on all men as worthy of supreme dignity and, perhaps more difficult, to persuade the lowly that they are not really lowly. As Samuel said to Saul, "Though thou be little in thine own sight, art thou not the head of the tribes of Israel?" In the eyes of God, every man is a prince, and every woman a princess.

Essentially, it was its emphasis upon the dignity of man that enabled Western religion to achieve the dominance it holds in the world today. In our time, the inability of men to share in this conviction may be the source of our deepest distress. The disprivileged of our country and of the world need self-respect; they need to believe in themselves. If we cannot help all men everywhere to recapture their sense of human dignity and individual worth, our failure may have consequences impossible to predict.

Law and Morals in the Hebrew Scriptures, Plato, and Aristotle

MILTON R. KONVITZ

IN mid-twentieth century the tension between enacted or positive law, and morals or a higher law, is one that has become visible to everyone familiar with the Nuremberg trials and the Eichmann trial; with the Universal Declaration of Human Rights, adopted by the General Assembly of the United Nations; the International Covenants on Human Rights, approved by the United Nations; the European Convention for Protection of Human Rights and Fundamental Freedoms, adopted by the Council of Europe; the American Declaration of the Rights and Duties of Man, adopted by the Organization of American States; the widespread resort to civil disobedience; the renewed dignity given to conscience by Vatican Council II; the resistance to the war in Vietnam, especially by church and synagogue groups, in the name of conscience; the expansion in the meaning and reach of the Bill of Rights of the United States Constitution effected by the Supreme Court, especially since 1954; the enlarged and deepened interest in the plight of the poor; the pressure on legislatures and courts to adapt the law to moral changes

1

brought about by technological advances—such as artificial insemination, the use of contraceptive devices, the transplanting of organs. This is only a partial bill of particulars which show the reasons for the deepening stress and strain between law and morals.

On the one hand there are those who cry for "law and order." Among them are men who are simply for the *status quo,* or really for the *status quo ante,* who want a restoration of "the good old days." Among them also are men who want to see the "law and order" changed, but only as the result of peaceful dissent and intelligent discussion. On the other hand, there are those who have their eyes on a new law and a new order, and who relegate existing law to the gross, material, non-value world, which they want to see subverted. They take their stand for morality and against the law.

Years ago Ahad Ha'am portrayed the essentials of this conflict in his essay on "Priest and Prophet." The priest is the man who seeks "not what *ought* to be, but what *can* be"; his battle is not against actuality—he fights in the name of actuality against its enemies. The prophet, on the other hand, is carried away by his idea; he is "essentially a one-sided man," for

> A certain moral idea fills his whole being, masters his every feeling and sensation, engrosses his whole attention. He can only see the world through the mirror of his idea; he desires nothing, strives for nothing, except to make every phase of the life around him an embodiment of that idea in its perfect form, . . . regardless of the conditions of life and the demands of the general harmony. (*Selected Essays,* translated by Leon Simon, Philadelphia 1912, pp. 130–132.)

The tension between law and morals and the complexity of relations between them are part of our intellectual and institutional history. They are perhaps ineradicable. We even lack a vocabulary adequate to describe the complexity of the problem. Our contemporary experience of it is rooted in ancient Hebraic and Greek categories, and we probably will come no nearer to its resolution than did ancient Israel, with its priests and prophets, or the ancient Greeks with their Plato and Aristotle.

I

IN THE HEBREW SCRIPTURES, the distinction between law and morals does not exist; or at least, it is not articulated. Neither is there a difference between religion and morals, nor any separation between religion and law. There is a single order of values which make a total claim on the people of Israel. By covenant, they became God's people. Their rights are all subordinate to God's rights; their duties are all subordinate to their duties to him; and these duties are all commanded by God, who made the law and whose will and nature fixed what is good and what is evil—what is allowed or commanded and what is prohibited. The same code provides what shall be the duties and the dues of the priests, the distinctions between clean and unclean animals, the rituals of purification of women, the test and treatment of leprosy, the definition and prohibition of incest, the duty to treat the stranger as an equal, and the requirement to have just balances and just weights. All duties, to whomsoever owed, are placed under the all-embracing commandment: "You shall therefore keep my statutes and my ordinances, by doing which a man shall live: I am the Lord . . . You shall be holy; for I the Lord your God am holy" (Lev. 18:5; 19:2).

Yet implicit in this single order of values is the need to differentiate, to classify, to establish an order of priorities, and above all to transcend the existing system and reach some higher sphere.

An example of transcendence is the dedication of the boy

Samuel, to abide "for ever" in the presence of the Lord at the temple at Shiloh. The Nazirites, with their life-long obligation to abstain from wine or strong drink and to wear their hair untrimmed—to symbolize their complete separation from the ways of the original peoples of Canaan and worship of the nature gods—are an example of the drive to transcend the socially accepted order and to try to reach what is assumed to be the spirit behind it. They exemplify a compulsion to absolutize values.

A more normal instance of transcendence is found in the story of Ruth. When Boaz observed Ruth gleaning in his field after the reapers, he instructed his young men to pull out some of the barley from the sheaves for her to glean. This was going beyond what the law required. It is an instance of what the Talmud later referred to as the principle of *lifnim mi-shurat ha-din,* which is interpreted as the duty not to insist on the strict law but to go beyond the letter of the law. The example and the principle point to an awareness of the existence of a moral law, higher than the existing law, which makes greater demands on the conscience. The law required only that Boaz was not to pick up the grain which fell from the hand of the reaper, nor to gather the grapes which dropped during the harvest—these belonged to the poor and not to Boaz (Lev. 19:9–10; Deut. 24:19–21). But when Boaz contrived that Ruth was to have as gleanings grain which the law held was his own, he certainly showed his feeling that there was a distinction between law and morals.

The prophets, with their sharp emphasis on what we today would call moral conduct, were feeling their way to an order of priorities among legal duties and to a distinction between law and morals. Thus Micah cried out:

He has showed you, O man, what is good
and what does the Lord require of you

but to do justice, and to love kindness,
and to walk humbly with your God (6:8).

Isaiah too felt that holiness meant to "seek judgment, relieve the oppressed, judge the fatherless, plead for the widow" (1:16–17). The rationale for these guidelines is the prophet's feeling that somehow man must put first things first, just as God does; for God says: "For I desire mercy, and not sacrifice; and the knowledge of God more than burnt offerings" (Hos. 6:6). Implicit in these judgments is the differentiation between law, morals, and religion—though the prophets would have denied vehemently that these spheres could ever be completely separated, even if only conceptually, one from the other.

II

PERHAPS THE STRONGEST ground for a differentiation between law and morals lay in the fact that the Hebraic mind seemed to work with two sets of categories:

1. The purely moral commandment: "You shall love your neighbor as yourself" (Lev. 19:19). The love commandment is often expressed in terms that point specifically to certain classes of persons as one's neighbors in a special sense: the widow, the orphan, the stranger, the poor and needy. The commandments to love these persons were given a religious provenance by the commandment to live one's life in imitation of God, to be holy as God is holy,

For the Lord your God is God of gods and Lord of lords, the great, the mighty, and the terrible God, who is not partial and takes no bribe. He executes justice for the fatherless and the widow, and loves the stranger, giving him food and clothing. Love the stranger, therefore, for you were strangers in the land of Egypt (Deut. 10:17–19).

These commandments are so sweepingly broad and so deeply moral that they cannot be confined in any legal enactments; they speak to the law in the heart (Deut. 30:14), the law written on the tablets of the heart (Prov. 7:3).

2. At the same time and equally pervasive is the positive law; the Sabbath day as a day of rest, for

> in it you shall not do any work, you, or your son, or your daughter, or your manservant, or your maidservant, or your ox, or your ass, or any of your cattle, or the stranger who is within your gates, that your manservant and your maidservant may rest as well as you (Deut. 5:14).

A similar law establishes the year of release, at the end of every seven years, when every creditor must release what he has lent to his neighbor (Deut. 15:1). In the same category is the requirement to build a parapet for one's roof, so that some one may not accidentally fall from it (Deut. 22:8); and the law relating to gleanings, and to leaving the corner of the field for the poor and the stranger (Lev. 19:9). All these are instances of legal duties which vest or entail legal rights in the beneficiaries. They are examples of what the Hebrew Scriptures speak of as *mishpat* or *tsedek*.

On the other hand, those moral commands that are general and are not reduced to specific enactments, that entail duties toward God which are fulfilled by love toward one's neighbor—such commands are referred to as *tsedakah*. While *mishpat* is directed negatively—a prohibition against wronging one's neighbor by depriving him of his rights—*tsedakah* looks to the positive realization of the good (S. R. Hirsch, commentary on Gen. 15:6, Deut. 15:8, and Psalm 72:3).

The moral and legal strands may intersect. An explicit example of interdependence is to be seen in the formulation of the law calling for the year of release. The rich man, knowing that the year of release is approaching, may refuse to lend to his needy neighbor; so that the benign purpose of the law may actually stand in the way of the rich extending credit to the poor. At this point the Bible calls upon the moral law, written on the tablets of the heart, to sustain the enacted or positive law of the year of release:

> Take heed lest there be a base thought in your heart, and you say, "The seventh year, the year of release is near," and your eye be hostile to your poor brother, and you give him nothing, and he cry to the Lord against you, and it be sin in you. You shall give to him freely, and your heart shall not be grudging when you give to him; because for this the Lord your God will bless you in all your work and in all that you undertake. For the poor will never cease out of the land; therefore I command you, you shall open wide your hand to your brother, to the needy and to the poor, in the land (Deut. 15:9–11).

In this guideline, law, morals, and religion are wonderfully interwoven. The commandment is one—establishing a year of release, when all debts are wiped out, and the poor are relieved of their grinding burden of debt and can look forward to a fresh start. But that single commandment, when looked at with our modern eyes, clearly has built into it categories which we tend to keep distinct and separate.

We should emphasize, however, that we are reading back into the ancient sources concepts and principles which came to be articulated only in modern times. The biblical and ancient rabbinic mind would have found it distasteful, and

perhaps even blasphemous, to separate conceptually or insti-
tutionally what God had joined together.

III

WHAT GOD HAD JOINED, according to the biblical theodicy,
was fact and value, evil and punishment, good deed and
reward. In so far as possible, the connection is to be effected
by the human agency of the ruler and his government. Their
essential function is to judge and to execute judgment, as
God's surrogates on earth. But what the human rulers and
judges might leave undone, God himself would do; for God
is the Supreme Ruler, the King of kings, and the all-wise and
omnicompetent Judge. God would use even nations as agents
to execute His judgments, lifting up a nation, using its power
and ambitions to cast down, to trample upon, and even
wholly to destroy other nations. Wicked men and nations are
held to strict account. Execution of judgment may be delayed; it may even be postponed for generations—but the day
of reckoning finally comes.

This Hebraic theodicy, made explicit by the eighth-
century prophets, puts law, morals, and religion into an
organic whole. Thus, every deed is subject to God's law, and
man lives in a law-centered and law-enveloping world, a law
from which there is no escape or hiding place. If the earthly
ruler will not execute God's law and judgment, then God
Himself will do it.

The theodicy encompassed the community as an entity. If
the group will live by God's commandments, then God will
send the rain in its season, and the people will have their
corn, wine, and oil, and the cattle will have grass, and everyone will eat and be satisfied. But if the heart of the people

will stray, then the anger of God will be kindled, and He will shut up the heaven so that there will be no rain, and earth will not yield her fruit (Deut. 11:13–17). The retribution may, however, come through "the rod of God's anger":

> Ah, Assyria, the rod of my anger,
>   the staff of my fury!
> Against a godless nation I send him,
>   and against the people of my wrath I command him,
> To take spoil and seize plunder,
>   and to tread them down like the mire of the streets.
>   (Is. 10:5–6)

But the individual, too, is directly subject to God's law, his judgment and punishment or reward. Immediately preceding the above-quoted verses, Isaiah foretells the curses that will come down upon the perverters of justice, the evil-doers:

> Woe to those who decree iniquitous decrees,
>   and the writers who keep writing oppression,
> to turn aside the needy from justice
>   and to rob the poor of my people of their right,
> that widows may be their spoil,
>   and that they may make the fatherless their prey!
> What will you do on the day of punishment,
>   in the storm which will come from afar?
> To whom will you flee for help,
>   and where will you leave your wealth?
>   (Is. 10:1–3)

Many of the Psalms emphasize the same theme of reward for good and punishment for sin and evil—the providential rule of man's world by the Creator and Ruler of that world:

Fret not yourself because of the wicked,
    be not envious of wrongdoers!
For they will soon fade like the grass,
    and wither like the green herb. . . .
Commit your way to the Lord;
    trust in Him and He will act. . . .
For the wicked shall be cut off;
    but those who wait for the Lord shall possess the land.
                                                    (Ps. 37:1–9)

The friends of Job, with the exception of Elihu, express the same belief. Eliphaz says to Job:

Think now, who that was innocent ever perished?
    Or where were the upright cut off?
As I have seen, those who plow iniquity
And sow trouble, reap the same.
                                                    (Job 4:7–8)

As we have noted, from the standpoint of an all-encompass-ing theodicy—which is a dominant biblical theme—there is no need for a differentiation among values, for distinction be-tween law and morals; because *all* acts are subject to the law of God, who will find a way to bring to judgment every man and every nation; "for all His ways are justice" (Deut. 32:4) ; "for the Lord is a God of justice" (Is. 30:18) ; "for all His works are truth, and His ways are justice" (Dan. 4:34) .

BUT THE BIBLE also provides a counterpoint to this theme, to this simple faith that could assert:

I have been young, and now am old;
    yet I have not seen the righteous forsaken
    nor his children begging bread.
                                                    (Ps. 37:25)

Experience challenges such naiveté. The critical voice cannot be altogether silenced in the face of the evidence that flagrantly contradicts this faith in Providence. "Why," cries out Jeremiah, "does the way of the wicked prosper? Why do all who are treacherous thrive?" (Jer. 12:1).

One explanation for the fact that the righteous often suffer is the belief, expressed by Elihu to Job, that undeserved suffering may be a form of moral education or discipline (Job 33:19–28). This would not, however, explain why the wicked prosper.

On the group or national level, Isaiah (or Deutero-Isaiah) made a similar attempt to solve this problem. His doctrine of the Suffering Servant implies the idea that a nation may suffer, not for its sins, but for the purpose of teaching mankind (Is. 52 and 53).

A much more daring line is taken by Psalm 73. The author candidly admits that he was envious when he saw the prosperity of the wicked. They enjoy good health; "they are not in trouble as other men are"; they speak with malice, and threaten oppression, and act arrogantly. "Behold, these are the wicked always at ease, they increase in riches." Though his spiritual torment continues, for rationally there can be no abatement of his perplexity, the psalmist does not fall into despair. He makes a staggering leap from the realm disclosed by his senses to a totally different level, from the I/world relationship to the level of I/God. In the face of the evidence of his eyes, he cries out:

> Thou dost hold my right hand. . . .
>   And there is nothing upon earth I desire besides Thee.
> My flesh and my heart may fail,
>   but God is the strength of my heart and my portion
>   for ever. . . .
> But for me it is good to be near God;
>   I have made the Lord God my refuge. . . .

The Psalmist does not see the work of Providence, "nevertheless" he believes; for the I/God relationship suffices as the strength of his heart, as his portion, as his refuge. The order of things is not changed; the righteous go on suffering, the wicked continue to flourish; the connection between deed and reward does not manifest itself; "nevertheless" life is justified, as long as man can say, "I am continually with Thee." To be near God is to live, to be far from God is to be spiritually dead—to be dead within the heart. To see things and events from the perspective of the I/God level is to free oneself from the need to find mechanical retribution operating in the world, it is to rise far above the worldly level of the friends of Job. For God's habitation is in the inner man, and not in the outer; his holy place is in the heart, and not in the market place.

The implications of this view are immeasurably great. For our purpose it is sufficient to see that it emancipates morality from the book-keeping approach which the theodicy necessitates. Law depends on utilitarian considerations and on external sanctions, but morality depends on God's judgment, which the heart will know. There is the law which men enforce, as God's agents; and there is the law, the higher law, the moral commandment, for which the only sanction is the conscience, or the heart.

The same resolution, through a "nevertheless," comes to Job when he is finally able to rise above his friends, his dung-heap, his suffering, and his devastating realization that Providence simply does not work in ways manifest to the physical eye. Job rises to another level of meaning, to the pure I/God level, where pomp, honor, prosperity, health—and degradation, dishonor, poverty, sickness—all the things that men may see, measure or count—simply do not matter. It is *there* that Job, stripped of his flesh, sees God (19:25–27). On the I/God level, the world and life have meaning—but a meaning that is visible only to the inner eye; and on any other level, though there may be all the sounds and trappings of life, since God is not there, there is only death. This is the wisdom that comes at last to Job, liberating him from ignorance, saving him from cynicism and atheism.

It is this kind of wisdom and liberation that is required in order to distinguish between law and morals. For as long as man is bound to a theodicy, then God's law orders every act and event; His law is perfect and will work mechanically to give each man his just deserts, and for each act his just reward. Such an order has no need of a differentiation between law and morals. But once the facts of life are faced, and it is recognized that, outside the realm where the policeman and the court have jurisdiction, there is no necessary tie between deed and reward, then a separate realm is needed for morality—a realm that only God's eye can penetrate, a realm in which man stands directly before God as his maker, ruler, and judge, a realm in which the outward signs of reward and punishment have no meaning.

IT IS ALSO PROBABLE that a distinction between law and morality was forced upon the Hebraic consciousness when the Jews came to live in exile, or under foreign rule in their home land. This comes out clearly in the maxim: "Render therefore to Caesar the things that are Caesar's, and to God the things that are God's" (Matt. 22:21). This doctrine assumes a difference between positive law, as the enactment of the state, and all other commandments—religious, moral, or legal—which emanate from God. A similar distinction probably underlies the advice offered by the prophet Jeremiah to the Jews who were in exile in Babylon (Jer. 29:1-7). As the Jews mingled with non-Jews, they were compelled to formulate a moral theory of man which, by implication, marked off religion, morals, and law as distinct spheres. Such a view of man's moral nature clearly appears in the talmudic tradition of the Laws of the Sons of Noah, which asserts that *all men* are commanded to observe seven fundamental principles. These prohibit idolatry (which was, in the Jewish tradition, always associated with immoral practices) , murder, theft, blasphemy, incest, and eating the flesh of living animals, and require the promotion of justice (Sanhedrin 56a) .

But, as we shall see later in this essay, always inherent in the Hebraic conception of positive law was the idea that while this law was an expression of good, of justice, of righteousness, nevertheless the law was transcended by the good, the just, and the righteous—a view of the relationship between law and morals which Plato and Aristotle would have found understandable and congenial.

IV

THE ANCIENT GREEKS, too, failed to differentiate between law and morals. Just as the Jews found divine sanction for the Chosen People and the Torah, so the Greek dramatists and philosophers found divine sanction for the Greek city-state and its laws. Their city of man was their city of God—a social order which embodied all that was best for man, or at least best for the Greek citizen. The city-state, writes Aristotle, "comes into existence for the sake of mere life, but exists for the sake of the good life" *(Politics,* 1252b–29) . Basic to the good life for the Greeks, as for the Jews, is the rule of law.

For the Jew, the teaching, the Law, Torah, "is a tree of life to those who lay hold of her; those who hold her fast are called happy" (Prov. 3:18) ; it was the Lord Himself who "became king in Jeshurun, when the heads of the people were gathered, all the tribes of Israel together" (Deut. 33:5) ; to obey the law was to be blessed—"If you obey the commandments of the Lord your God, . . . then you shall live

and multiply, and the Lord your God will bless you. . . ."
(Deut. 30:15–16) .

Socrates, in prison, condemned by the Athenian jury to die
by poison, praised the laws and constitution of his city, and
held fast to them with his last breath. He heard the laws say
to him that by their virtue they had given him his very life,
for by their power his father had married his mother; it was
the laws that directed them how to bring up their son and
educate him. Indeed, Socrates was the child of the laws, their
ward, and their servant; and he would sooner drink the cup
of hemlock and die than destroy his country's laws by breaking them (*Crito,* 50a–51c) .

The laws had their origin in ancient customs and traditions, behind which was the will of the gods. "All human
laws are fed by the one divine law," said Heraclitus (*Frag.*
114d–k) . It was this belief that gave Antigone the strength
to defy the decree of Creon. "It was not Zeus who gave the
order," she shouted at Creon. He, and not Antigone, was the
one who violated the law; he, and not she, was the criminal.

> Nor did I think that your pronouncements were
> So powerful that mere man could override
> The unwritten and unfailing laws of heaven.
> These live, not for today and yesterday
> But for all time. . . .
>
> *(Antigone* 440–449)

The rule of law, as conceived by the Greeks, in theory
excludes no phase of life or conduct from its province. Its
reach is coextensive with tradition and custom, institutions
which historically encompassed the totality of man and society. There is no room in this view for any differentiation
between morals and law.

But as in the case of Hebraic thought and experience, a

critical element gradually penetrated into the accepted theory, so that in due course philosophical analysis began to point to a differentiation between law and morals. There was nothing explicit in the process. There was a groping, a reaching out, a positing of elements which could later be interpreted as implicitly involving a differentiation, and possibly even a separation, between law and morals.

In Plato's *Republic,* the law is clearly subordinate and accountable to the supreme Form, the Good. The purpose of the law is the production of men who are altogether good. To have such law, philosophers must be kings, and kings must be philosophers. Although this view merges law and morals, the merger is possible only in the ideal state, in which the philosophy of the good life and the art of statecraft coalesce in the same persons. The implication is that in a society that falls short of the ideal, the law, when judged by the ideal moral order, will be found wanting. Thus there is an implied differentiation between law and morals.

Since the ideal social order is beyond human attainment, Plato's *Laws* constructed a society that would be subject strictly to the rule of law. In its formative stage, this society would select the best laws under which the people could live and be ruled; but once the code of laws was instituted, there were to be no departures from it. Easy and hard cases alike were to be decided according to the promulgated law. The ideal or moral element was to be kept out.

It was either/or to Plato: either the moral, ideal, intellectual judgment decides, or the decision is made in strict accordance with the law. Philosophy can justify only the former method; expedience can justify only the latter. In a crucial passage in the *Laws,* Plato says:

> No law or ordinance whatever has the right to sovereignty over true knowledge [of Good]; 'tis a sin that

[moral] understanding should be any creature's subject
or servant; its place is to be ruler of all, if only it is
indeed, as it ought to be, genuine and free.

This is the voice of pure reason, of reason as it listens only to
the Form of the Good. It is the voice heard in the *Republic;*
it leaves no room for law except for law as the enforcement of
the moral judgment.

But we are not finished. The above passage goes on to
say:

But, as things are, such [moral] insight is nowhere to be
met with, except in faint vestiges, and so we have to
choose the second-best, ordinance and law *(Laws,* 875).

For the second-best system, then, the moral judgment is
important only as the code of laws is being prepared at the
founding of society. But the moral judgment pretty well
exhausts itself in this constitutional and legislative process.
Once enacted, the law has no concern with anything outside
its own order. Moral wisdom brings the code of laws into
existence; but the laws do not look before or after; they see
only themselves.

THE REASON FOR Plato's preference for the rule of wisdom, if
that were possible, is succinctly stated in the *Politics:*

There can be no doubt that legislation is in a manner
the business of a king, and yet the best thing of all is not
that the law should rule, but that man should rule,
supposing him to have wisdom and power. Do you see
why this is? . . .
Because the law does not perfectly comprehend what is
noblest and most just for all and therefore cannot en-

force what is best. The differences of men and actions, and the endless, irregular movements of human beings, do not admit of any universal and simple rule. And no art whatsoever can lay down a rule which will last for all time. . . .

But the law is always striving to make one. . . .   (294)

The law, in other words, should ideally be indistinguishable from the moral wisdom. Moral wisdom will be flexible; it will respond to the infinite variety of human beings, human needs, human situations, human changes. The law cannot achieve this ideal; it will enact what is for the general good but not what is good for each particular case. Laws, some of them written and some of them unwritten, are in a general form, intended for the majority, and only roughly do they meet the cases of individuals (*Ibid.*, 295). Since the laws are based upon long experience, and upon the wisdom of counsellors who have recommended them, and persuaded the multitude to enact them, it follows that to allow either an individual or the multitude to break the law in any respect would be a far greater crime and more ruinous error than any adherence to an imperfect law could be (*Ibid.*, 300).

While Plato recognized that harm could come from making trifling acts into crimes, he was not satisfied with setting any limit on the omnicompetence of the rule of law. He saw in the exclusion from the reach of the law

an evil for the public as a whole, for while the frequency and triviality of such faults makes it both improper and undignified to penalize them by law, they are a real danger to such law as we do impose, since the habit of transgression is learned from repetition of these petty misdeeds. Hence, though we are at a loss to legislate on such points, silence about them is also impossible (*Laws*, 788).

Yet Plato provided for the regulation of almost every conceivable aspect of life from cradle to grave. It did not occur to him that the effect of placing almost every human action under the law may be the attrition of the moral sense and the loss of human freedom and responsibility. Even a well-trained dog is permitted a large measure of liberty for spontaneous play. Plato recognized that extraordinary moral wisdom is required for the preparation of the code of laws. But once the code is promulgated, he makes no provision for keeping the moral sense alive in the citizens or in their rulers. All are to live strictly under the rule of law, and any act contrary to law is to be punished by death (*Politicus,* 297). "For nobody," says Plato, "should be wiser than the law" (*Ibid.,* 299), that is, once it is agreed that the rule of the wise must give way to the rule of law, once it is agreed that the best order is impossible and must give way to the second-best. Plato left no room for a combination of wisdom and law, for compromise, for accommodation, for an order of society, institutions and thought based on both law and morals.

However, as we shall see later on, some serious qualifications to this conclusion must be made. After all, Plato's idealism was too deeply felt, and too widely pervasive of his thought, to warrant a formulation of jurisprudence that might serve as a model for Hobbes, Austin, or Kelsen. Plato could be an absolute idealist in the *Republic* but he could never be, in any dialogue, an absolute positivist. Indeed, as we will see, his ultimate resolution of the problem of the relation of law to ideal was not in essence different from the biblical position.

V

PROBABLY WITH AN EYE on Plato, under whom he had studied for twenty years, Aristotle faced up to the choice between the rule of law and the rule of man, and chose the former. In a famous passage in the *Politics,* Aristotle writes:

> He who commands that law should rule may thus be regarded as commanding that God and reason alone should rule; he who commands that a man should rule adds the character of the beast. Appetite has that character; and high spirit, too, perverts the holders of office, even when they are the best of men. Law [as the pure voice of God and reason] may thus be defined as "Reason free from all passion" (*Politics,* 1287a) .

If faced with a choice between the *Republic* and the *Laws,* Aristotle would choose the latter; not, however, as the second-best, but as the best; for even the best of men, the philosopher-kings, cannot be free from appetite and high spirit.

In fact, however, Aristotle did not see the need for the rule of law to be as absolute, as all-encompassing, as Plato in the *Laws* thought it had to be. Indeed, always keeping in mind the mean or the middle-way as the best disposition, and the mixed polity as the best government, Aristotle could not have been expected to choose one extreme or another, either the rule of law or the rule of man. His choice was for an open-ended, and not an enclosed, rule of law. Basically, then, Aristotle would prefer the approach of Plato as formulated in the *Laws,* provided the formulation expressly left room for some open doors and windows; but he would reject without hesitation the line of thought in the *Republic* that led to the rule of the philosopher-king.

What open doors and windows does Aristotle provide to go with the rule of law? The answer to this question will show the subtle interplay of law and morals in Aristotle's thinking.

First, there is the distinction between legal justice and natural justice. Legal justice is justice according to law; it is achievable in a state among citizens whose relations are regulated by law and who enjoy free and equal status. In such a polity, the administration of the law means the discrimination between what is just and what is unjust. To act unjustly means to appropriate too large a share of what is good, and too small a share of what is evil.

> This is why we do not permit a man to rule, but the law; because a man rules in his own interest, and becomes a tyrant; but the function of a ruler is to be the guardian of justice, and if not justice, then of equality (*Nicomachean Ethics*, 1134b).

Legal justice is conventional, and is therefore variable. But once the law is settled one way or another, its binding force is not reduced by the fact that its origin was institutional. A rule, says Aristotle, is conventional

> that in the first instance may be settled in one way or the other indifferently, though having once been settled it is not indifferent; for example, that the ransom for a prisoner shall be a mina, that a sacrifice shall consist of a goat and not of two sheep. . . . (*Ibid.*)

Are all rules of justice merely conventional? No, there is also natural justice, following laws of nature that are immutable and that have validity everywhere. Rules of justice are variable, yet there is such a thing as natural justice. What Aristotle means, I believe, can be made clear by an example. It is by natural justice that murder is prohibited and punished. No society can treat homicide indifferently, and agree that legal justice shall look the other way when a human being is killed. It is, however, a matter of convention whether the punishment shall be death, life imprisonment, or imprisonment for a number of years. The definition of murder and its breakdown into classes or grades—willful or negligent, first degree, second degree, the distinction between murder and manslaughter, and the punishment of each grade or type—these are all variable, though the law against murder is a matter of natural justice. This, I think, is what Aristotle means by his statement that the laws of natural justice are immutable and are valid everywhere, yet all rules of justice are variable.

In the *Rhetoric,* Aristotle speaks of "particular" laws, those established by each people in reference to themselves; and of "general" laws, those based upon nature. "In fact," Aristotle continues,

> there is a general idea of just and unjust in accordance with nature, as all men [are] in a manner divine, even if there is neither communication nor agreement between them. This is what Antigone in Sophocles evidently means, when she declares that it is just, though forbidden [by a "particular" law], to bury Polynices, as being naturally just: "For neither today nor yesterday, but from all eternity, these statutes live and no man knoweth whence they came." And as Empedocles says in regard to not killing that which has life, for this is not right for some and wrong for others, "But a universal precept, which extends without a break throughout the wide-ruling sky and the boundless earth" (*Rhetoric,* 1373b).

Although this statement might be somewhat reduced in value because of its possible forensic context, nothing can be asserted against the import of the statement in the *Nicomachean Ethics* that there seem to be some acts which a man cannot be compelled to do, and rather than do them he ought to submit to the most terrible death: for instance, we think it ridiculous that Alceaeon in Euripides' play is compelled by certain threats to murder his mother! But it is sometimes difficult to decide how far we ought to go in choosing to do a given act rather than suffer a given penalty, or in enduring a given penalty, rather than commit a given action; and it is still more difficult to abide by our decision when made, since in most of such dilemmas the penalty threatened is painful and the deed forced upon us dishonorable, which is why praise and blame are bestowed according as we do or do not yield to such compulsion (1110a).

This statement could not have been made in its context unless Aristotle had in mind some such distinction as that between conventional, enacted, or particular laws, and laws of natural justice. His statement assumes the existence of some kind of higher law, or a morality which transcends positive law. Aristotle might have cited here the example of Antigone, without necessarily approving her invocation of the higher law under the circumstances; or he might have cited the use made of the higher law by Socrates when he related to the jury the instances in which he ran the danger of facing the death penalty rather than obey unconscionable superior orders, or when he said to the jury:

Where a man has once taken up his stand, either because it seems best to him or in obedience to his order, there I believe he is bound to remain and face the danger, taking no account of death or anything else before dishonor. . . . Gentlemen, I am your very grateful and obedient servant, but I owe a greater obedience to God than to you. . . . And so, gentlemen, I would say, You can please yourselves whether you listen to Anytus [the prosecutor] or not, and whether you acquit me or not; you know that I am not going to alter my conduct, not even if I have to die a hundred deaths (*Apology*, 28c–30a) .

BESIDE CLASSIFYING LAW and justice as conventional and natural, Aristotle also classifies justice under two other headings: the unwritten kind, and the kind according to law. From the context it would appear that Aristotle meant to distinguish between justice according to morals, and justice according to law. The examples he offers make this clear. On the one hand, he says, there is the usual type of business contract, when it is clear that there is a *quid pro quo,* involving either an exchange on the spot or future delivery. On the other hand, there is the "moral type" of agreement in which a gift or other service is given "as to a friend." Since the latter transaction is not on stated terms, it often generates misunderstanding, for the giver may in fact expect to receive an equivalent or greater return, as though he had made a loan and not a gift. The reason for this is

> that all men, or most men, wish what is noble but choose what is profitable; and while it is noble to render a service not with an eye to receiving one in return, it is profitable to receive one (*Nic. Ethics,* 1162b–1163a) .

Although Aristotle is admittedly not precise in his use of the terms "written" and "unwritten" in the *Nicomachean Ethics,* it is hard to see how Barker could interpret the terms so that "unwritten" becomes merely the "customary." (Ernest Barker, *The Politics of Aristotle,* 366.) In the *Rhetoric* Aristotle repeats the same classification: the just is measured according to laws that are written, or according to those that are unwritten. One kind of unwritten justice, he says,

> arises from an excess of virtue or vice, which is followed by praise or blame, honor or dishonor, and rewards; for instance, to be grateful to a benefactor, to render good for good, to keep one's friends, and the like . . . (*Rhetoric*, 1274a).

There is, it seems clear, an unwritten law that belongs, not to the law enforced by the state with rewards and penalties, but to the moral sphere, where the sanctions, if any, are left to public opinion.

But there is still another kind of unwritten law, one which is within the positive legal order and which, therefore, does entail sanctions enforced by the state. This is a type of law which bridges the sphere of morality and the sphere of enacted law. Aristotle calls it *epikeia* or equity. The *locus classicus* of the notion is in the *Nicomachean Ethics* (1137a), where Aristotle defines equity as the correction of the law in cases in which the law is deficient by reason of its generality. In addition to the legally just, there is also then, the equitably just, which is a correction of the former.

There is a need for equity, because a law must always be drafted as a universal proposition; but life produces unusual or unanticipated sets of facts, and the judges will feel that these ought not to be subsumed under the generality of the enacted law. The judges will, in these circumstances, seek to correct the omission from the enacted law by writing into it what the legislator himself would have said, had he known what the judges know.

As we have noted, Aristotle states in the *Rhetoric* that there are two kinds of unwritten justice. We have already mentioned one kind, that which arises from an excess of virtue or vice, which is followed by honor or dishonor. The second kind of unwritten justice is the equitable, or that which "goes beyond the written law," that which was omitted in the written law. Aristotle's elaboration in the *Rhetoric* clarifies the notion of equity:

> Actions which should be leniently treated are cases for equity; errors, wrong acts, and misfortunes must not be thought deserving of the same penalty. Misfortunes are all such things as are unexpected and not vicious; errors are not unexpected, but are not vicious. . . . And it is equitable to pardon human weaknesses, and to look, not to the law but to the legislator, not to the letter of the law but to the intention of the legislator; not to the action itself, but to the moral purpose; not to the part, but to the whole; not to what a man is now, but to what he has been, always or generally; . . . to prefer arbitration to the law court, for the arbitrator keeps equity in view, whereas the dicast looks only to the law. . . . (*Rhetoric,* 1374b) .

In a later passage in the same treatise, writing specifically of forensic oratory, Aristotle says that when the written law is against one's case, then we should argue from the general—meaning natural—law, and from equity,

> as more in accordance with justice; and we must [then] argue that, when the dicast takes an oath to decide to the best of his judgment, he means that he will not abide rigorously by the written laws; that equity is ever constant and never changes, even as the general law, which is based on nature, whereas the written laws often vary (this is why Antigone in Sophocles justifies herself for

having buried Polynices contrary to the law of Creon, but not contrary to the unwritten laws) : "For this law is not of now or yesterday, but is eternal. . . ." (*Rhetoric,* 1375a) .

Students of Aristotle do not agree as to where equity was meant to be located—within the legal order or outside it. For the purposes of our discussion, it is not imperative that we take a definite stand on this issue. For us it is enough to note that the concept allows Aristotle to build a bridge from law to morals, so that law could at times be transcended or could transcend itself. On the one hand, equity has a legislative function, permitting the judge to act in place of the legislator, to write into the enacted law a provision that would cover the omitted case. This would seem to put equity within the legal order itself. On the other hand, equity suggests a transcendence of the enacted law to natural justice. This suggests that equity is in the moral sphere, but is imported into the legal order to fill a vacant space or to displace a legal enactment.

The answer as to the proper location of equity will come more easily, I think, if one will consider the primary question of the relation of law to justice—a topic which affords us an opportunity to see the essential unity in the legal-moral thought in the Hebrew Bible, Plato, and Aristotle—the topic to which we now turn.

VI

IN THE HEBREW BIBLE, as we have seen, the law embraces the whole life of man and of the community; but there is room left for the good which exceeds the measure commanded by the law. Yet the law itself commands its own transcendence by placing before man and society the ideal of holiness: "Be holy. . . ." (Lev. 20:7). For the law is Torah; it is law but it is also teaching, instruction, since behind the legal code is God the Lawgiver and the Judge. Torah is teaching about God, and His ways and His wishes; it is God's plan or constitution for Israel. Torah is, in its most pervasive sense, God's instruction. The study of Torah is itself a basic commandment: "These words which I command you this day shall be upon your heart. You shall teach them diligently to your children, and shall talk of them when you sit in your house, and when you walk by the way, and when you lie down, and when you rise" (Deut. 6:6–7). Torah is, therefore, both law and religion. As religion, Torah reveals something of the nature of God, its author. But the revelation of God's nature is made through the law which He gave to Israel. Thus law and religion are inextricably intertwined.

The most fundamental characteristic of the law, and of God, is justice, or more correctly, righteousness. Whatever righteousness may mean, its most enduring meaning is the quality that makes for what is *right*. The law is perfect because it flows from God who is always *right*, and because it points to what is *right* for man. God does not turn out codes of law as a machine may turn out pins or nails; God's laws bear His imprint; they disclose His justice, His righteousness. "And what great nation is there, that has statutes and ordinances so righteous as all this law [Torah] which I set before you this day?" (Deut. 4:8). The theme is repeated with many variations: "The law of the Lord is perfect . . . the precepts of the Lord are right . . . the commandment of the Lord is pure . . . the ordinances of the Lord are true and righteous altogether" (Ps. 19:7–9). One could quote hundreds of passages which express the theme; but perhaps nothing in the Bible does this more fully or more movingly than Psalm 119 with its 176 verses—a rapturous, sometimes even sensuous, love song to the law. The following three verses (62–64) are typical:

> At midnight I rise to praise Thee,
>   because of Thy righteous ordinances,
> I am a companion of all who fear Thee,
>   of those who keep Thy precepts.
> The earth, O Lord, is full of Thy steadfast love;
>   teach me Thy statutes!

The law, then, points to God, its author; it points to goodness, to justice, to righteousness. The virtue of the law is not simply in its lawness, for other people too have their laws, as they have their gods. But the Torah is God's law; as *His* law, it points to His justice, His righteousness. The law is, therefore, inherently transcendent. It is worthy of being law because it partakes of justice, of righteousness; and yet it allows itself to be transcended by justice, by righteousness.

> And I will restore your judges as at first,
>   and your counselors as at the beginning.
> Afterward you shall be called the city of righteousness,
>   the faithful city.
> Zion shall be redeemed by justice,
>   and those in her who repent, by righteousness.
> (Is. 1:26–27)

It is because justice or righteousness includes observance of the law, and at the same time points to that which transcends the commandments, that the prophets, when they castigated the people, seldom spoke of the commandments but spoke rather of justice and righteousness, or gave unmistakably clear examples of moral injustice and oppression, which are a denial of righteousness. Thus Amos accuses the nation

  because they sell the righteous for silver,
      and the needy for a pair of shoes—
  They that trample the head of the poor into the dust of
      the earth,
      and turn aside the way of the afflicted; . . . (2:6–7)

To those who heard him, it was sufficient for Amos simply
to say, without offering any elaborate bill of particulars:

  Seek good, and not evil,
      that you may live;
  and so the Lord, the God of hosts, will be with you,
      as you have said.
  Hate evil, and love good,
  and establish justice in the gate; . . . (5:14–15)

It was precisely because the law pointed to something
within itself and yet also beyond itself—justice or righteousness—that Job could be portrayed not as a Jew, but as "a man
in the land of Uz," who was "blameless and upright, one who
feared God, and turned away from evil" (1:1). When he
recalled the events of his past life, Job could defend himself
by asserting (29:14), "[I] put on righteousness, and it
clothed me; my justice was like a robe and a turban." The
Hebrew readers of *Job* did not find it strange that when this
gentile thought of examples of justice and righteousness, he
could say:

  I was eyes to the blind,
      and feet to the lame.
  I was a father to the poor,
      and I searched out the cause of him whom I did not
      know.
  I broke the fangs of the unrighteous,
      and made him drop his prey from his teeth. (29:15–17)

Thus, centuries before Paul told the churches of Galatia that it was possible to transcend the distinction between Jew and Greek, slave and free, male and female, the Hebrew Scriptures had unmistakably taught the same lesson in transcendence, only what they had in mind was not justification by faith (Gal. 3:23–29) but justification as exemplified by the life of "a man" named Job.

It may be that after the exile in the sixth century B.C.E. the prophets could no longer point to the neglect of the poor and needy through non-observance of the particular commandments relating to gleanings, dedication of the corners of fields, the sabbatical year, and similar "welfare" provisions, since these laws were binding only in the land of Israel; and so the prophets were compelled to go beyond these specific commandments to the more general moral principles of justice and righteousness. The fact, however, is that it seemed to make no difference to the prophets whether they addressed Jews in Babylonia or in their homeland. They hardly ever thought of the specific commandments, not even of the Ten Commandments; their cry always was that righteousness, and only righteousness, redeems a man and exalts a nation, therefore, "Let justice roll down as waters, and righteousness as a mighty stream" (Amos 5:24). They did not, of course, mean to downgrade the Ten Commandments or the code of laws, let alone to imply that they were abrogated. This would have been a repudiation of the Torah. Just as the specific enactments concerning the poor, for example, assumed a commitment to the more general moral principles of justice and righteousness, so the moral principles imply their implementation through specific, detailed provisions. The genius of the Hebrew Scriptures is that, despite its diverse authors and subjects, it constantly interweaves the general and the specific, the legal enactment and the moral principle, the law in the books and the law in the heart, the letter and the spirit, the law as enactment and the law as teaching.

VII

In PLATO, the Form of the Good plays the role that righteousness plays in the Bible. The law is, or should be, nothing less
than an emanation from the Good, and the closer it approxi-
mates this ideal Form, the better it is. The main effort of the
Republic is to show this.

In the parable of the Cave, human beings appear chained,
with their faces to the wall. In back of them the cave has an
opening; outside the cave and at a distance, there is a blazing
fire. The prisoners, watching the wall, see the shadows of the
things that pass outside the opening of the cave; and they see,
too, their own shadows. It is these shadows that the prisoners
accept as the truth. One of the prisoners is released, and
eventually he discovers the sun as the source of light and as
somehow the creator of the shadows. Having seen the truth,
he no longer wants to go back to his place in the cave; but he
is taken back, and he is now a misfit. As he tries to free others
from their illusions and lies, they punish him and finally they
kill him.

The sun is, of course, the Form of the Good, which is the
ultimate creator of all things and of all truth. The purpose of
the *Republic* is to project a society in which the man who has
seen the sun will be accepted as the ruler: the philosopher-
king. Such a society is an embodiment, as it were, of the Form
of Justice. While justice is a virtue of the soul, it is also the
virtue of a *polis* in which the philosopher is king. The good
polis is the good man writ large. The laws of the good *polis*
are true to the Form of the Good.

The dominant position of the moral, and the dependence
of the law on the moral, are clear in the *Republic*. The *Laws*,
because it projects a law-centered society, presents at first
blush a problem as to the role of the moral; however, on

closer examination it becomes apparent that even here the law is subordinate to and dependent on the moral. For though the city imagined in the *Laws* will not be ruled by a philosopher-king, its constitution and its code of laws are the work of a philosopher-statesman and his associate commissioners. The rule of law in this imagined city is justified only because the city's code of laws is an expression of the philosophic, moral mind; its author is one who has seen beyond the shadows on the wall to the sun which is the creator of all things and truths. The code of laws is as close to the Form of the Good as anything other than the philosopher-king can be. Just as in the *Republic* the law may be said to be assimilated into the moral, so in the *Laws* the moral may be said to be assimilated into the law. In each instance the Good remains preeminent and the generator of all values.

The moral function performed by the philosopher-lawgiver appears clearly in the requirement that the laws be introduced by ethical preambles which will teach the citizens the moral reasons for their enactment. The legal code as a whole has such a preamble or prelude (*Laws,* Bk. V), which is intended to teach that, after his gods, the most divine thing a man has, and what is most truly his own, is his soul; that a man must above all else, advance the interests of his soul; that excess of wealth and property will breed public and private feuds; that we should leave our children rich in reverence but not in gold. It is on these and similar moral truths that the legal code is based; it is these truths that it seeks to advance (*Laws* 726–734).

Many of the specific laws also have their own preambles (e.g., *Laws* 741, 772–3, 870), which attempt to appeal to the citizen's reason and emotions. For the laws must aim not only to order the polity, and not only to produce virtue in the soul of the citizen, but also to teach. Indeed, the code of laws is a great text-book in religion, morals and politics; for "any man who treats of law in the style we are adopting, *means* to educate his fellow-citizens rather than [merely] to lay down the law to them" (*ibid.,* 857). The Curator of Law and Minister of Education are to instruct the schoolmasters to teach the code of laws to their pupils (811). This is hardly different from the view that Torah is both law and teaching!

And so, though in the second-best polity there is to be the strict rule of law, yet law and morals remain in intimate symbiosis, as though they are body and soul, man and God, the law of the state and the law of nature—things dissimilar yet like one another, different and yet the same.

VIII

AT THE END of the *Nicomachean Ethics* (1179b–1181a), Aristotle writes what is in effect an introduction to *Politics.* Having discussed happiness and virtue, friendship and pleasure, has he completed his investigation? Perhaps yes, says Aristotle, if all men could be depended upon for nobility of character and genuine love of what is noble. The fact is, however, that most men are amenable to fear rather than honor, and abstain from evil not because it is base but because of the penalties it entails; passion can generally be stopped, not by reason, but by force.

The young must, of course, be educated in virtue, but this means in part that they must be brought up under right laws; and these laws are as necessary for adults as they are for the young. Obviously referring to Plato's *Laws,* Aristotle says that while the lawgiver ought to encourage and exhort men to virtue on moral grounds, he must also impose sanctions for disobedience. Men's lives are, therefore, to be regulated by the moral intelligence and by a code of laws; but the law itself is a rule that emanates from wisdom and intelligence, and that has compulsory force. There must be a public order established by law, "and only good laws will produce good regulations" (1180b). Legislation is thus a branch of political science; laws are a product of the art of politics. Ethics is, therefore, by extension, a part of politics. But the reverse proposition is just as true: Politics is a part of ethics. A code of ethics needs a code of laws; and a code of laws assumes a code of ethics.

For one thing, law aims at justice, and justice can at times be achieved through equity rather than the strict law, through the spirit rather than through the letter of the law, through reliance, as it were, on an understanding of the "preamble"—written or unwritten—rather than solely upon the enactment itself. There must be the rule of law, but the *aim* of law must not be overlooked, its connection with justice (in the non-jural, moral sense) must be kept in view. The goal of the laws and of the rule of law is to make the citizens "good by training them in habits of right action—this is the aim of all legislation" (*Nich. Ethics,* 1103b).

Thus society needs a code of laws as teaching, for the formation of good habits and virtuous character; it needs the code of laws for its specific provisions for justice in social relations; it also needs the "general" justice which is provided for by the laws of nature, by equity. Law is, therefore, thoroughly intertwined with morals; the rule of law is not altogether separable from the need of men and society to aim at the good, to seek and fulfill the demands of justice and righteousness. For it must always be remembered that the purpose of the state is not mere life but the *good life*—"a good quality of life" (*Politics,* 1280a); and it must "be cardinal issue of goodness or badness in the life of the *polis* which always engages the attention of any state that concerns itself to secure a system of *good* laws well obeyed" (*Ibid.* 1280b). What conclusion is to be drawn from this?

The conclusion which clearly follows is that any *polis* which is truly so called and is not merely one in name, must devote itself to the end of encouraging goodness. Otherwise, a political association sinks into a mere alliance, which only differs in space from other forms of alliance where the members live at a distance from one another. Otherwise, too, law becomes a mere covenant— or (in the phrase of the Sophist Lycophron) "a guarantor of men's rights against one another"—instead of being, as it should be, a rule of life such as will make the members of a *polis* good and just. . . . The end and purpose of a *polis* is the *good life,* and the institutions of social life are means to that end *(Ibid.,* emphasis supplied) .

IX

IN EACH SYSTEM of thought that we have considered, there is simplicity and complexity: law and morals are one, and yet are not one; the rule of law is sovereign, yet there is, in some sense, a higher law, a morality, a general or universal law, which no particular law may contradict; the law is good, yet it aims at goodness, justice, righteousness; there is goodness immanent in the law, yet the law must be transcended, at least at times, in order to achieve the goodness at which the law aims; the law is good in itself, yet it is subservient to the ideal of the social order, which is to make the people a holy nation, a just people, a righteous people; the law is the result of a covenant, an agreement, yet it is not, if it is truly law, *merely* conventional, for it was covenanted *because* it was good; the law is coercive, it imposes pains and penalties, yet it is Torah, it is teaching, it is wisdom in living, it is *etz ḥayyim,* a tree of life—it "will enable all sorts of men to be at their best and live happily" *(Politics,* 1324a) , its object is "supreme virtue" or what "we may call . . . complete righteousness" *(Laws* 629) ; it is a compendium of regulations but also a textbook in virtue, righteousness, or holiness; the code commands "law and order," but the order must be a just order or the law is not "right" law.

In the relations between law and morals, whether in the Hebrew Scriptures or in Plato and Aristotle, immanence and transcendence are both involved. The ideal must take some tangible form in the here and now; the ideal must somehow become intrinsic in the existing, living order; facts in some way must themselves be holy and good and true and beautiful. Yet the ideal is always promise rather than achievement; it is beyond; it is the object of our quest; it belongs to a higher order; it is yet to emerge; it is the city of God and not the city of man. And still: through love, through knowing which is a form of action, through teaching which is a form of possession and creation, through action which is a form of loving, knowing and teaching—the particular and the universal come to possess one another; conventional justice and natural justice, the human and the divine embrace one another. Together they are one, and yet each is separate; but each needs and seeks the other. There remains paradox, contradiction—and reconciliation; for the real is always itself, and yet infinitely more.

The Ethics of the Pharisees

LOUIS FINKELSTEIN

IN a time of constant and accelerating social and technological change, with consequent challenge to the moral order, it may prove instructive, perhaps even helpful, to consider similar, if lesser, challenges of another age, and the manner in which its intellectual leaders met them. The society with which the present paper is concerned is that of Jerusalem as it developed into the metropolis of Judah in pre-exilic times, and again, after its destruction and restoration under the Maccabees half a millennium later.[1] The men who responded

---

Page numbers of books noted without further identification may be referred to in the following editions:

Mekilta, ed. Horowitz-Rabin, second ed., Jerusalem, 1960.
Mekilta d'R. Simeon b. Yohai, ed. I.N. Epstein–E.Z. Melamed, Jerusalem, 1955.
Sifra, ed. I.H. Weiss, Vienna, 1962.
Sifre, Numbers, ed. Horowitz, Leipzig, 1917.
Sifre, Deuteronomy, ed. L. Finkelstein, Berlin, 1939; reprinted New York, 1909.

[1] It is evident from Scripture (II Kings 22:14) that before the time of King Josiah, Jerusalem had developed a "second quarter." Archeological research confirms this information. However, even after this expansion, the population of the city could hardly have exceeded four thousand souls. On the return from the Exile, Jerusalem was once more only a hamlet, and Nehemiah had to cast lots to exhort or compel one-tenth of the re-established community to dwell in Jerusalem (Neh. 11:1ff.) . By the time of the Maccabees, however, the

39

to the moral and spiritual problems of Jerusalem's market place in the first period of its expansion were the Prophets; those who led it in the second period were the Pharisaic Sages, who further developed ideas inherent in Prophecy.

Some aspects of the thinking of these ancient religious and intellectual geniuses can be better appreciated now when so much has been learned about primitive man and the evolution of human culture. Early tool-making *Homo-sapiens* might well have destroyed himself through conflict within his clans and tribes, had he failed to invent tabus and other binding customs protecting each individual from the aggression of his immediate neighbor and kinsman. Rivalry with his fellows, hunger for food, for sex-life, for possessions, and above all for primacy, would have imperiled the existence of all primitive societies, had they not created sanctions protecting father against son, and son against father, brothers against one another, and sisters from their siblings. The fact that all known human societies, no matter how primitive, possessed such sanctions is sufficient indication of their role in the preservation of the species. Groups lacking them apparently have disappeared.

---

city had begun to grow, and it was greatly expanded under Herod.

The influence of an urban environment on the thought and personality of city dwellers, however, depends less on the city's absolute size than on the station of its population. It is the fact that the city draws to itself the boldest among the unlanded population, and the most pleasure-seeking among the landowners which creates the tension between the groups.

In many countries, as in Palestine for the most part, towns were simply agricultural settlements, where the farmers of a particular district lived together for protection, as they did in medieval England, but the tensions under discussion, which led to revolutions against the governing classes and challenged the established authority of custom, tended to develop in commercial centers, where traders met people from other regions and countries. (See Henri Frankfort, *Civilization in the Near East,* Bloomington, 1931, pp. 52ff., 57ff. and note 2. Cf. further V. Gordon Childs' works there cited.)

The tensions which might have led to civil strife in Jerusalem were averted (except in rare instances) by the teachings of the Prophets, and their disciples, the Pharisees. (See discussion of this subject in *The Pharisees, the Sociological Background of their Faith,* third ed., pp. 82ff., 627ff. [hereafter referred to as *The Pharisees*].)

In some regions the power of the early tabus over men's minds and behavior declined as towns developed. This was probably due in part to the constitution of the urban population in those parts of the world. In the first instance, their cities were settled by wealthier individuals who could live from the toil of other people. But ultimately, the towns also attracted the poorest people, those who had no land and obtained their livelihood through service to the rich land-owners and aristocrats. These newcomers were among the boldest, most adventuresome, independent, and intelligent of the unlanded peasantry, who refused to remain on the land as little more than serfs. Thus the population of the city's market place tended to consist of people who were, in effect, pioneers.

Even though these ancient towns were, for the most part, mere hamlets, the type of person drawn to them, and the close contrast between wealth and poverty, necessarily created tensions of a type quite new in the world. Both among the affluent and the poor, urban life encouraged skepticism regarding the validity of the tabus which peasant children were taught to fear. The city bred hatreds and competitiveness, crime and oppression, from which kinship groups living in close proximity in the country were comparatively free. Thus, urban teachers in various parts of the world found it necessary to seek a "rational" substitute for the primitive tabus which were being challenged and ignored. In Jerusalem, this task fell first to the Prophets, and then to the Pharisees.[2]

The Ethics of Love for Man

THE PRIMARY TASK of the Prophets of Jerusalem and Samaria (the latter while it existed, encountered precisely the same

---

[2] See *The Pharisees*, pp. 1ff., and *New Light from the Prophets*, London, 1969, pp. 12ff.

problems as Jerusalem) , and of the Pharisees, was thus to discover a surrogate for the moral force exerted among agricultural groups by clan and family kinship. For this purpose, the Prophets and Pharisees had recourse, in the first instance, to their basic idea that the whole human species is a single family, whose Father is the one God. They dreamed of a time when this truth, obvious to them, would be recognized by all men, who would act accordingly. There would emerge a world in which the wolf would lie down with the lamb, and the leopard with the kid, no harm ensuing to the weaker at the hands of the stronger. Nation would not bear sword against nation; nor would men learn war anymore.

In this world-nation-state, God would be not only King, but also Father. Everywhere men would love Him as their Parent, and obey Him as their Monarch.

The faith in the emergence of a world society to be governed by God alone, is suggested frequently in Scripture, as well as in Rabbinic literature. (This doctrine must be distinguished from the belief in a future human Messiah reigning over all the world, and from the belief that Israel will be governed directly by the Divine rule and that all other nations will be subject to it. These beliefs will be considered below.)

One of the most impressive expressions of the hope for the coming of the Divine Kingdom uniting all men as equals, occurs in a prayer still recited on Rosh Hashanah, imploring God to establish His Kingdom over all the earth: "Our God, and God of our fathers, do Thou reign over all the earth with the honor due Thee. Reveal Thyself in the majesty of the greatness of Thy strength, over all those who dwell in the world, Thy land. So that everything made will know that Thou hast made it, and everything created will know that Thou hast created it." In a simpler but no less emphatic form, this prayer was recited in the ritual of the Holy Land, as preserved in a probably original text found in the *Genizah* manuscripts.[3] The date of composition of this prayer can scarcely have been later than the fourth century B.C.E., as is evident from the fact that its form violates a rule set down at approximately that period.

The Pharisee's faith in this future world society, united in love and reverence for God, enabled him to endure the present, with its wars, injustices and tensions. In his own behavior, however, he did not have to await the realization of this vision. He enrolled as a citizen of the Divine Kingdom even amidst the prevailing nationalism and petty rivalry in the city for status, power, and wealth, and assumed the relevant duties and responsibilities as if the Kingdom of God were already existent.

He had to regard every man, no matter what his background or station in life, as his brother. With this conviction in his heart, he could overcome the divisiveness which city life engendered. As Rabbi Akiba was to put the matter centuries after the origin of Pharisaism, "Scripture com-

---

[3] See J. Mann, in *Hebrew Union College Annual* II, 1925, p. 329. The date of the authorship of this prayer may be deduced from the use of the term *aleph lamed* in its opening strophe, in place of the Tetragrammaton. Had the Tetragrammaton been employed originally, it would have been replaced with the cipher *aleph dalet* when the pronunciation of the Name ceased to be customary in the synagogue, which occurred in the fourth century. Thereafter there was no occasion for those who hesitated to pronounce the Name in the synagogue to resort to the cipher *aleph lamed*. See *Tosefta Berakot* 6 (7) .20, ed. Lieberman, p. 39, and my discussion of the subject in *New Light from the Prophets*, p. 9, as well as in *Conservative Judaism*, XXIII, Winter 1969, pp. 25ff. (The *baraita* also occurs with some variants in *Yer. Berakot* 9.1,1d.)

In contrast to this prayer for the Kingship of God, as the early Pharisees and the Hillelites conceived it, one may cite the prayer, apparently emanating from Galilee (I. Elbogen, *Der. jued. Gottesdienst*, p. 142), which reads: "Impose fear of Thee upon all Thy works, and reverence for Thee on all that Thou hast created; so that all beings shall hold Thee in awe, and all creatures shall worship Thee. Thus they will become a single society to do Thy will, with a complete heart." The prayer continues with the petition that the Lord may reign in Zion and bring honor and glory to His people. While this prayer was also recited in the Holy Land (*Monatsschrift* LV, 1911, p. 597; *Hebrew Union College Annual* II, 1925, p. 329), it seems to have arisen among Shammaitically-minded Galileans (see above), and for that reason stresses the importance of the fear of God rather than love for Him. (See below, pp. 51, 81.)

mands: 'And thou shalt love thy neighbor as thyself; I am
the Lord (Lev. 19:18) .' The verse is to be interpreted: 'I the
Lord created him [you must love him].' "[4]

In order to be reminded each day of one's membership
in the Divine Kingdom, he read Deuteronomy 6:4-9 both
morning and evening:

> Hear, O Israel, the Lord our God, the Lord is one. And
> thou shalt love the Lord, thy God, with all thy heart,
> and with all thy soul, and with all thy might. And these
> words, which I command thee this day, shall be upon
> thy heart; and thou shalt teach them diligently unto thy
> children, and shalt talk of them, when thou sittest in thy
> house, and when thou walkest by the way, and when
> thou liest down, and when thou risest up. And thou
> shalt bind them for a sign upon thy hand, and they shall
> be for frontlets between thine eyes. And thou shalt
> write them upon the doorposts of thy house, and upon
> thy gates.

This twice daily ceremony was described in Rabbinic
times as "the acceptance of the yoke of the Kingdom of
Heaven."[5] It is not known when that term was introduced,
but it certainly described the meaning of the ritual correctly.
To stress further his citizenship in the Divine Kingdom, the
Pharisee wore on his arm and forehead small leather boxes
containing parchment on which these verses from Deuteronomy, and related passages, were inscribed. He also placed
such parchments on his doorposts.

The commandment to love God and not merely obey Him,
required one to be so devoted to Him that one also loved

[4] *Abot d'R. Natan* I, ch. 16, ed. S. Schechter, pp. 32f. where, however, the text
has been corrupted. For the correct reading, see the citation in my *Mabo
le-Mesiktot Abot ve-Abot d'R. Natan* (hereafter, simply *Mabo*) , p. 47.
[5] Cf. *Mishna Berakot*, 2.5. See many similar passages, e.g., *Sifre*, Deuteronomy,
31, p. 54, line 5.

His creatures for His sake. One refrained from dealing unjustly with others lest one offend Him. More affirmatively, one strove to help others because this was pleasing to Him. Through complete preoccupation with God and His desires, man would come ultimately to see the world as He saw it.

The Prophet and the Pharisee could hope that, imbued with this doctrine, their disciples' behavior would be marked by respect not only for one another but also for their neighbors; that they would overcome clan, tribal and national chauvinisms; that they would develop affection for rich and poor alike, for the stranger no less than for the Israelite; that steps would be taken toward the emancipation of women from the degradation which they suffered among the frequently polygamous peasantry; and that even the lot of slaves would, under their influence, be ameliorated. The Kingdom of God would consist of persons deriving from all classes and groups.

In a stirring and instructive image, a Rabbinic Sage commented on the suffering of God when pain is inflicted on man, even one guilty of a crime. "When a person [convicted of a capital offense] suffers, what does God say?" the Rabbi asked. "[God says:] I have a severe headache! I have severe pains in my arm!" the Sage replied in a bold anthropomorphism, justified only by the need to stress the infinite value of even the most depraved of men. All people are children of God; all are His subjects; all are citizens of His Kingdom.

The Ethics of Holiness

THE ACHIEVEMENT OF LOVE for one's fellowman, despite all differences of family background, status, wealth and education, required not only the conviction that God is the universal Father and King, but other concepts which would help repress the hatred and jealousy engendered by competitiveness and greed. Hence, among the urban Pharisees, the concept of the Divine Kingdom was supplemented by the conviction that pleasures and possessions were, in their very nature, ignoble, demeaning and unworthy of man.

"It is a tradition of the Pharisees," ran a Sadducean taunt, "that they deny themselves pleasure in this world. And yet in the future world [of which the Pharisees conceived, as will be seen below] they will have nothing!"[6] Josephus similarly reported that "The Pharisees consider human pleasure of little value, and despise the delicacies in life. They follow the conduct of reason, and what that prescribes as good for them to do. And they think they ought to strive earnestly to observe reason's dictates in practice."[7] (Josephus, however, apparently was speaking only of one Pharisaic faction, for in this time some Pharisees were wealthy and lived in accordance with their means.)

The Pharisees considered the rejection of the goods and ambitions of the temporal world part of their effort to achieve holiness. Thus they reinterpreted the primitive concept which equated holiness with what was tabu and considered the holy a source of peril, holding that, on the contrary, what was holy brought blessing to the individual, the people, and mankind. The holiness of God Himself inhered in His transcendence of all selfish desire. The command of Scripture, "Be ye holy, for I, the Lord your God, am holy" (Lev. 11:44) was interpreted to mean, "Just as I am holy, so you must be holy; just as I am above [mundane] desire, so you must be above [mundane] desire."[8] The word used to express the

---

6 *Abot d'R. Natan* I, ch. 5, ed. Schechter 13b.
7 Josephus *Antt.* XVIII, 1.2. See Loeb Classics Ed. *Josephus* IX, pp. 10–11, notes *b* and *c*.
8 *Sifra, Shemini, perek* 12.4, ed. Weiss 57b. Cf. also *Sifra, Qedoshim,* beg. 86c, where the command "Be ye holy" is interpreted "Be ye *perushim.*" This interpretation is given by Nahmanides in his commentary on Lev. 19:2. According to him, the word *perushim* means "separated" and indicates abstinence from unworthy action and speech, not specifically forbidden in Scripture. He holds that the name "Pharisees" was given this group apparently because of their self-denial in this regard. He accepts this interpretation of the Scriptural command to "be holy" as precise and literal.

notion of being above and beyond desire was *parosh,* literally, "a Pharisee." The comment should therefore be rendered, "Just as I am a Pharisee, so you must be Pharisees."

(In other contexts, this early interpretation of the term "be ye holy" is expanded and softened, as it were. Thus *Mekilta*[9] explains the Scriptural verse, "And ye shall be unto Me a kingdom of priests and a holy nation" (Exod. 19:6) not as a promise, but as a command. According to *Mekilta,* it meant, "Holy and sanctified, separated [*perushim*] from the peoples of the world and their idolatries." This was, apparently, the interpretation of the verse by affluent priestly groups who, as we shall see, rejected the principle of complete self-denial.)

Thus, the very word "Pharisee" was taken to connote the self-denial which the Sadducean taunt and Josephus' report described as only one element in Pharisaic doctrine. In other contexts, the title "holy" was often associated with this self-denial. We are told that "Anyone who practices self-denial even in one specific respect, may be called *qadosh* (holy)."[10] R. Phineas b. Yair, enumerating the steps by which mankind might achieve the return of Elijah and the Resurrection, included *perishut* (self-denial) as one such means. *Perishut,* he maintained, was necessary to achieve *qedushah* (holiness) ; holiness was necessary to achieve humility; and all three were essential elements in progress toward Elijah and the Resurrection.[11]

---

9 *Mekilta Jethro, Bahodesh,* ch. 2, p. 209. Cf. *Mekilta d'Arayot, Sifra, Qedoshim, perek* 9.2, 91d, where the Scriptural expression "Sanctify yourselves, therefore, and be ye holy" (Lev. 20:7) is explained as referring to "sanctification of separation [*perishut*] from idolatry." According to this *baraita,* as according to *Mekilta, perishut* does not signify self-denial at all. Perhaps the interpretation given in these passages replaced the older one when the Hellenistic culture threatened the survival of Judaism. The Pharisees—or at least some of them—then accepted into their membership all who rejected the culture "of the nations of the world and their idol worship."

10 *B. Ta'anit* 11a.

11 Mishna *Sotah* 9.15; and parallel passages.

R. Akiba employed the word *perishut* in the same sense when he said, "Vows offer support for *perishut*";[12] that is, the practice of self-denial will be encouraged and made easier through a binding vow. Obviously, R. Akiba considered *perishut* meritorious and a step toward holiness.

R. Akiba's disciple, R. Meir, used to advise his disciples, "Purify yourself and sanctify yourself from all sin and transgression, and I [i.e., the Deity] will be with you everywhere."[13]

According to an anonymous teacher, "One who sanctifies himself a little [through exertion of his own initiative and will-power] will be helped to sanctify himself greatly [through the help of Heaven]."[14] The verse "For thou art a holy people unto the Lord, thy God," (Deuteronomy 14:21) is interpreted as a commandment: "Sanctify thyself, so that thou shalt be a holy people."[15]

The more prosperous, priestly faction of the Pharisees

---

[12] Mishna *Abot* 3.13.

[13] *B. Berakot* 17a.

[14] *B. Yoma* 39a. In later times, the term "holy" came to be used mainly in relation to sexual self-denial or self-control, or in the achievement of a feeling of service to God even in the sex act. (See, e.g., *B. Yebamot* 105b; and cf. *B. Shebuot* 18b, which deals with the reward awaiting those "who sanctify themselves" at the moment of copulation. For a further discussion of this meaning of "holiness," see Professor Louis Ginzberg, *Legends of the Jews,* V, p. 319, n. 312; and Kauffmann Kohler, in *Jewish Encyclopedia,* under *Holiness.*)

To what extent the word *qadosh* is used in this ethical and moralistic sense in Scripture itself, need not concern us here; but doubtless some passages suggest this very connotation. The word *tumah,* "defilement," clearly is used both in Scripture and in Talmudic works to suggest moral as well as ritualistic impurity. Thus, *Sifra,* commenting on the verse, "And he shall make atonement for the holy place, because of the uncleanness of the children of Israel" (Lev. 16:16) , remarks: "One might consider in this context three types of impurity, that of idol worship . . ., that of sexual offenses . . ., that of bloodshed. . . . Lest one suppose that this goat is offered as atonement for these defilements, Scripture says, etc." (*Sifra, Ahare, perek* 4.1, ed. Weiss 81c.) As defilement is the opposite of holiness, it was almost inevitable that this connotation of *tumah,* should lead to a similar and opposite definition of *qedushah.*

[15] See *Sifre,* Deut. 104, p. 163; and cf. *ibid.,* 97, p. 138.

naturally rejected the Pharisaic attitude toward earthly pleasures and possessions as unholy and improper. God was, indeed, above all mundane desire, but that was not a Divine attribute: it was the essence of God's Divinity. The holiness of material things and human beings, as well as of the angels, consisted in their being dedicated to Divine purposes. But this Divine purpose need not be rejection of human satisfactions by man; in some instances, it might be their fulfillment.

THE CONTROVERSY within Pharisaism regarding the meaning of holiness was most clearly articulated in relation to the Sabbath and Festivals. According to R. Eliezer and the School of Shammai generally, these days are to be kept holy "through provision of [special] food, drink, and clean clothes."[16] They held that one was required to fulfill the commandment to "remember the Sabbath day to keep it holy" (Exod. 20:8) throughout the week. This could be done by setting aside, each day, some special viand for the Sabbath day. We are told that Shammai himself followed this practice, which was rejected by his colleague, Hillel.[17] The Hillelites held that the holiness of the Sabbath was unrelated to special foods, drink, or fine clothes. Some of them also denied that one

---

[16] So an anonymous comment in *Sifra, Emor,* par. 12.4, ed. Weiss 102b; cf. *Mekilta Bo,* ch. 9, p. 30; and *Mekilta of R. Simeon, ibid.,* 12.16, p. 18. The opening phrase of the passage in *Sifra* corresponds to that given in the name of R. Eliezer, somewhat earlier *(Sifra, Emor,* par. 11.1, ed. Weiss 101c). It seems clear that the whole *baraita* in *Sifra,* par. 12.4, also emanated from him, as did that in *Mekilta of R. Simeon.* This would be in accord with the general Shammaitic approach to the holiness of the festivals as shown in the discussion in the text, and in the references given in the next note. Probably the *baraita* in *Mekilta of R. Ishmael* derived from R. Nehunya b. Hakkanah, his teacher, as did so many other *beraitot* in the midrashim of the School of R. Ishmael. (Cf. my discussion of the subject in *Hanoch Albeck Jubilee Volume,* pp. 352ff.)

[17] *Mekilta Jethro,* ch. 7, p. 229, in the name of Eleazar b. Hizkiah b. Hananyah b. Garon, one of the leading Shammaites of the last days of the Second Commonwealth. Cf. *Mekilta of R. Simeon* 20.8, p. 148; and *B. Bezah* 16a; also see notes of Horowitz on the passage in *Mekilta.*

had to prepare for the Sabbath throughout the week. For the School of Hillel, the commandment to "remember the Sabbath day to keep it holy" meant only that one recited a blessing at the beginning of the Sabbath, thanking God for having granted Israel this holy day, when one rose above all earthly desire and concentrated on things of the spirit.[18]

R. Akiba, following this view, interpreted the verse "Therefore the Lord blessed the Sabbath day and hallowed it" (Exod. 20:11) as follows: "He blessed it with the *manna;* and He hallowed it with [the requirement that one recite] a blessing [for it]."[19] That is, He blessed it with the double portion of the *manna* which descended for the Israelites in the Wilderness on Friday, to provide for their Sabbath needs. But the food provided for the Sabbath was, significantly, identical in quality and in quantity with that for every other day. God hallowed the day through the imposition of the commandment that one should enjoy its serenity and be grateful for it.

R. Ishmael, also adhering to the view that holiness meant a rejection of earthly pleasures and concerns, agreed that the blessing that God provided for the Sabbath inhered in the provision He made for a double portion of the *manna* on Friday. But for R. Ishmael the sanctity of the Sabbath consisted in the fact that no *manna* descended on that day. Holiness thus meant nothing more than rejection of earthly wants, precisely in the manner ascribed to the Pharisees as a group.

---

[18] Thus R. Eleazar b. R. Zadok reports that his father (who followed the customs of the School of Hillel, although he was a Shammaite—*Tosefta Sukkah* 2.3, ed. Lieberman p. 261) used to "recite a short prayer on the Sabbath eve" ending with the doxology "Blessed art Thou, O Lord, Who dost sanctify Israel and the Sabbath" (*Tosefta Berakot* 3.7, ed. Lieberman p. 13; and cf. *Tosefta Kifeshutah*, ad loc., p. 34, as well as Professor Lieberman's note on *Tosefta Sukkah* 2.3, in *Tosefta Kifeshutah, ad loc.*, p. 855.)

[19] *Mekilta Jethro, Bahodesh,* ch. 7, p. 231, and see also *Bereshit R.,* ch. 11. beg., ed. Theodor p. 87.

R. Akiba would not agree that mere obedience of the commandment to refrain from work on the Sabbath day symbolized holiness of the day. After all, many Mesopotamian pagans also refrained from work on the Sabbath day. He defined its holiness in the fact that the people of Israel enjoyed the rest provided by the Sabbath, devoted it to the worship of God, and blessed Him for His gift of the Sabbath to them.

The disagreement between the Schools of Shammai and Hillel concerning the meaning of holiness, particularly in relation to the Sabbath and festivals, apparently is reflected in Scripture itself. To counter the widespread pagan notion of the Sabbath as a day of ill-omen, Deutero-Isaiah insisted that its holiness inhered in the fact that it is a delight (Is. 58:13). His words are ambiguous. They may be interpreted as defining "the delight" of the Sabbath precisely as R. Ishmael did, in the prohibition against mundane labor and mundane concerns. But they may also imply that one should make the Sabbath delightful through special provision of food, drink, and clothes.

Certainly, Ezra interpreted the holiness of Rosh Hashanah precisely as did the Shammaites four centuries later. When he read the Torah to the people on the first day of Tishri and they all wept, hearing that the day was to be kept holy, Ezra said to them, "Go your way, eat the fat and drink the sweet, and send portions unto him for whom nothing is prepared; for *this day is holy unto our God Lord;* neither be ye grieved, for the joy of the Lord is your strength" (Neh. 8:10).

Following this definition of holiness, the Hillelites believe that the sanctity of the priests consisted not in any superiority granted them over the rest of the people, but rather in selfless dedication to the service of God and to the atonement of His people's sins. This, of course, was not the view of the priests themselves, whether Pharisees or Sadducees! They held that their "holiness" meant that they were "separated" from the people, in the sense of being above them.

The Pharisaic prayers and benedictions always stressed that God "sanctified" the people of Israel through the *commandments* imposed upon them. The Sadducean view was that the holiness of Israel was one of *status,* rather than function.

THE PHARISAIC REINTERPRETATION of the concept of holiness, which transformed it from its primitive connotation of tabu and danger into a concept of creativeness, happiness, and faith was certainly a major achievement in ethics and theology. It enabled man to think of God as both holy and beneficent, of religion as a source of strength in time of trouble, and of the injunctions of the Law as blessings intended for man's betterment.

Echoes of more primitive views are by no means lacking in various parts of Scripture and even in Rabbinic literature. But once the Pharisaic insight had been proclaimed, religion ceased to be, at least for the urban and intelligent, a source of fear and became a faith, a hope, an encouragement in times of sorrow.

On the other hand, the Sect of the Judean Wilderness also accepted the Pharisaic interpretation of holiness as dedication to the community and to one's fellowmen. Thus the Scroll of the Sect of Damascus, after enumerating various ethical obligations incumbent on every individual, summarizes its teachings in the exhortation "to love everyone, his brother, as himself, and to strengthen the hands of the poor, the needy and the stranger, and to seek each one the welfare of his brother." Those obeying these prescriptions are called "those who walk in these things in the *perfection of holiness,* according to all the ordinances of the community."[20]

Angels were called "holy ones", apparently because they were, like God, utterly selfless, devoted and devoid of personal ambition or desire for the satisfaction of the senses. But the holiness of the angels, of God, and of man at his best, was not merely negative. It also implied an affirmative hunger to create, to give, to help. This interpretation of Divine holiness is manifest clearly in one of the most ancient paragraphs of the *Amidah.* It reads, according to the older text used in the Holy Land, "Holy art Thou, and Thy Name is awe-inspiring; and there is no god besides Thee. Blessed be Thou, O holy God."[21] It seems evident that the purpose of this affirmation was a denial of Persian dualism, as many writers have suggested. Before uttering any petition to God, the leader of the Pharisaic congregation had to articulate his acceptance of Prophetic monotheism. He did so through his assertion that the two opposing forces, ascribed in Zoroastrianism to different divinities, were really united in the same God. God was awe-inspiring; this was as far as the Prophets and the Pharisees could accept ascription to Him of the traits which Persian dualism associated with Ahriman. But He was also, and primarily, beneficent, possessing all the goodness associated in Zoroastrianism with Ormuzd. If "holiness" in this paragraph connoted anything but loving creativeness and mercy, the prayer would lose all meaning. (In the Babylonian Jewish liturgy, apparently, fear that the prayer might seem a concession to the prevailing religion led to the omission of the term "awe-inspiring." Nothing

---

20 See *Zadokite Document* 8.21, ed. Schechter p. 7; ed. C. Rabin VII, (XIX), p. 27; and R. H. Charles, *Apocrypha and Pseudepigrapha of the O.T.* II, p. 815. Cf. also *ibid.,* 9.31–33. For the text, see *Jewish Quarterly Review,* N.S. XVI, 1925, p. 145.

21 For the date of the origin of this benediction, and its relation to the dangers of assimiliation to Zoroastrian dualism, see *New Light from the Prophets,* p. 126.

but the goodness and love of God was appropriate in this context.)

The Ethics of Anonymity[22]

IN OUR AGE, when even very promising students frequently sacrifice the opportunity for future achievement and fulfillment as scholars, philosophers and leaders, through hunger for youthful recognition and fame; when national leaders unashamedly forget the basic good of their country in their desire for certain reelection and posthumous fame; when it has become a commonplace to say, "Praise me or blame me, but don't ignore me," it may be of special interest to study a way of life which recognized the perils inherent in the desire for primacy, power and fame, and was aware of the thirst for further recognition which even partial fulfillment of this desire stimulates.

The discipline of the Pharisees required them not only to abstain from the search for contemporary or posthumous fame, but to avoid it whenever possible and to court anonymity. The desire for fame was held inconsistent with the Pharisaic doctrine of the immortality of the soul (to be discussed below) and with the utter selflessness implied in love for God and in the concept of holiness. That the Pharisees actually insisted on such anonymity cannot be doubted. The practices characteristic of them, the Prophets whom they followed, and the Rabbis who succeeded them until the second century C. E., all demonstrate this fact. Only

---

22 Most of this section of the paper was published in *Conservative Judaism*, vol. XII, no. 4, Summer 1958, pp. 1ff., and is reprinted here by permission. In that version, following other writers, I frequently referred to the early Pharisees as "Hasideans" as I also did in other works. However, it is now clear that Pharisaism came into existence long before the time of the Maccabees, as is usually supposed. (See discussion of this subject in *Conservative Judaism*, vol. XXIII, no. 2, Winter 1969, pp. 25ff.) The Hasideans were clearly a different group whose characteristics I hope to discuss in another context.

in a later age did the norm fall into disuse and become almost obsolete.

Apparently, it is because of the norm of anonymity that so little is known about early Pharisaism and its central institution, the Great Synagogue.[23] Not one of its leaders during the long period from Ezra until Simeon the Righteous (a matter of over three hundred years) is known to us by name.

The anonymity of the Men of the Great Synagogue bears no analogy to the oblivion which surrounds primitive authorities in almost every other tradition, such as the early judges who founded the British Common Law.[24] The members of the Great Synagogue did not originate a tradition; they appeared in the midst of it. They were extremely conscious of history, and they were also profoundly aware of the role of the individual in the historical process. The names of their foremost teachers could have been forgotten by admiring circles of disciples and followers only as a result of a deliberate decision.

Apparently, posthumous fame seemed no more rational an aim of life to the Pharisees than contemporary popularity. They had outgrown pagan identification of name and self, and had no wish to be known by name in future generations.[25] Like the Prophets before them, the Pharisees sub-

---

23 The character of "the Great Synagogue" and its role in the history of Judaism in general, and of Pharisaism in particular, is still only inadequately explored and understood. For some suggestions regarding it, and a partial bibliography, see my discussion in *Ha-Perushim ve-Anshe Keneset ha-Gedolah* (hereafter, *Ha-Perushim*).

24 Professor E. Bickerman has maintained that similar anonymity characterized the early teachers of the Greek philosophical schools, and concludes that the phenomenon was unrelated to any specific Pharisaic view. However, the argument below seems to me to show conclusively that it was felt that being mentioned by name was an improper tribute to a great, saintly teacher. One is reminded of the rule which obtained in much later times, namely that it is not proper to set up a memorial for the righteous. Their works are their memorials. (*Yer. Sheqalim* 2.7, 47a.) For further evidence that the anonymity of scholars and saints was deliberate, see below.

25 For the identification of name and self in early biblical and in other primitive thought, see *The Pharisees*, p. 169, and literature there noted.

mitted to the pseudo-immortality of history only when necessary for the service of God. Indeed, under such circumstances, they would even accept contemporary fame. But as a goal in life, historical immortality seemed not only an illusion, but also sinful. They did not seek recognition among mortals, but before God Himself. They wanted Him to accept them as His dedicated servants. Nothing less sufficed.

Precisely because thirst for contemporary and posthumous fame is so common, anonymity became a distinctive symbol of the Pharisees' dedication to God.

They probably knew that this desire for anonymity linked them to the Prophets, though this aspect of Prophecy has been virtually unrecognized in modern times. Because most of the Prophets whose speeches have survived are all identified by name, we forget that the overwhelming majority of writers of prophetic works were unnamed in the historical record.

The Books of Isaiah, Jeremiah, Ezekiel, and the Twelve, whose authors are identified, are the exception rather than the rule. No authors are recorded for Joshua, Judges, Samuel, Kings, Ruth, Esther, Lamentations, most of the Psalms, Job, and Chronicles. The Midrash suggests that works ascribed to well-known Prophets include anonymous portions.[26] On the other hand, the Talmud holds (with apparent justice) that when the name of a Prophet's father is recorded, the latter, too, probably belonged to the prophetic circle.[27] If so, there were many Prophets, noteworthy in their time, whose words have been either lost or included in the works of others.

In at least two instances it can be demonstrated that this

---

[26] Thus, according to R. Simon, Beeri the father of Hosea was a Prophet, the real author of Is. 8:19–20; but because the two verses could not form a book, they were interpolated into the Book of Isaiah. See *Vayyiqra R.* 6.7, ed. M. Margoliot p. 162; and *ibid.* 15.2, p. 322.

[27] *B. Megillah* 15a.

anonymity was deliberately chosen. The name of Deutero-Isaiah must have been a household word in his day and it scarcely could have been forgotten, except through his own determination or that of his disciples. Malachi (perhaps to be read as in the Septuagint *malako,* "His messenger") presumably was a title given a Prophet who wished to be anonymous.

The derogation of either contemporary or posthumous fame among the early Pharisees was such that no objection was raised to the ascription of one's own work to another author, preferably an earlier one. Designation of authorship was a pedagogic device, to be used when helpful to further man's spiritual development. Human beings were not considered originators of the inspiration which came to them; it belonged to God.

Just as the Pharisaic principle of anonymity can be traced back to Prophecy, so did it pervade the Talmudic period. From the time of Simeon the Righteous (ca. 200 B.C.E) until the end of Herod's reign (4 B.C.E.), the names of two or three scholars at the utmost are recorded for each generation. A few more are recorded in the period following Hillel and Shammai. But for centuries after Simeon the Righteous, most of the Rabbinic tradition was transmitted with deliberate anonymity.

The prayers of the early synagogue liturgy, comparable to the Psalms in beauty and inspiration, are almost all anonymous. Only accidentally did we discover that Rab, in the third century C.E., compiled special prayers for Rosh Hashanah. The great contribution of Rab and other scholars to the revision of the older texts of the prayers for use in Babylonia, was reconstructed only through critical studies.

The tradition of anonymity exercised an almost equally great influence on the record of legal opinions and decisions in Talmudic times. While the name of an editor or compiler of an ancient Rabbinic work is mentioned occasionally, and while R. Johanan, in the third century C.E., transmits reliable information concerning the authorship of some especially important Rabbinic texts,[28] almost all the compilations of ancient laws and *aggadot* remain anonymous or pseudonymous.

In view of these facts, one can hardly doubt that the Founding Fathers of Pharisaism, like the various Biblical authors, *sought* anonymity precisely as did the *Hazon Ish*[29] and the *Hafetz Hayyim*[30] in the twentieth century. The latter saints seem to have been unaware that they were anticipated in their desire for anonymity by several millennia; but their motivations were precisely those of their early predecessors, namely to give expression to their supreme and utterly selfless love for God.

IN THE LIGHT OF THESE REMARKS, it may seem strange that Ezra, an outstanding figure in early Pharisaism and perhaps the founder of the movement, is not only well-known to history, but that a portion of his memoirs has been preserved. The inconsistency, however, is more apparent than real. Ezra himself clearly followed the tradition of Prophetic and Pharisaic anonymity. His memoirs tell us virtually nothing about his great achievements, which have to be reconstructed from other sources. Indeed, the book bearing his name leaves the impression that his life was a failure. So little is recorded of him that Ben Sira, rejecting the Pharisaic traditions about him, omitted him from his list of the famous "fathers of old" (Eccles. 44:1ff.).

The Biblical and Talmudic references to Ezra's personal

---

28 *B. Sanhedrin* 86a.

29 Rabbi Abraham Isaiah Karelitz, one of the foremost Talmudists of the twentieth century; d. 1954.

30 Rabbi Israel Meir ha-Kohen, a leading scholar of Lithuania in the early part of the twentieth century; head of the *yeshivah* in Radin, Poland; d. 1933.

life and works, which flouted the norm of anonymity, were justified by the purpose they had to serve. In his native Persia, Ezra occupied a distinguished position. Even if we reject the suggestion of H. H. Schaeder[31] that he was a member of the Imperial Cabinet, Ezra surely was one of the most celebrated Jews in the Persian Empire of his time. His memoirs show that he was on terms of relative intimacy with the Great King himself. We may assume that he lived a life of comfort and perhaps luxury in the imperial capital. All this he rejected in order to cast his lot with his struggling brethren in Jerusalem, to labor with them and, when necessary, to quarrel with them in order to establish in the Holy Land a spiritual community devoted to Torah.

Ezra's memoirs were transmitted to later generations, apparently in order to give encouragement to the Pharisees by showing how this distinguished scholar and statesman, descended from a high priestly family, associated himself with the Pharisaic movement and sought to advance its cause.

The rule of anonymity was thus, from the beginning, not held to be binding under all circumstances. It was an expression of complete devotion to God, to be followed except when the service of God required identification of a person by name. That is why the principle was relaxed when Simeon the Righteous became head of the Great Synagogue. The association of the famous High Priest with Pharisaism was a signal triumph for the movement, to be proclaimed as widely as possible, and to be recalled by future generations.

Simeon's leadership of the Pharisees may have had other immediate and practical implications. Antiochus III had granted the Jews a charter, recognizing the Torah as the law governing them in the land, and apparently giving Pharisaic scholars legal status as "scribes of the Temple."[32] The High

---

[31] *Esra der Schreiber*, Tuebingen, 1930.
[32] Josephus, *Antt.* XII.3. (138ff.) ; Loeb Classics Series, *Josephus*, VII, pp. 71ff.; also notes of R. Marcus in Loeb Classics, *loc. cit.*, pp. 751ff. For further discussion of the issues raised here, cf. what I wrote in *Ha-Perushim*, pp. 78ff.

Priest's presidency of the movement was probably indispensable to this arrangement, and almost certainly greatly encouraged it.

Contemporaries, for all their wisdom, scarcely could have anticipated that Simeon's leadership of the comparatively obscure Pharisaic Great Synagogue would be far more impressive to future generations than his High Priesthood. From the viewpoint of the third century B.C.E., Simeon's presidency of the Great Synagogue conferred distinction on it, but none on him.

Once the departure from custom had been made, and the name of the head of the Great Synagogue had been transmitted in the oral record of the Pharisees, the precedent had to be followed for his successors as well. Moreover, if the association of Simeon with the Great Synagogue was in some way connected with the Charter of Antiochus III, the head of the Pharisees had become, in effect, a governmentally recognized official. He was the chief scholar of the Temple; he was authorized, doubtless, to identify the other scribes who were to be free from Imperial taxation. His court was a recognized tribunal for interpretation of the Law and adjudication of disputes, as required by the Charter of Antiochus.

Thus it came about that Antigonus of Socho, successor to Simeon the Righteous as head of the Great Synagogue, was remembered by name. When, after his death, and during the Maccabean revolt, the two wings of Pharisaism became separate schools, the head of each was recorded by name. This apparently is how the "pairs" of scholars who headed Pharisaism from the rise of the Maccabees until the end of Herod's reign came to be remembered.

The men called *Ben Bag Bag* and *Ben He He* in the Talmud and described as disciples of Hillel probably assumed these curious names as pseudonyms to avoid posthumous fame. And it is significant that, in recording a number of incidents in which "a certain saint" figures, the Talmud re-

marks that the term always applies either to R. Judah ben
Baba or R. Judah ben R. Ilai.[33] Apparently, in relating
stories of saintliness it was felt to be incongruous to identify
the central figures. Perhaps other circumlocutions employed
in the Talmud to describe nameless scholars, such as "a
certain old man," were designed to avoid personal identification of particularly saintly people.

The anonymity cultivated by the Pharisees was adopted by
fringe groups as well. Thus the Sect of the Judaean Desert
never mentions its founder by name, but calls him only "the
teacher of righteousness." The authors of such works as the
Book of Jubilees, the Enoch writings, the Testaments of the
Twelve Patriarchs, Judith, and Tobit, all followed the tradition of anonymity.

In fact, during the five centuries from Ezra until the fall of
Jerusalem (70 C.E.), a period of vigorous literary creativity,
only one author is known by name, Jeshua ben Sira, the
writer of Ecclesiasticus. Standing outside Pharisaism, opposing its teachings and rejected by it, he apparently sought, or
at least accepted, the name-immortality which Pharisaism
condemned. In the light of this difference between his views
and those of the Pharisees, his ode in praise of the fathers of
old may be particularly significant. It is, perhaps, intended
in part to document the view that immortality in history is
awarded the good and denied the wicked. There was, for ben
Sira, no other immortality.

THE SELFLESSNESS reflected in the Pharisaic doctrine of anonymity was not confined to individuals; it applied to groups
and institutions as well. The Pharisees did not identify
themselves as a group with a specific name. They apparently
described themselves as the *keneset* ("the Assembly" or "the

---

[33] *B. Baba Qamma* 103b.

Congregation") .[34] They were called *Perushim* by opponents who considered them heretics.[35] Nor, so far as we know, did the Essenes (or the Sect of the Judaean Desert which was probably identical with them) have proper names for their respective groups. The Damascus document identifies the sect from which it emanated only as "those who entered the covenant," and "those who left the land of Judaea to settle in Damascus."

THE TRADITION of anonymity was abandoned to some extent after the fall of Jerusalem in the year 70 C.E. The destruction of the authoritative center of religious guidance for the community left the people confused by a welter of contradictory local traditions. The institutions of Jerusalem, both the Temple and the authoritative "courts" of the Pharisees, had ceased to exist. The population of the capital was dispersed. The endless variety of opinions might well lead to skepticism regarding the authority of any of them. To overcome the threatening chaos in the religious and spiritual life of the people, it became customary to associate transmitted opinions with particular authorities. Each community and

---

[34] Mishna *Bekorot* 5.5; *Zabim* 3.2; and cf. *Ha-Perushim*, p. 32, also Hanoch Albeck, in his *Additions and Appendices* to the sections in the Mishna mentioned.

[35] The view held by Nahmanides that the *Perushim* were called by that name because of their partial asceticism (see above, note 8) has been widely advocated by modern writers. Yet the fact remains that, except in passages where the word may refer not to the Pharisaic group but to self-denial and asceticism, the term is applied to the Pharisees, in Rabbinic works, almost exclusively in quotations from the words of their opponents. Moreover, the word *perushim* in the sense of "heretics" actually occurs in *Tosefta Berakot* 3.25, ed. Lieberman p. 18. Professor Lieberman, in *Tosefta Kifeshutah, ad loc.*, p. 53, accepts this reading of the word, without however necessarily agreeing that it meant "heretics," or that the term was used of the Pharisees by their opponents in other contexts. Professor Louis Ginzberg, in his great *Commentary on the Yerushalmi*, III, p. 284, following earlier writers, would emend the word to read *posheim*, meaning "sinners," a reading which actually occurs in the parallel passages in *Yer. Berakot* 4.3.8a. See, however, my discussion of the subject in *Ha-Perushim*, p. 119.

indeed each individual Pharisee might now choose the scholar he would accept as his authority. "Let us begin," said the assembled Talmudic Fathers in Yabneh, "with Hillel and Shammai."[36] Thus opened the era in which ascription of maxims to specific authorities became a virtue instead of a vice.

However, so little weight attached to this innovation that transmitters sometimes deliberately confused the record, attributing to one scholar the statement of another.[37] The purpose of such changes usually was to win acceptance for a view which one considered right. From the time of R. Akiba onward,[38] this practice was denounced as misleading, but traces of it abound in extant Rabbinic literature.

Throughout the Talmudic period, a clear memory survived of the time when anonymity had been the rule. Thus we are told that King David once said, "I have a tradition, going back to the Academy of Samuel of Ramah, that a scholar who risks his life for the words of the Torah may not be quoted by name."[39] For that reason, maintains the Talmud, projecting its own views on an earlier generation, a decision obtained at risk of life and brought to David was transmitted anonymously. The Talmud says, "This is what is meant by the words of Scripture, 'But he would not drink thereof but poured [the water] out unto the Lord' (II Sam. 23:16)." "Water" signifies Torah, and "pouring it out before the Lord" means giving it with complete dedication, that is, anonymously.

That this tradition was not a figment of a Babylonian aggadist's imagination but was part of the Pharisaic view of

---

36 *Tosefta Eduyot*, beg.
37 Cf. Professor S. Lieberman, in *Tosefta Kifeshutah*, IV, p. 52, and references there given.
38 Cf. *Sifre*, Deuteronomy 188, p. 227.
39 *B. Baba Qamma* 61a.

life, can be demonstrated from the Mishna. The Mishna[40] records a norm brought by R. Hanina of Ono "from prison," i.e., transmitted by R. Hanina from R. Akiba during the latter's imprisonment by the Romans after the rebellion of Bar Kokeba. The curiously oblique reference to R. Akiba in the Mishna was not a rhetorical device. R. Akiba was not named in this passage because he had risked his life in giving information to R. Hanina for transmission to the other scholars. He was no longer alive when the norm was recorded, but violation of the principle of anonymity would, under the circumstances, have been an offense to his memory.

According to R. Jose ben Halafta, R. Hanina shared the same peril as R. Akiba. Hence, in his discussion of the incident, R. Jose omits the name of R. Hanina too. "We told the messenger," began R. Jose in recording the argument he gave against the views of R. Akiba.[41]

Despite later association of norms with individuals, anonymity was used consciously by the editors of the Mishna to indicate approval of particular views. "R. Judah the Patriarch accepted such and such an opinion, and therefore taught it anonymously,"[42] the Talmud occasionally remarks.

Only toward the end of the Tannaitic period do we hear of any emphasis on the need to associate norms with the people who handed them down. Thus, in the *baraita* known as *Qinyan Torah*[43] and published in many prayer books as

---

[40] *Gittin*, ch. 6, end. On the other hand, another decision given by R. Akiba while in prison is clearly recorded in his name (Mishna *Yebamot* 12.5). The Mishna does not state that R. Akiba offered the decision while in prison, but it is clear from the discussion in *Babli* and *Yerushalmi, ad loc.*, that this is precisely what happened.

[41] Mishna *Gittin, loc. cit.*

[42] Cf. e.g. *B. Hullin* 85a.

[43] The additional chapter was needed because the treatise was read on the Sabbaths between Passover and Shabuot. The purpose was to indicate the authority of the Pharisaic scholars which in this treatise is traced back to Moses. As Mishna *Abot* contains only five chapters, while six Sabbaths intervene between Passover and Shabuot, a sixth had to be added. The whole ritual was necessary to affirm the correctness of the Pharisaic view that Shabuot occurred on the fiftieth day after the first day of Passover, and not

the sixth (supplementary) chapter to Mishna *Abot,* we are told[44] that one of the forty-eight qualifications needed to acquire knowledge of the Torah is the transmission of a saying in the name of its author. The author of the *baraita* seems to have felt that this assertion required some documentation, although he offered none for the other qualities he considered indispensable to effective learning. Therefore he added: "For you have learned that he who repeats a statement in the name of its author brings redemption to the world, as is implied in the verse, 'And Esther told the King thereof in the name of Mordecai' (Esther 2:22)."

The Ethical Implications of Study

THE ACHIEVEMENT OF UNIVERSAL LOVE for one's fellow man was not an exceptional state of being to be sought only by exceptional people. Pharisaism held that it could be man's normal condition, and sought to restore to mankind the joy of complete integration with God and participation with Him in the creation of a constantly improving world.

Selfless love for one's fellow man, however, frequently must be preceded by transformation of personality and character; the translation of the ideal into wise daily behavior always requires development of judgment and creative initiative in the service of God. Unfortunately, codes of conduct, no matter how detailed and helpful, often prove inadequate to the task, for life rarely conforms to preconceived patterns. In any given situation, choices have to be made between alternative and conflicting values. The "holiness" of Pharisaic doctrine implied maturity, adequate to discern the right path to be followed in uncharted areas.

Each day, every man sits in judgment, often unconsciously,

---

on the fiftieth day after the Sabbath of the Passover week. See my discussion of the subject in *The Pharisees,* third ed., pp. 650ff.
44 Section 6.

participating with God in further creation of the world, or frustrating His will through destructive decisions. Each judgment is momentous, based on the weighing of opposing factors and the reduction of human complexities to the simplicities of right and wrong.

Scholastic brilliance and disciplined logic do not suffice for this formidable task. Lytton Strachey's analysis of the relations of Francis Bacon to Lord Essex may help illustrate this point. (I cite the example without necessarily accepting Strachey's version of the problem or his solution, having no access to material bearing on them. But the point he makes appears to me correct. Clever argument, based on sheer ingenuity and not resulting from disciplined education in ethics, in the discernment of right from wrong, may mislead one, and help transform a simple problem of morals into confusing and fatal complexity.)

Lord Essex was about to be tried for high treason. Francis Bacon, who had been his friend and beneficiary of his kindness, was asked to serve as one of his prosecutors. "He had no hesitations or doubts," writes Strachey. Other minds might have been confused in such circumstances, but Bacon could discriminate with perfect clarity between the claims of the Earl and the claims of the Law.

> Private friendship and private benefits were one thing; the public duty of taking the part required of him by the State in bringing to justice a dangerous criminal was another. It was not for him to sit in judgment: he would merely act as a lawyer—merely put the case for the Crown, to the best of his ability, before the Peers. His own opinions, his own feelings, were irrelevant. It was true, no doubt, that by joining in the proceedings he would reap considerable advantages. From the financial point of view alone the affair would certainly be a god-

send, for he was still pressingly in debt; and, besides
that, there was the opportunity of still further ingratiat-
ing himself with the man who now, undoubtedly, was
the most powerful personage in England—his cousin,
Robert Cecil. But was that an argument for declining to
serve? It was nonsense to suppose so. Because a lawyer
was paid his fee did it follow that his motives were dis-
reputable? There was, besides, one further complication.
It was clear that it would be particularly useful for the
Government to number Francis Bacon among its active
supporters. The Earl had been his patron, and was his
brother's intimate friend; and, if he was now ready to
appear as one of the Earl's accusers, the effect upon the
public, if not upon the judges, would be certainly great;
it would be difficult to resist the conclusion that the case
against Essex must be serious indeed since Francis Bacon
was taking a share in it. If, on the other hand, he refused, he would undoubtedly incur the Queen's dis-
pleasure and run the risk of actual punishment; it might
mean the end of his career. What followed? Surely only
a simpleton would be puzzled into hesitation. The responsibility for the Government's acts lay with the Government; it was not for him to enquire into its purposes.
And if, by doing his duty, he avoided disaster—so much
the better! Others might be unable to distinguish between incidental benefits and criminal inducements: for
him it was all as clear as day.

Never had his intellect functioned with a more satisfactory, a more beautiful, precision. The argument was
perfect; there was, in fact, only one mistake about it, and
that was that it had ever been made. A simpleton might
have done better, for a simpleton might have perceived
instinctively the essentials of the situation. It was an

occasion for the broad grasp of common humanity, not for the razor-blade of a subtle intelligence.

PHARISAISM turned to instruments other than brilliance and logic to help man in his ethical decisions. The Pharisees looked to profound and indefatigable study of Scripture to help mold character. For them, study of the word of God was more than a ritual, a natural act of worship, a symbolic declaration of faith in Revelation. Preoccupation with Torah had ethical and pragmatic importance. In the maze of life, study of Torah leads to what Scripture calls Wisdom. The student will acquire skill in ethical decision-making primarily through study under the saints of his time. He becomes familiar with the opinions and practices of his teachers which he may adopt as norms, but even more important, he masters their approach to human problems, and develops the ability to apply their methods to his own moral perplexities.

Moreover, the formation of character and personality was considered a never ending task. From the moment of birth until death, one's character and conduct continually had to be examined and improved. The more one immersed oneself in the complexities of Torah, the more sensitive one became to what is right, and the less likely one was to fall into error.

No less important than the direct helpfulness of study for the discovery of righteousness was its indirect influence, exerted through the joy such discovery always imparts. The joy of Torah study had as its corollary a detachment from the temporal life—its petty concerns, its silly pride in transient success, and its equally silly pain in momentary failure—that is indispensable both to serenity and to the good life. Just as it was possible to share God's holiness through conscious negation of earthly goods, so it was possible to share His serenity through creative study of Torah.

Because the Pharisee saw study of Torah to be an indispensable element of existence, he could not help but imagine that the Deity Himself engages in this study![45] Perfect as God is, He too tastes the ineffable joy of creative learning of Torah. Beyond the physical universe which He has created for physical beings, He is constantly creating universes of Torah with more and more complex insights into the problems of human relations, and revelations concerning their perfection. Surely, once one had conceived of the Deity, despite His perfection, as engaged in study (as well as in teaching Torah to those who die in childhood),[46] one could not seek satisfaction in any lesser aspiration or ambition.

Because the study of Torah was considered valuable not only as a means of making man socially more responsible, but also of providing him with an otherwise unattainable happiness, the School of Hillel (and their predecessors) held that everyone—even the poorest of the poor—should be encouraged to devote himself to this discipline.[47] The student might suffer pangs of hunger, he might weaken his body, his life might be shortened, but only through study could he obtain in this world the bliss otherwise to be had only in Paradise. He might have to deny himself the happiness of a married home (as Ben Azzai did, for many years);[48] or he might have to deny his wife and children some basic needs (as R. Akiba, with their consent, did);[49] but he (and his family) would be more than recompensed.

The School of Shammai rejected this whole conception.[50] They held that study was the prerogative of the well-born, the wealthy who could afford it, the strong who possessed the

---

45 *B. Aboda Zara* 8b.
46 *Ibid.*
47 Cf. *Abot d'R. Natan* I, ch. 3; II, ch. 4, ed. Schechter 7b.
48 *Tosefta Yebamot* 8.7, ed. Lieberman, p. 26, and parallel passages. Later, Ben Azzai married the daughter of R. Akiba (*B. Ketubot* 63a).
49 *B. Ketubot* 62b.
50 *Abot d'R. Natan, loc. cit.*

energy for it, and the brilliant who could master the Torah. But the School of Hillel said, "One teaches anyone; for many sinful people who came to study the Torah turned out to be righteous saints."[51]

THE STUDY OF TORAH was particularly helpful in the administration of civil justice in cases where the judge had to weigh the opposing values and claims of the litigants. Study of Biblical and Pharisaic jurisprudence was, therefore, especially valuable in the development of ethical acumen. The Pharisaic judge, seeking to know the will of God in the case before him, sharpened his own intellect and that of his disciples by reviewing the methodology needed for such inquiry. The decisions of earlier judges could be questioned, argued and reappraised. The Pharisee struggled, like all upright judges, to rise above all personal motivation. He tried as far as possible to serve as the spokesman of the Divine. "Whoever wishes to achieve wisdom," said a Sage of later age, "should devote himself to the study of the civil law; for there is no branch of the Torah above it, because it is like a never-failing fountain."[52]

While study of juristic decisions might be particularly helpful in preparation for the moral life, the student would also profit from earlier decisions dealing with ritual. Because such decisions generally present fewer complexities than those of jurisprudence, study of ritual questions served as introduction to the broader and deeper disciplines of the ethical life. Learning to serve God selflessly, one might also learn to serve man selflessly.

Perfection of self and pursuit of the good life, however, would be beyond the reach of the most competent man, if he had to plan every act, weigh it in the scales of merit, and

---

51 *Ibid.*
52 Mishna *Baba Batra,* end.

assay its relation to the right. Fortunately, the Torah provided guides and offered specific instruction in many areas of conduct.

The system of ritualistic and juristic obligations prescribed in the Pentateuch and elaborated in the Oral Tradition constituted an indispensable road map for the traveller through life. When the Sabbath approached, the Pharisee did not have to decide for himself exactly when the holy day began nor just what labor might be performed on it. In the area of commerce, he did not, in general, have to analyze to what extent he might attract custom to himself and away from his neighbor without acting improperly. Such issues had been worked out in sufficient detail to enable him to concentrate on more subtle problems. The Torah, and especially the Oral Tradition, presented to the Pharisee specific norms of recommended ethical behavior, although these were usually less precise than those of ritual and juristic law, were flexible and subject to varying applications and interpretations, and were not enforceable in the courts of law.

THE PHARISEES also taught that in order to study effectively one needed not only a teacher, but also a colleague.[53] A fellow student was important in helping to criticize one's intellectual efforts and, even more, in translating intellectual achievement into moral decisions.

Discovery of the reality about ourselves, which is obvious to others yet usually concealed from us, presents one of the most formidable challenges to the ethical life. The Pharisee knew that he was blind to his own failings, and that he, like other people, idealized himself in a form quite unrecognizable to anyone else.

Professor Higgins, in G. B. Shaw's *Pygmalion,* is puzzled because though in his own estimation he was "a shy, diffident

---

53 Mishna *Abot,* 1.6.

sort of man" who had "never been able to feel really grown-up and tremendous, like other chaps," he was widely considered to be "an arbitrary, overbearing, bossing kind of person." In the Talmudic tradition, Shammai doubtless believed that he obeyed his own maxim to receive everyone with a ready and pleasant welcome. But that was not the appearance he gave, according to numerous observers whose descriptions of Shammai have been recorded in the Talmud.

Man must do more than summon the energy to discover what seems to be the right and to pursue it. He also has to overcome a bias in his own favor. Having lived with himself all his life, he has become accustomed to his own failings and readily accepts them. Indeed, he may be a sinner in the very area in which he regards himself as a saint. Through a peculiar quirk of personality, one frequently projects one's faults on others, thinking he is free of guilt because he denounces it.

The Pharisees taught that a colleague who restored one's humility rather than fed one's arrogance, who loved one's best self and did not cater to one's worst, was the best and most creative of friends.

THE THREE ELEMENTS in Judaism distinguished by Pharisaism, namely, intellectual preparation for decision-making, obedience to ritual and juristic norms, and acceptance of traditional ethics, were summarized by Simeon the Righteous in his famous apothegm, "The world stands on three pillars: on the Torah, on the ritual, and on deeds of loving kindness."[54] The "Torah" stressed by Simeon the Righteous is more than technical scholarship. It is hard to suppose that the High Priest considered simple study of the Law as an inherently more important element in the triad of Jewish service to God than the Temple ritual over which he pre-

---

54 *Ibid.*, 1.3.

sided. The value attached by Simeon to Torah suggests that for him the word meant precisely what is suggested in the present argument—the mastery of the science of the good life.[55] This comprehensive Torah basically precedes both ritual and ethical norms.

The study which the Pharisees recommended was not an academic discipline which might bring one a doctorate or departmental promotion. Its goal was not merely the satisfaction of curiosity, nor did it cater to one's vanity. It was the Pharisaic analogue of the Chinese suggestion that one try to reform the world beginning with oneself. In the Pharisaic tradition, the scholar and the saint were indistinguishable. Nothing but true saintliness could stimulate the search for scholarship which eschewed normal rewards of talent; on the other hand, as Hillel indicated, the saintliness that the Pharisee sought could be attained only through such study. For this reason, Pharisaic study never became specialized. Nothing human was alien to it. The study of physiology, of zoology, of the physical world, of man's character, of the economy, and even of the techniques of crime, were all relevant to it. Somewhere or other, they touched on the issues of right and wrong. All knowledge was grist to the Pharisee's mill. Every scrap of information might end up as a footnote, so to speak, in his discussion within himself or with his colleagues, about right and wrong.

---

55 The issue whether greater importance attaches to study, because it leads to general personality and character education, or to the observance of specific rituals, came to a head in the famous conference held during the Hadrianic persecutions when, at first, the observance of the commandments was forbidden, but study was not. Many scholars then felt that it was better to flee to the lands of the Diaspora where one could fulfill the rituals, rather than remain in the land of Israel which was still the main center for the study of the Torah. (See *Sifre*, Deuteronomy 41, p. 85, and cross-references there given.) However, the basic issue had developed much earlier, and was the subject of continuous argument between the Schools of Shammai and Hillel throughout many generations. (See *Ha-Perushim*, p. 11, and references there given.)

"I have never heard it maintained," remarks A. E. Housman, in a memorable passage in one of his lectures, "by the wildest enthusiast for Classics that the standard of morality or even of amiability is higher among classical scholars than among men of science." This he says after implying that science itself does little or nothing to improve men's sensitivity to what is right. But for the Pharisee, study which lacked the goal of raising the standards of morality and amiability would be a waste of time. Sheer technical and highly specialized erudition and brilliance would scarcely advance the real fortunes of either scholars or mankind. The Pharisee, therefore, would not find it at all astonishing that a generation such as ours, which boasts more scientists and research scholars than the total of all who had lived in preceding generations, is also marked by bitter anti-intellectualism and by disillusioned, idealistic youth. Scholarship which did not have saintliness (the solution of moral problems) as its goal was, for the Pharisee, "the wisdom of the nations," superfluous at best, and perilous at worst.

Philosophical and Theological Foundations for the Ethical Life

THE PHARISEES RESORTED to several basic philosophical and theological concepts to enable their followers to achieve universal love for their fellow men. The doctrine of the Fatherhood and Kingship of God and the Pharisaic reinterpretation of the concept of holiness have already been discussed. These views led to the emergence of others which provided further stimuli for the life of righteousness, self-denial, and service to mankind.

One of the most important of these doctrines was that of man's immortality.

Pharisaic contempt for the joys of physical life as well as the aspirations and possessions of the temporal world, almost implied the rejection of the body as the essential element in man. If man shared God's holiness in being superior to bodily hungers, this was so because the human personality shared the very nature of God, and was part of a realm of being to which these hungers were alien. If man belonged to this realm of existence, he could not be subject to death. His body might perish and moulder in the earth, like that of animals. But the body was simply a prison in which the spirit was confined during physical life.

This doctrine of the Pharisees may have derived from similar ideas of Socrates and Plato, but this is by no means certain. Whether the doctrine was indigenous or not, it enabled the Pharisee to develop, from his concept that the essence of life was study of Torah, the view that physical existence on earth was essentially a process of education, that life was, in fact, a school from which the spirit is graduated at death into a Heavenly Academy of which God, the angels, and the saints of earlier ages are members.[56] Life beyond physical existence was conceived as admission to a fellowship of scholars who, over endless eons, devote themselves indefatigably and happily to that which the Pharisee so much enjoyed on earth—study of Torah.

The doctrine of the immortality of the soul conferred on every human being supreme dignity and importance. It reduced concern with the inevitable troubles and frustrations of mundane existence to the level of petty and childish querulousness. It also destroyed consciousness of difference of status. Nothing that one might achieve in this world could make one proud, and nothing that one might lack could make one feel inferior to one's neighbor. In the eyes of God, all human spirits were equal in their value and their significance.

Perhaps the early Pharisees already had concluded that

---

[56] See Professor Louis Ginzberg's *Legends of the Jews,* Index, *s.v. Academy, heavenly,* and *Heavenly Academy.*

immortality was the special reward and prerogative of the saintly and the scholarly. Certainly this view was held by later Talmudic scholars. If the world was a school, one might expect only those who benefitted from its opportunities for education to be admitted into the Heavenly Academy. But the early teachers, at least, seem to have been unaware of even this differentiation among people. Everyone appears to have been considered significant in the eyes of an all-merciful, forgiving Father.

The doctrine of human immortality is not mentioned in the Pentateuch or the Prophets. There seem to be some references to it in the Psalms[57] and the Book of Job;[58] and it is specifically mentioned in the Book of Ecclesiastes.[59]

Apparently, the early Prophetic teachers feared that any reference to the survival of man's spirit as an entelechy, independent of the body, might encourage the sometimes obscene rituals associated with ancestor worship and with worship of the dead in general. However, the silence of the Pentateuch and the Prophets concerning the doctrine of immortality should not mislead us into acceptance of the view that early teachers rejected it or were unaware of it. On the contrary, the occasional negations of the doctrine of immortality in Scripture indicate clearly that the idea was widespread. But perhaps it was held appropriate for discussion only with the confines of the Prophetic and Pharisaic academies, and was not to be taught to those likely to misunderstand or misinterpret it.[60]

WHILE THE DOCTRINE of the immortality of the soul was congenial to the moral and ethical conditions of Jerusalem's market place, it could hardly be understood in aristocratic

---

[57] Cf. Ps. 73:16; also Ps. 114:16 (where the doctrine apparently is rejected).
[58] Job 13:15.
[59] Eccl. 3:21.
[60] Cf. discussion of the subject in *New Light from the Prophets*, pp. 4ff.

circles and among the rural populace, even among those ultimately attracted to Pharisaic doctrine. In these groups, the
concept of the after-life took on a totally different form,
namely, that of the future resurrection of the righteous. The
roots of this doctrine might be sought in very early ages of
human civilization. Indeed, belief in life-after-death apparently was held by primitive man in pre-historic times. He
might not have been able to formulate this doctrine in a
verbal proposition, but the manner in which he supplied the
bodies he buried with eating utensils showed that he considered them alive in a special, perhaps dormant, condition.
In Egypt, bodies of the members of royal and aristocratic
families were embalmed, perhaps to be preserved for a future
existence. Zarathustra held that the dead would come to life
when the present eon ended, and a better world would come
into existence. Perhaps even earlier, Isaiah had proclaimed
the future resurrection of the dead as part of the revelation of
the Divine Kingdom.

The concept of the resurrection among the provincial
Pharisees differed from that of most other ancient people in
its association with Divine judgment, when the righteous of
the world would be awakened to eternal bliss, and the wicked
would be condemned either to non-existence or to torment.

In Talmudic Judaism, the mutually inconsistent concepts
of immortality and the resurrection were combined.[61] There
is evidence that in the School of Hillel, the doctrine of
human immortality alone was accepted, and that the entire
theology of the Day of Judgment, the punishment of the
wicked in the future world, and the resurrection of the dead,
was rejected. The School of Shammai, on the contrary, held
fast to the notion of a future resurrection, a Day of Judgment, with the condemnation of the wicked to eternal tor-

---

61 See *Mabo*, pp. 215ff. for further discussion of this subject.

ment, of the majority of mankind to some period of punishment, and of the saintly alone to ultimate resurrection.[62]

The doctrine of the resurrection of the dead, while providing support for certain aspects of Pharisaic ethics, did not involve the negation of the pleasures of the temporal world nor of its ambitions. Those deprived of happiness in the present world might be comforted with the thought that they would be offered appropriate compensation for their suffering in the Messianic times. The rural and aristocratic Pharisees might regard the future Divine Kingdom as one in which God would indeed reign, but in which a Davidic or Aaronid descendant would be His viceroy, while Israel would at last come into its own as the ruling people of the world. Certainly, there was nothing in the doctrine of the resurrection of the righteous to lead one necessarily to ascribe special dignity to every neighbor, or to negate the importance of status and possessions in the present world.

Thus, the concept of the resurrection of the righteous was entirely congenial to those converts to Pharisaism from rural and aristocratic groups who could not share its basic rejection of the goods and ambitions of the temporal world.[63]

Both Pharisaic views, adopted by the Talmudists and indeed by all the religions of the Western world, exerted a profound, although not decisive, influence on human conduct through many generations. As is well known, Maimonides, in his *Guide for the Perplexed,* mentioned only the doctrine of man's immortality. In his other writings, however, he also

---

[62] See *Abot d'R. Natan* I, ch. 41, end, ed. Schechter 67a. It seems obvious from the tradition, transmitted by R. Jose, that only the Shammaites held the view that in the Day of Judgment there would be a division of people into three groups—the righteous, to enjoy immortal bliss; the wicked, to suffer eternal torment; and the middle group, to suffer some punishment, preparatory to complete forgiveness. The School of Hillel held that all transgressions are forgiven at death. That is why they held, too, that no sin-offering might be sacrificed on behalf of one who had died; whereas the Shammaites held that it might. (See discussion of the subject in *Hanoch Albeck Jubilee Volume*, pp. 355f.)

[63] Cf. discussion of this subject in *Mabo*, pp. 213ff.

accepted the belief in the resurrection, giving the doctrine varying interpretations at different periods in his life.

No LESS IMPORTANT than the eschatological doctrines of man's immortality and resurrection was the view that having done wrong, man could, if he so desired, obtain complete forgiveness from God, who would then transform even errors or transgressions into meritorious behavior. Even when an act was in itself irreversible, repentance was necessary and indispensable to man's life. For it was only through man's continual awareness of his tendency to err that he could educate himself to avoid wrong-doing and become ever more righteous, more holy, more God-like, throughout his life.

Thus, just as disdain for possessions, status and pleasures enabled the Pharisee to be oblivious of the frustrations of life, so the concept of repentance enabled him to escape the burdens of remorse and regret for the inexorable past. No matter how deeply conscious he might be of God's perfection and his own imperfection, he need not sink into unhappiness because of unwitting or even willful wrong-doing. A merciful Father would provide him with full pardon for any transgression.[64] One might regret youthful error, and even be conscious of all the evil which followed in its train, without morbid sense of guilt or even (to use Maimonides' word) of "shame." Man begins life as an imperfect being; that is inevitable. The issue is whether he will use his years on earth to perfect himself, for perfection in Pharisaism was a process rather than a condition. Thus it was possible for one sage to maintain that "One hour of the bliss of the future life is better than all of temporal existence; and yet one hour of repentance and good deeds during existence is better than all of the future life."[65]

---

[64] See Maimonides, *Hilkot Teshubah*, particularly 1.3; but cf. *Mekilta Jethro, Bahodesh*, ch. 7, p. 228, and parallel passages there noted.
[65] Mishna *Abot* 4.17.

CLOSELY ALLIED with the Pharisees' doctrine of human immortality was their concept of Providence and freedom of the will. As Josephus indicates, the Pharisees believed in a degree of free will,[66] but they maintained that virtually everything man does has been foreseen and therefore preordained by God. (Only in the second century C.E. did R. Akiba formulate the paradoxical principle, "All is foreseen, but freedom is granted [man].") [67]

The Pharisaic negation of man's freedom was a necessary element in their philosophy of life. They did not regard failure in the market place, or poverty, as something for which an individual should blame himself. One's economic condition, like one's state of health, intellectual capacity, longevity, or vigor, were determined at birth. According to R. Akiba,[68] they were determined by heredity. While the Pharisees frequently spoke in praise of the dignity and importance of labor,[69] even of menial work, they regarded it simply as part of one's duty to participate in the maintenance of civilized life, and not as a virtue in itself, because it led to profit.

Thus, the Pharisee who found himself a failure in the market place could live with himself quite happily, conscious, of course, of his poverty, but not blaming himself in any way. On the contrary, he could trust that all would be well, for man's fate was in the hands of God. On the other

---

[66] Cf. discussion of the subject in *The Pharisees*, pp. 195ff. and references there given.

[67] Mishna *Abot* 3.15.

[68] Mishna *Eduyyot* 2.9. See further, such passages as *B. Niddah* 16b, where we are told that one's economic condition, one's vigor, and other qualities are determined at birth; and *B. Ta'anit* 25a, where the story told of R. Eleazar implies the belief that one's economic status is determined neither by one's efforts nor one's merits, but by the period in which one happens to live. According to R. Hanina, Israelites (like everyone else) are subject to fate. (This statement was disputed by R. Johanan, *ibid.*) Examples of such views may be multiplied.

[69] Mishna *Abot* 1.10; 2.2; 3.7 *et al.* Cf. also *Abot d'R. Natan* I, ch. 11; II, ch. 21, ed. Schechter 22a ff. and parallel passages there noted.

hand, success was not to be ascribed, even in one's mind, to one's own cleverness and wisdom, but to the mercies of God. In times of danger, one did not lose oneself in panic; in success, one still had to remember that were it not for Divine protection all one's talents might lead to disaster.

Only in one area of life, did the Pharisees believe that freedom of the will prevailed—in the choice between following the path of righteousness or leaving it.

The Pharisaic doctrine reflected the views of a group which held that (a) no one had a right to look down on a person who had failed in life; (b) no one had a right to feel that one's follies (except in the area of ethics and religion) had contributed to his disaster; (c) one ought to make the study of the good life one's main concern, and one's remunerative labor secondary to it; (d) in one's decisions and activities, it would be folly to violate the Divine Will which required one to act justly, in an attempt to improve one's lot in the temporal world; for one could not know whether any particular decision would be beneficial to one's fortunes, whereas the evil which one perpetrated could not be doubted.

As ALREADY OBSERVED, the early Pharisees, and indeed their successors for many generations, went even further. They held that prosperity, longevity, and other temporal blessings were preordained and were not affected even by the merit of one's deeds. It was easy for the Pharisees to accept this view because of their contempt for the world's goods.[70] But to the majority of the Jews, and even to the members of the affluent and rural groups who were attracted to Pharisaic ranks, the doctrine that all of life (except one's way of life) was preordained, seemed to destroy all notions of human accountability and responsibility.

---

70 See above, p. 48.

The early Pharisees and their Hillelite followers did not deem it necessary to suggest that the wicked who prospered in this world were doomed to suffer in the future life. They held that man should serve God out of love for Him,[71] and were quite content to accept the doctrine that "the world is judged with mercy, and not according to the majority of one's deeds."[72] They also hold that immortality was the portion of every man, with very few exceptions;[73] and that death atoned for any but the most heinous transgressions.

They refused to ask the questions raised by Job, namely, why he suffered. Nor did they see merit in the answers given by Job's friends, namely, that he suffered because he deserved it. They believed that it was useless to explore the reasons for human agony, and particularly for the disasters which came upon the righteous, no less frequently than on the wicked. Misfortunes are part of life and must be accepted as expressions of Divine Love.

This portion of early Pharisaic doctrine was rejected by the Shammaitic and pre-Shammaitic scholars who held that worship based on fear of God is superior to worship based on love for Him,[74] and that no matter what may be the portions of the wicked and the righteous in temporal life, the scales would be balanced on the Day of Judgment.[75]

---

[71] See above, p. 43.

[72] The maxim of R. Akiba, Mishna *Abot* 3.15. As found in most prayer books, this passage reads: "The world is judged with mercy; *and everything is according to the majority of one's deeds.*" The reading found in some printed editions of the Mishna is an emendation of copyists who could not bear to ascribe to R. Akiba a view which seemed heretical to them, namely that the world is not judged according to the majority of the deeds. However, see variant readings cited in the Romm edition of the Mishna; in *Tosafot Yom Tob;* and in Charles Taylor, *Sayings of the Jewish Fathers*, pp. 27, 48, 61, 89, 96, 97, 132.

[73] For a discussion of the subject and an analysis of the passages involved, see *Mabo*, pp. 213ff.

[74] See *Abot d'R. Natan* II, ch. 10, ed. Schechter 13b; and Schechter's notes *ad loc.* Cf. discussion of the passage in *Mabo*, pp. 32ff.

[75] See above, p. 76.

On the other hand, quite aside from the fundamental issue of the theodicy, the combination of the doctrines of Providence and freedom of the will, which was basic to Pharisaism, was beyond the comprehension of the peasantry and many members of the urban aristocracy. The Sadducees could not believe that their affluence and good fortune were unconnected to their own superior merit, or at least to the superior merit of their ancestors. Neither could they agree that their successes were simply accidents, and not the result of their wisdom and cleverness. Thus they denied the Pharisaic view that all is preordained, and stressed, instead, the doctrine of man's complete freedom.[76]

The simpler peasantry, out of whose ranks the Essenes were drawn, shared the Pharisaic view that poverty was neither the fault of man nor a reflection of God's anger at man's impiety. However, they sought to escape the Pharisaic paradox by preaching a doctrine of complete predestination which left no room for freedom of the will. In their opinion, they were the chosen ones, the elect, who had to undergo hardships in this world, but who would be rewarded with endless bliss in another life. Even their piety was not of their own choice. They had been selected for their calling, and had been assigned the tasks devolving on them in this world, as well as the rewards which awaited them in the future.[77]

The logical paradoxes and contradictions involved in some of their doctrines evidently gave the Pharisees themselves no concern. As already observed, the Talmudic authorities and their successors found it possible to accept both the view that man's soul is immortal, and the principle of the physical resurrection of the dead. We shall examine presently an even

---

[76] See *The Pharisees,* pp. 195ff., and references there given.
[77] Cf. Josephus, *Antt.* XIII, 5.9; and see discussion in *The Pharisees,* pp. 254ff. Cf. now, *Manual of Discipline* of the Sect of the Judaean Desert, 3, 1.16; 4, 1.24; etc.

more difficult concept basic to Pharisaism, which the simple peasant or urban aristocrat found difficult to accept, namely, that mutually contradictory teachings were both right. Thus, the combination of the notion of man's freedom with that of Divine Providence, which has troubled philosophers in so many ages, was quite congenial to the Pharisees. Like some modern physicists, they were willing to agree that if reality seems paradoxical, we must accept that fact and not endeavor to explain it away.

ONE MAY READILY TRACE the influence of all three Pharisaic notions—man's immortality, the power of repentance, and the combination of the notions of man's freedom of will and Divine Providence—on later thought and culture. Yet later generations, in their penchant for logical simplicities and their aversion to recognizing paradoxes as truths, generally have wavered between full acceptance of the Sadducean doctrine of absolute freedom, and the Essene doctrine of absolute determination. The successful industrialist or military hero rarely admits that his share in his achievement is at most minuscule. The Moslem and the Calvinist deny any element of choice in human affairs. A descendant of the Pharisees who aspires to be their disciple may be forgiven for considering this a pity; for both doctrines have caused great and unnecessary grief to unfortunate, innocent men and women. Parents whose children have in some degree failed, are endlessly haunted by the blame they feel. And those who feel themselves condemned to failure are frequently deprived of the sense of initiative which, whatever it might achieve, would itself be a source of comfort to them. Indeed, some of the major disasters which have marked the twentieth century may be ascribed to Marxist determinism which (although Karl Marx probably was totally unconscious of the fact) was a lineal descendant of the doctrines of the Essenes and the Apocalyptists of the Second Jewish Commonwealth.

The Ethics of Pluralism

ONE OF THE MOST CURIOUS and significant characteristics of Pharisaism was that it was not a unified system at all. As already observed, there were at least two schools of thought considered equally valid by all Pharisees, who viewed both as the words of "the Living God."[78] The rural and urban Pharisees disagreed on such theoretical issues as the meaning of holiness, and the immortality of the soul versus the resurrection of the body, as well as on such fundamental problems as the nature of Divine Revelation,[79] laws of marriage and divorce,[80] and an endless number of rituals including those dealing with permitted and prohibited food. Nevertheless, we are told that Pharisees permitted marriages between members of the opposing groups,[81] did not hesitate to eat in one another's homes,[82] and generally followed the principle that the rules of each system were those which its followers ought to obey.[83]

Indeed, until the time of the Maccabees, teachers of the two factions taught their disciples both systems of theology and Law.[84] And until the excitement and panic of the revolt

---

[78] *Yer. Berakot* 1.7, 3b.

[79] See *Sifre*, Deuteronomy 83, p. 148, notes; and cf. A. J. Heschel, *Torah Min Hashamayim*, II, pp. 146ff.

[80] Mishna *Yebamot* 1.4; *Qiddushin* 1.1; *et al.*

[81] Mishna *Yebamot, loc. cit.;* and parallel passages.

[82] *Ibid.*

[83] See *B. Yebamot* 14b; and cf. discussion by Professor Saul Lieberman in *Tosefta Kifeshutah, Yebamot,* p. 8.

[84] Cf. *B. Temurah* 15b where we are told that until the time of Jose b. Joezer, the Torah was taught "as Moses" had given it—i.e. there were no differences of opinion. This cannot mean that there were no differences of practice, for the differences between the Schools of Shammai and Hillel, as well as those recorded in the names of later scholars, surely had their roots in very ancient

against Rome, in the last days of the Commonwealth, neither group tried to impose uniformity of practice on the nation at large.[85]

The early Pharisees were not troubled by the question of how it was possible to accept the validity of diametrically opposed views. They had received both traditions from earlier generations and were content to accept the paradoxical doctrine that in giving His commandments to His people, God had permitted diversity of interpretation. On a practical

---

traditions. It means rather that all scholars taught their disciples both systems. That is, apparently, what is meant by the statement that until the time of Jose b. Joezer, the leaders were *eshkolot;* thereafter, there were no more *eshkolot* (*B. Temurah loc. cit.,* Mishna *Sotah* 9.10). The term is interpreted to mean "a person who has everything" (*B. Temurah loc. cit.*). It seems probable that Rabban Johanan b. Zakkai sought to revive this ancient tradition, teaching his disciples both systems of Law. This appears to be the meaning of the tradition preserved in *Abot d'R. Natan* I, ch. 14, ed. Schechter 29a, and *Abot d'R. Natan* II, ch. 28, ed. Schechter 29b, and parallel passages which affirm that Rabban Johanan b. Zakkai had mastered every part of the Oral Tradition. This would seem to be slight praise, indeed, for the outstanding scholar of his age, unless we assume that, unlike all other scholars, he mastered both the Shammaitic and the Hillelite traditions. This would seem to be the implication of Mishna *Abot* 2.8 as well, according to which "Rabban Johanan b. Zakkai received the tradition from Hillel *and Shammai,*" and this despite the fact that he was an ardent Hillelite. It would also explain the curious fact that one of his disciples, R. Eliezer b. Hyrkanos, turned out to be the leader of the Shammaitic faction in the following generation, while another disciple, R. Joshua b. Hananya, held the same position among the Hillelites.

85 The first effort to impose the views of one School on the whole community apparently occurred when the Shammaites, on the eve of the revolution against Rome in the year 66 C.E., found themselves in the majority. Hence they issued the famous Eighteen Decrees, concerning which see Mishna *Shabbat* 1.4 and *B.* and *Yer. ad loc.* Apparently, R. Gamaliel's harshness toward those who deviated from his teachings was due to his desire to create a uniform tradition which was to be eclectic, with both Shammaitic and Hillelite elements. The decision taken in Yabneh, establishing the Hillelite tradition as the authoritative one, came about as a result of the recognition that it was necessary to introduce uniform practices among Jews after the Temple was destroyed and the future was so uncertain. The majority of the Academy in Yabneh being Hillelite, the view of that School prevailed. (See *Tosefta Yebamot* 1.13, ed. Lieberman, p. 4; *Tosefta Kifeshutah;* and parallel passages.)

level, they accepted the validity of local interpretations of the ancient tradition, recording both for future generations.

Some of the differences between the Pharisaic factions concerned issues far more fundamental than those which divided Pharisaism from either Sadducism or Essenism. Yet the Pharisees considered the latter systems unauthorized and objectionable, and took vigorous steps to prevent their acceptance among the people. Inevitably, the question arises: Why should the Pharisees, so willing to encourage independent thought and conduct within their own group, have been so intolerant of deviations by the Sadducees and the Essenes?

THE ANSWER MUST BE SOUGHT not in the individual issues raised by these sects, but *in their attitude toward Pharisaism.* It is not only in the Gospels that the Pharisees are described as hypocritical; the charge was made, as Professor David Flusser has pointed out, as early as the organization of the Essene sect.[86] The simple peasant found the sophisticated Pharisaic paradox impossible to accept. Their insistence that two contradictory views were both equally correct, although the follower of one faction was bound by the customs of his ancestors, did not make sense to the rustic. He concluded from their very tolerance that the Pharisees did not take religion seriously, indeed, that they were hypocrites. This view was reinforced by their suspicion of the Pharisaic civility in conversation, their polished manners, and their general urban behavior, all of which seemed alien and artificial to the farmer.[87]

Thus, it came about that the Essenes substituted for the Oral Tradition of the Pharisees, which perpetuated the contradictory views of their factions, written codes. These in-

---

[86] See *G. Allon Memorial Volume,* p. 136.
[87] Cf. *The Pharisees,* pp. 97, 837, notes 48–52.

cluded such works as the Manual of Discipline and the Damascus Document, as well as the earlier Book of Jubilees.[88] The Pharisaic scholars were condemned as transgressors of the very Law which they preached, and in the name of which they taught the people.

The equally simple-minded, but far wealthier, priestly Sadducees rejected the Pharisaic system with similar vigor, because according to them, the interpretation of the Torah was entrusted not to the lay Pharisaic scholars, no matter how learned, but to the Temple priests, no matter how ignorant. It was probably the Sadducees who gave the Pharisees their name, *Perushim,* meaning sectarians, for they regarded rejection of their own priestly views and authority as sectarianism.[89]

It was the refusal of the Sadducees and the Essenes to accept scholarly Pharisaic interpretation of the Law and validation of opposing views, which compelled the Pharisees to declare them "in error"[90] or followers "of another way."[91] Their actual rejection by the Pharisees did not occur until the rise of the Maccabean state, when a consensus concerning the practices to be accepted by the nation as a whole had to be agreed upon.

Recognition of diverse and inconsistent interpretations of the Law as being equally valid, continued to be characteristic of Pharisaism throughout the generations. Passionate adherence to the traditions which one had imbibed in one's childhood and youth, in one's parental home or at school,

---

[88] As the reader will observe, I accept the general consensus according to which the Sect of the Judaean Scrolls were, in fact, the Essenes, or at least a particular group of Essenes.

[89] Cf. *Ha-Perushim,* pp. 24ff.

[90] See the reference to "those in error" in the prayer *Habinenu* (*B. Berakot* 29a).

[91] Cf. the discussion by Professor Saul Lieberman in *Tosefta Kifeshutah, Berakot,* p. 122; and in *Proceedings of the American Academy for Jewish Research* XX, pp. 395ff.

remained an integral part of the Pharisaic tradition in Talmudic and post-Talmudic times; and it existed together with an equally passionate determination to respect the opposing views of those reared in them.

When Sir Isaiah Berlin remarks, in his *Four Essays on Liberty* (p. 167),

> One belief, more than any other, is responsible for the slaughter of individuals on the altars of great historical ideals—justice or progress or the happiness of future generations, or the sacred mission or emancipation of a nation or race or class, or even liberty itself, which demands the sacrifice of individuals for the freedom of society. This is the belief that somewhere, in the past or in the future, in divine revelation or in the mind of an individual thinker, in the pronouncements of history or science, or in the simple heart of an uncorrupted good man, there is a final solution.

he is, *mutatis mutandis,* echoing the underlying thesis of Pharisaism.

From the point of view of the Pharisees, it was possible that what was right in the market place of Jerusalem might be wrong in the hamlets surrounding the capital city.[92] What might be commendable for a wealthy aristocrat might be wicked for a beggar. They left it to their teachers to work out specific judgments and evaluations. Indeed, the whole Talmud is an effort to discover what is right under one set of circumstances and yet wrong under another, and at the same time whether diverse and contradictory views can be reconciled logically and made into a coherent whole.[93]

---

92 Cf. *The Pharisees*, pp. 780ff., and *Sifre,* Deuteronomy 146, p. 200, where we are told that although the "pillars" were beloved in the days of the Patriarchs, they were objectionable in the time of their descendants.
93 *The Pharisees,* pp. 780ff.

Many of the Pharisees and their disciples concluded, at different times, that the variety of accepted opinion and judgment imperiled the survival of the faith and the people. However, it is probably this very flexibility that enabled both the Jewish faith and Jewish people to endure the harsh persecutions of the Middle Ages and the continuous challenges to Judaism throughout the centuries.

IN A TIME when means of rapid communication and transportation are transforming all mankind into a single community, with close juxtaposition of differences in economic status, educational and cultural background, and traditional custom—precisely as they were in the Athens of Solon, the Rome of the Gracchi, and the Jerusalem of the Pharisees—the mutual respect and cultural pluralism urged by the Pharisees, may be an important element in the avoidance of ultimate worldwide revolution.

The hungry African or Asian sees movies reflecting the luxuries of the affluent West. Too often, he loses his self-respect together with his faith in his own tradition. Of the traditions of the West, he chooses only the outer accouterments, just as Near Eastern Asians adopted from the conquering Greeks of Alexander's time, not Homer and Euripides, but the far more easily mastered exercises and habits of the *gymnasia,* so repellent to their forefathers. Similarly, the Occidental often finds it difficult to appreciate profundities and values inherent in the great Eastern civilizations of China, Japan and India. But those ancient civilizations, "backward" as they may seem to the pleasure-seeking, overindulged Occidental, have their own invaluable merits and are possibly indispensable to the real happiness and fulfillment of the peoples which have given them birth.

Statesmanlike planning for the future begins with the acceptance of human civilization as pluralistic and complex, with the recognition that, rooted in differing surroundings and exposed to differing conditions, the human mind has created for different peoples modes of thought and behavior congenial and necessary for them. To impose foreign value systems on people is to injure their souls. In the spirit of the Pharisees, the values of both Western and Eastern civilizations must be viewed with a combination of passion and detachment; with passion by those who are heirs to this genius, and with detachment enabling those in love with their own traditions to recognize the right and duty of others to bestow equal love on their own civilization.

Conclusion

WHATEVER ELSE Pharisaism may have to teach us in the intellectual and moral turbulence of our time, one lesson which we may derive from it is pre-eminent. It is that, for many people, perhaps even the vast majority, the satiation of the basic physical hungers of life are less important than the satisfaction of life's spiritual hungers—to serve, to create, to know, to lead a meaningful life.

This insight of Pharisaism is amply documented, on the one hand, in the clinical observations of psychiatrists and, on the other, in the rise of modern nationalism in developing nations and their rejection of the most benevolent paternalism by outside powers. Every parent can observe the child's desire, from nursery age through late adolescence, to take risks which are his own, his willingness to suffer hardships and reject help from any quarter, in order to feel that he, too, can create and contribute and serve. Perhaps these moral and spiritual hungers reach their greatest intensity in adolescence. In adulthood, many a scholar and scientist has pursued his work under trying conditions, without expectation of reward and often without expectation of recognition, driven merely by the desire to understand, to know, to create systematic structures of recorded fact out of seemingly chaotic occurrence. Many a philanthropist has performed for others menial labor which he would disdain doing on his own behalf.

The tragedy of mankind in the twentieth century seems to be that even many of its creative spirits have lost the joy which has always been the birthright of the creator. This deprivation seems to be due entirely to the astonishing rise of concern with immediate monetary returns, rapid recognition, and the achievement of power. In the search for these gains, altogether dissociated from the real pleasures of creation, the latter often is forgotten completely. Thus, those who should be the moral and spiritual leaders of the age are themselves competitors in the market place, and cease to lead because they are not morally in the van of the community.

The tragedy is compounded by the world-wide substitution of the modern nation-state for the ancient family, clan or tribe, as the prime claimant for human loyalties. Even when the individual is able to overcome his personal hunger for power, he simply transfers that hunger to the nation-state of which he is part. In this manner, he satisfies both his craving to serve and his craving to dominate. He serves his particular people, and as part of it, he finds fulfillment in the expectation that he will achieve primacy in the world.

That was, indeed, as far as many of the rural-aristocratic faction in ancient Pharisaism could move toward selflessness. But this was a negation of the doctrines of the School of Hillel as well as of its predecessors and its successors. For them, mankind as a whole was God's people. The Pharisees' loyalty to the Jewish people was only part of a greater and deeper loyalty to mankind. They conceived of Israel as a "kingdom of priests and a holy people" (Exod. 19:6), in the sense that their people was to be a priest-people, dedicated to the service of mankind, precisely as the individual was simi-larly dedicated to the welfare of his fellow man.

The Pharisees did not seek to do away with different peoplehoods and nationalities. But they wished to teach every nation, beginning with their own, that the goal of the indi-vidual man must be creative service to a transcendent cause, and that the goal of the nation and of the nation-state must likewise be service. They rejected the notion that only mem-bers of the people of Israel possessed immortality of the soul. That attribute was shared by every righteous person.[94] A late second century Sage, echoing earlier teachers of his group, held that a Gentile who lives in accordance with the Torah is above the High Priest who ministers in the Temple.[95]

Without for a moment detracting from the urgent need to prevent man's physical annihilation through expansion of his numbers and the pollution and exhaustion of the earth's natural resources; without questioning the need for a re-assessment of the social and political structures which proved so useful in simpler stages of human development but which may need adjustment to the complexities of modern techno-logical civilization; should we not also seek a meaningful pursuit for the mind of man, which would bring him joys similar to those which study of Torah provided the descend-ants and disciples of the Pharisees in their darkest hours? Does the social responsibility of science end with efforts to undo what has already been done? Would it be beyond the power of modern humanistic research to discover how simple men and women can find fulfillment in creative art and service to others? For twenty centuries, the followers of the Pharisees dwelt on what Professor Jeremias used to call "a

---

[94] *B. Sanhedrin* 105a; *Tosefta, ibid.* 13.2, ed. Zuckermandel p. 434; and cf. *Mabo,* p. 223.
[95] *Sifra Ahare (Mekilta d'Arayot)*, *perek* 13.13, ed. Weiss 86b; *B. Sanhedrin* 59a.

portable territory," namely, the Torah, their tree of life. Can we not discover an analogous tree of life for all our children —in the West and in the East? Might not this be a realistic moral equivalent of war, such as William James sought in his day, but which has thus far eluded us?

The question of the survival of mankind in these perilous times may depend in part on the reply to these questions. The Pharisees managed to preserve their own people; might not some echo of their doctrine enable humanity to survive the greater dangers it faces now, and is apparently destined to face with increasing urgency in the generations to come? Has not the time come for a resurgence of the Pharisaic combination of passion for the truth and recognition that no matter how strong one's convictions may be, alternative views may still be right in the eyes of God? Do we not need to revive, even in this age of such widespread want, the passionate love for wisdom and understanding which marked even the poorest of the Pharisees?

Above all, do we not have to revert to the Pharisaic doctrine, which saw ultimate evil in the suffering of any individual person, no matter how debased, whatever his background, status or lack of knowledge, and recognized ultimate good in the fulfillment of the individual person, whoever he or she might be—for all are the beloved children of the One God.

Doubts About Justice

WALTER KAUFMANN

This paper is dedicated to the memory of Martin Luther King Jr., who fought injustice, embodying and teaching pride, courage, gentleness, and unconquerable freedom from resentment—"out of the mountain of despair a stone of hope."

I

REFLECTION on justice has been close to the heart of Western philosophy at least since Plato; it has been prominent in British moral philosophy; and it attracts some of the best minds today. But most contemporary moral philosophers are as blind historically as were Plato and Kant, Hume and Mill. Nor does it accord with current etiquette to state at the outset why one is interested in the topic one writes about.

My interest in justice is twofold. First, it is existential. I have found myself in situations—or to use less existentialist terminology, on committees—where it was my task to try to make just distributions. As we distributed coveted admissions to a small percentage of students who wished to do graduate work, or raises and promotions to younger colleagues, or Fulbright grants to colleagues all over the country, I found most philosophical discussions of justice oddly irrelevant. Many other authors must have been in comparable situations, but for the most part their writings on the subject do not show it. The point is not that they do not mention such prosaic situations, but rather that these situations point up limitations of otherwise acute analyses of justice.

This reason might suffice, the more so because the existential interest extends far beyond the relatively trivial instances I have mentioned. The moral issues between avowedly capitalistic and avowedly socialistic countries revolve around justice—or at least injustice. So does the civil rights crisis at home. If we include so-called retributive justice, we may add that the central crisis in penology and criminal law for more than a generation now concerns the question whether we should not be better off if we abandoned the very idea of retributive justice, concentrating instead on deterrence and reform. Nothing more needs to be said to establish the importance of the subject of justice.

Even so I have another reason for dealing with it. In 1952 I laid aside a project in social philosophy for other studies, but my work during the next fifteen years has brought me again and again to the brink of justice. A single example will suffice. The relevance of Nietzsche and existentialism to ethics is a commonplace, but references to both by British and American moral philosophers are scarce and usually incredibly ill informed. The time has come to continue what Nietzsche and some of his successors have begun. Still, I shall not deal with their ideas about ethics; I shall concentrate on developing some of my own. But before attempting a detailed analysis of justice, I shall try to sketch our historical context.

II

I WANT TO DISTINGUISH three phases of the current crisis in morality. This is not to say that there are only three, but since I merely want to suggest in broad outlines at what historic juncture we are standing now, it would be foolish to even mention more than three.

The first phase is *the growth of moral skepticism*. This is so familiar that it should suffice to enumerate a few of its elements.

1. For the majority of mankind, religion has lost its authority in moral matters. In the United States, God is still invoked occasionally to back up conflicting positions that were reached in the first place without the benefit of the clergy or the Bible. But even those who still invoke the Bible or their own religious tradition usually pick and choose what they find morally acceptable. A moral conflict between God's commands and their own conscience seems unthinkable to most of our contemporaries. They assume that if even they can see that something is wrong, God must see it too; and if the Bible or tradition does not bear this out, then somebody must have got God wrong. Thus God's name is used in vain. When it is invoked in moral matters, we are almost always confronted with a ritualistic redundancy.

2. Not only has religion lost its authority in moral matters; our whole way of thinking has become anti-authoritarian. This is largely due to the rise of science and more important than the battles between science and religion that are commonly associated with Galileo's name and Darwin's. We have learned the habit of asking: What precisely does this mean? What speaks for it, what against it? What alternatives are available and which are to be preferred? Once these questions become instinctive enough to be directed also toward moral statements, we have moral skepticism. The development of the social sciences has done its share to make this explicit.

3. Increased social mobility has also contributed to this development. Rare is the American family in which all children live out their lives in the town in which they were born. Young people encounter many different environments and are exposed to different mores. Travel is becoming ever

more widespread. All this helps to make unthinking absolutism rarer and rarer among the young, while moral skepticism is gaining ground. Had we stopped with the second
point, it would stand to reason that the trend must be far
more advanced among professors, and especially philosophers, than among students. In fact, this is not so: our moral
philosophers tend to be more conservative than many of their
students. This is due, at least in part, to the fact that many
older men lived in a more stable environment when they
were young, under the tutelage of parents and teachers who
were still closer to absolutism, while those who are students
now cannot recall stability, having been born into a world
wounded by Auschwitz and Nagasaki.

Not only has war eroded moral standards, but service in
armies of occupation has accelerated the growth of moral
skepticism. So has the fact that more and more people live in
big cities where—though not quite as much as in an army
abroad—one can get away with behavior unthinkable in a
small home town.

4. Both the atrocities of our time and the vast anonymity
of metropolitan life have contributed to a widening sense of
futility among young people. Millions have come to feel that
they no longer count and that what they do or don't do will
make no difference. Many have gone beyond moral skepticism into moral nihilism. From the reasonable position that
whatever they do may not make any difference a million
years hence, and perhaps not even 100 years hence, they infer
fallaciously that therefore it makes no difference. In fact,
what we do or do not do may make a tremendous difference
to us and our fellow men right now.

So MUCH for the first phase, the growth of moral skepticism.
The second phase is *skepticism about law*. As for *natural law*,
the collapse of any widespread belief in that is implicit in the

growth of moral skepticism. The very concept of natural law
is not widely familiar: philosophers, lawyers, and theologians
know it; few others do. Not only is the concept mildly
esoteric, but the idea that a single moral law is binding on all
men, regardless of historical period or geography, no longer
seems plausible to most educated people. The Roman Catholic church still clings to this notion, but few except Catholics
do; and many Catholic theologians defend the Inquisition by
saying that it was justified in its time but would not be justi-
fiable today. The ferment within Catholicism today does not
need stressing.

There remains *positive law*, the law actually in force in a
state. The man who did most to promote skepticism about
the moral authority of positive law was Hitler. Whatever one
may think of the many war crimes trials from Nürnberg to
Jerusalem, they did their share to convince millions that
upholding and obeying the law of the state in which he lives
is not always every citizen's moral duty. What a few had
learned earlier from Sophocles' *Antigone,* Thoreau, Tolstoy,
or Gandhi, large masses of people learned from the Nazi
experience. Not only is disobedience to positive law sometimes defensible; there are times when it is a duty.

Politicians point to the loss of respect for the law to
inveigh against it. One can also try to comprehend it as part
of a larger development, as a second phase that takes us
beyond the growth of moral skepticism. Instead of deploring
it one can applaud at least some movements of civil disobedience. But the question remains in what cases civil disobedience is defensible, and when it is morally a duty.

The easy way out is to introduce natural law at this point,
saying: We may, or even ought to, disobey positive law
whenever it comes into conflict with natural law. By beginning my account with the growth of moral skepticism and the
collapse of natural law, I meant to suggest that those who are

counseling us to take this way out are advising us to return to the womb. We can no more return to such naive absolutism than "a flying bird can re-enter the egg shell from which it has emerged"—to quote Tolstoy's words from his *Reply to the Edict of Excommunication* issued against him by the Russian Orthodox church.

Another way out is more popular today: We are told that we may, or ought to, disobey unjust laws, because justice takes precedence over law. With that we come to the third phase of the crisis in morality: *doubts about justice.*

The growth of moral skepticism (phase 1) is one of the most striking features of the twentieth century. In the nineteenth century such skepticism was still rare, and few grasped its implications as clearly as Nietzsche did. Since his death in 1900, moral skepticism has gradually permeated the atmosphere in which we live. Skepticism about law (phase 2) was still rare in 1950, but the civil rights movement and the war in Vietnam are fast making it part of our climate of opinion. Doubts about justice (phase 3) are not yet widespread in any articulate form, and most of our moral philosophers have not reached them yet. At this point I cease to describe what *has* happened and attempt instead to lend a hand to what should happen.

Nietzsche's Zarathustra says: "What is falling, we should still push. Everything today falls and decays: who would check it? But I—I even want to push it" ("On Old and New Tablets," section 20).[1]

---

[1] The student rebellions of 1968 should be seen in this perspective. Many of the rebels had not only lived through skepticism about morality and law but were close to nihilism and despair. Few had reached conscious doubts about justice. But their often alarming self-righteousness did not depend on having seen the face of justice. Sure of the injustice of existing arrangements, they were eager to fight, if not destroy, "the establishment." *Their* application of Zarathustra's dictum was marred by the impatience of youth. They need to be reminded how important it is to evaluate alternatives—and how those who helped to topple the wretched Weimar Republic cleared the way for Hitler.

III

It is unworthy of a philosopher to invoke as an authority what he takes to be the wave of the future. It is not difficult to name trends that we ought to oppose, and it is even easier to enumerate trends that invite neither resistance nor assistance. But the concept of justice is a focal point of the confusions inherent in traditional morality. It looks preeminently objective, even absolute; it seems mathematically precise and not subject to emotion, preferences, or momentous decisions. Both the ancient Hebrews and the ancient Greeks considered justice the sum of the virtues: the just man was for both the good man. To question justice is to probe the very heart of morality, and a critical analysis of the concept of justice might be the fulfillment of the critique of morality attempted but never consummated by Nietzsche, early positivism, and existentialism.

Attempts to mount the bandwagon of history are common and contemptible. But some awareness of historical developments and of the ways in which the meanings of familiar concepts have changed is desirable, albeit rare. It is widely taken for granted that justice is a timeless idea, yet it could be shown that the meanings modern philosophers associate with justice were quite unfamiliar not only to Homer but even to Aeschylus; and Aristotle distinguished that justice which is the sum of the virtues from that justice which is a part of virtue.[2]

This is not the place for a history of the concept of justice, but at the very least we should distinguish four stages in its development. In the *first,* justice was tied to custom, and injustice meant a violation of tradition. In the *second,* justice

---

2 *Nicomachean Ethics,* Book V. 1 and 2.

was the sum of the virtues. This meaning still bears a close relationship to the first stage. In the *third,* justice became a particular virtue. At the cost of some oversimplification, we may associate these three stages with Homer, Plato, and Aristotle, allowing for the presence at each stage of the beginnings of the next one. Aristotle distinguished distributive and rectificatory justice and associated the latter with restitution (not with retribution) ;[3] he also expressly denied that justice could be reduced to reciprocity.[4] At the *fourth* stage, justice is no longer primarily, if at all, a virtue but rather a quality of laws, of arrangements, of distributions, and at one time also, though less and less so, of punishments.

My thesis can be expressed in an extremely simple way: *Punishment can be unjust but never just; and distributions can be unjust but, with the exception of simplistic cases, never just.* Many writers seem prepared to allow the first half of this thesis but proceed as if the collapse of retributive justice were irrelevant to "justice," or at least to distributive justice. *The central point of my paper is to contribute to the collapse of distributive justice.*

It is a commonplace that it is easier to preach morals than to give reasons for morals. It is also easier to praise distributive justice than to bury her. Indeed, it is easier to give reasons for clinging to the concept of distributive justice than it is to expose what is wrong with it.

Not many passages in religious literature are as moving as Isaiah's "seek justice [*mishpat*], correct oppression; defend the fatherless, plead for the widow" (1.17). Among the few that are is Amos' similar but slightly earlier outcry (5.21 ff.). The importance of the concept of justice in modern reform movements has been immense, and though great cruelty has often masked itself with the name of retributive justice, it is

---

3 *Ibid.,* 2–4.
4 *Ibid.,* 5.

possible that even more good has been done in the name of distributive justice. Moreover, it seems far better to call alms *tsedakah* (justice), as Jews have done traditionally, than to parade as charity attempts to mildly ameliorate incredible injustices.

The case for clinging to the concept of distributive justice probably rests mainly on three points. The appeal for justice is rhetorically immensely powerful. It does not hurt the self-respect of those who receive. And it *seems* to be an irreducible principle that cannot be given up without inviting distributions against which our moral sense rebels. Of course, this moral sense has a history and was influenced decisively by the Hebrew prophets; but so was mine.

If my aim were to persuade, the best strategy would be to begin with an attack on the concept of retributive justice, mobilizing your humane feelings against retribution and revenge, pointing up what seems wrong with this concept, and then to let the concept of distributive justice die of the aftereffects. But in one short paper there is not time enough to deal with both, and the case against retributive justice is much more familiar and needs less to be restated. Indeed, retributive justice is no longer a sacred cow; she may be attacked with impunity. But even some philosophers who find her utterly repugnant or "quite incredible"[5] still consider distributive justice the quintessence of morality or at least, along with benevolence, one of "the two 'cardinal' moral virtues."[6] One might suppose that the two were not that different; that both consisted in meting out to men what they deserve; and that both might die of the realization that this cannot be done.

Since I must limit myself, I shall confine my attention to the more attractive sister, in an attempt to show how con-

---

[5] William Frankena, *Ethics* (1963), p. 59.
[6] *Ibid.*, p. 50.

fused she turns out to be on close inspection. So much for preliminaries. Let us now distinguish two conceptions of just distribution and call the first *material* and the second *formal*.[7]

IV

MATERIAL CONCEPTIONS of justice tell us what should be meted out to each. One formulation, mentioned already in the first book of Plato's *Republic*, suggests that justice consists in giving each his due. In Latin: *suum cuique*, to each his own. The trouble with that definition is that it is circular and vacuous. What is due a man is indeed what justice requires to be given to him; but as long as we do not know what justice requires or what would be just, it does not help us in the least to be told *suum cuique*. The concepts of "due" and *suum* (his own) are derived from a prior conception of what is just, and as long as we do not know what is just these notions are void of content and hence of no help.

This is not the time to examine, one by one, the conceptions of justice advanced in Plato's *Republic* and in ethical and legal literature since his time. Instead of dealing very briefly with a great many suggestions, let us deal in detail with one—*that justice consists in giving each what he deserves*[8] —and then ask whether a few other, especially prominent suggestions represent improvements on this formulation.

The most suggestive comment on this definition of justice is Hamlet's: "Use every man after his desert, and who should 'scape whipping?" (II.2). These words remind us how inseparable distributive justice is from retributive justice. Like *suum cuique*, this definition covers retribution no less than the distribution of good things. And the good men deserve is

---

[7] We shall get to the formal conception in section VIII.
[8] Because I accept this definition and have some notion of what justice is, I can say that punishment can be unjust but never just, etc.

as incalculable as the suffering they deserve—if indeed it makes any sense to say that a man deserves to suffer.

It is impossible to say how much income Dr. Cutter, the surgeon, deserves; or Professor Wisdom; or this carpenter; or that miner; or what kind of housing each deserves; or how much free time per day, per week, per year. Neither does it make sense to label any particular distribution of such goods among doctors, teachers, carpenters, and miners "just." Suppose a college can admit only one-fifth of the students applying for admission. It would be preposterous in almost all cases to say that 800, and only 800, deserved to be admitted, and that the decision of accepting these particular students, while turning down the rest, was just.

Instead of immediately invoking the traditional abstractions—equality, ability, need, or merit, to which we shall get around in due time—let us begin by considering a little more concretely what might conceivably be relevant to the determination of desert in a vast variety of cases. We shall distinguish eight categories, most of them with many subclasses. This can be done more easily in a chart, but it is essential here and now to communicate some idea of the complexity of the matter. The first category is

I.   *What one is:*
     A. by birth:
          1. ethnic group
          2. social class.

To consider such matters conceivably relevant is not necessarily inhumane or reactionary. In India, for example, members of the so-called depressed classes are held to deserve preferred treatment in some cases, such as university admissions, partly to offset the disadvantages that have beset them from birth, partly because a society is desired in which all classes have some representation in the higher-level occupations. (Since this paper was written, the same practice has been introduced in the United States.) Other subclasses of this category are:

      3. sex (e.g., females are widely held to deserve exemption from being drafted into the armed forces)

      4. place of birth (relevant, e.g., in deciding who deserves the advantages that go with citizenship)

      5. physique

      6. citizenship

      7. relationship to the distributor.

Some of these matters may not be determined by birth, and other matters are considered according to their status, not at birth but

    B. at the time of distribution:

      1. profession

      2. rank

      3. age

      4. health

      5. intelligence

      6. other potential

      7. character

      8. residence

      9. membership

      10. beliefs (perhaps relevant for a bishop)

      11. motivation.

So much for what one is. Next let us consider

  II.   *What one has:*

    A. property (land, money, shares, goods)

    B. family

    C. friends

    D. claims.

Instead of commenting on each subclass, let us proceed to

III.   *What one has done:*
   A. education (1. formal, and 2. informal)
   B. military service (length, experience, exploits, decorations, highest rank attained)
   C. civilian occupations:
      1. kinds
      2. length
      3. experience
      4. achievements.

To give some idea of the complexity of determining this one small point of a man's achievements in a single civilian occupation, let us mention some of the things involved in distributing raises among professors:

   a. teaching, where we still have to distinguish
      α. levels (such as introductory, upper-class, and graduate courses) and
      β. techniques (such as lecturing, conducting discussions, supervising independent work, and laboratory sessions) . Next we have
   b. publications, where we must again distinguish
      α. levels
      β. quantity
      γ. reception (e.g., reviews and comments)
      δ. impact
      ε. probable long-range importance
   c. unpublished research
   d. discussion with colleagues
   e. administrative work.

All this comes under III.C.4 and concerns no more than a man's achievements in a single civilian occupation. He may have achieved a great deal in other civilian and military occupations before becoming a professor, or he may be competing with others who have. Depending on what is being distributed, his rank and age and several of the other points already mentioned, or still to be mentioned, may be relevant too. For example,

    D. other accomplishments:
        1. public service, including offices held
        2. private service (e.g., lives saved)
        3. extracurricular activities, publications, lectures, etc. And in some contexts one might also take into account
    E. sufferings (one may deserve compensation)
    F. crimes (which may end "what one has done").

IV.   *What one is doing:*

Here one might distinguish, for example,

    A. professional work (not to be confused with I.B.1. profession; for a man may be doing his boss's work)
    B. public life
    C. in one's family
    D. on one's own.

Now we are ready to consider needs. Let us distinguish

V.   *What one needs for oneself:*

    A. for subsistence
    B. for comfort
    C. for some project
    D. for optimal development, and

VI.   *What one needs for one's dependents:*

with the same four subclasses, on whose vagueness we shall soon have to say something further.

VII.   *What one desires:*

Although this is ignored in most discussions, it is relevant in many cases unless we assume that a man often deserves

something as a reward that in fact he does not desire at all.
Finally, there is still

VIII. *What one has contracted:*
There is no need for subheads here or for further categories; the eight suggested here with their subclasses suffice to
show how impossible it is to measure what men deserve. With
that, the material conception of justice breaks down. But
before we turn to consider what might be called a formal
conception of justice, let us consider *some objections to our
analysis.*

V

IT MIGHT SEEM that our analysis, for all its complexity, is still
not nearly complex enough. For we have assumed for the
sake of the argument that justice consists in giving each what
he deserves, and "desert," as Joel Feinberg has shown, "represents only a part, and not necessarily the most important
part, of the domain of justice."[9] Thus a man may "deserve"
an honor or office but not qualify for it, and in that case
justice does not require that he receive it.

Even as Aristotle distinguished that justice which is the
sum of the virtues from that justice which is a part of virtue,
we should distinguish that "giving each what he 'deserves' "
which represents the material conception of justice as a whole
from that "desert" which is merely one consideration among
others. Feinberg's point concerns "desert" in the narrow
sense, while we have been considering "desert" in the other
sense, which is so generous and inclusive that his point is
easily taken care of in my chart, under claims one has (II.D)
or what one has contracted (VIII). If neither heading did
suffice, one could easily expand the chart. So far from damag-
ing my case, that would actually be grist to my mill.

---

9 "Justice and Personal Desert" in *Nomos VI: Justice* (1963), p. 70.

My thesis that distributions can be unjust but hardly ever just is not reducible to the claim that merits and needs conflict, and that any attempt to do justice according to one is bound to violate the other. Let us consider *merit* first.

Some writers suppose[10] that if only we were willing to take our stand on merit alone, our system, though morally objectionable, could be made to work. In our present system, it has been said, the right to vote is quite independent of merit; but—and here I quote—"This kind of arrangement would look like whimsy or worse, like sheer immoralism, if the only values recognized in our political community were those of merit."[11] In fact there is such a *crisscross of merits* that it makes excellent sense to say: People's merits are not equal but nevertheless cannot be arranged in any single scale; hence a merit system, while workable in some very limited contexts where criteria can be clearly specified, is unworkable in other contexts. When it comes to the right to vote, it may be *the least evil* to give every adult one vote, provided he is, say, over eighteen and able to read the ballot.

To consider merit relevant in this and many other contexts is not unjust, nor does justice demand that people who know nothing about the issues be allowed to vote. To deprive people of the vote on grounds of size, weight, hair color, or skin color *is* unjust, but no particular system can claim to be just. One might call the least unjust "just," but in practice one cannot be sure of any system that it *is* the least unjust.

It is one of the aims of my complex chart to show vividly that there *is* a crisscross of merits and that the popular notion that conflicts arise only when we heed both merits and needs is false.

---

10 E.g., Gregory Vlastos in "Justice and Equality," in *Social Justice,* ed. Richard B. Brandt (1962) , p. 46.
11 *Ibid.,* p. 45.

V I

It might seem that our analysis is needlessly complex and could easily be reduced to a simpler model. Instead of distinguishing eight categories, one might distinguish merely three: merits, abilities, and needs. But this model is too simple and has to be supplemented in two ways.

First, much of what we have included under what one is, has, is doing, desires, and has contracted is relevant to just distribution but has no place in the tripartite model. Place of birth, citizenship, and residence are almost universally considered relevant to the distribution of offices and of the right to vote, and it is far from evident that this is unjust. Relation to the distributor is almost universally considered relevant to the distribution of goods in a will, and again it is not evident that this is unjust. But none of these considerations are reducible to merits, abilities, and needs.

Secondly, these three categories are not as simple and unambiguous as the fact that there is one word for each makes them sound. In the case of merit, we have shown this. In the case of *need*, we obtained two categories by distinguishing what one needs for oneself and what one needs for one's dependents, and then divided each into four more subcategories: for subsistence, for comfort, for some project, and for optimal development. On reflection, these four are still utterly unclear. What is literally needed for *subsistence* is so pitifully little that it is generally understood that this is *not* what is meant; but what *is* meant is *not* understood.

Comfort is equally unclear and obviously involves a crucial subjective component. Once one is used to certain things—cigarettes, television, so many meals a day, such and such furniture, a car, or perhaps several cars in the family, a W.C., or perhaps three full bathrooms, two-day weekends, a month in Florida every winter, a three-month summer vacation, a forty-hour work week or perhaps no more than six hours teaching a week—one is apt to be uncomfortable without these things. It is thus possible to make every member of a group comfortable while the distribution of goods is strikingly unequal, and it is even possible for the person with fewer needs and goods to be more comfortable than some who have far more goods but "needs" that outstrip their possessions. Needs are not fixed data but can be created, cultivated, and—though this is much more difficult—diminished and even eliminated.

What is "needed" for a *project* is often far from clear: foundations are frequently persuaded that extremely questionable needs are authentic; and more often than not, they assume that the significance of a project is proportionate to the claimed need for money. This widespread assumption is obviously silly and vicious. Moreover, does not justice require a weighing of the needs for the completion of various projects and a comparative ranking of how much each project is needed?

If we want to give each enough for his *optimal development*, how do we determine what a man needs for that? To answer the last two questions, we require a decision about goals—an idea or vision of man and society as we should like them to be.

Ultimately, every attempt to spell out a material conception of justice involves a decision about the kind of society we want. It is an abiding testimony to Plato's genius that, although he was the first philosopher to deal with justice at book length, he recognized this crucial fact. It is a central fault of many discussions of justice since his time that this point is overlooked.

VII

IT MAY SEEM as if one material conception of justice did not involve any ultimate value judgments. For there are some who would disregard differences in merit and need, taking their stand on *absolute equality*. Again, the meaning of equality is not as simple as one might suppose. Is it considered just to give each the same, regardless not only of his needs and desires, his merits and his ability to make use of what he is given, but also of what he already has (E.1)? If food is distributed, for example, is it just to give equal amounts to those who have plenty and those who have nothing? If this suggestion were rejected as palpably unjust, need would be reintroduced. But it might still be argued that absolute equality really means that all should be equal *after* the distribution has been made, or at least as nearly equal as the distribution can make them. In that case, those who *have* would receive nothing till all havenots had received as much as *they* have (E.2).

Although this system is not followed in any civilized country anywhere, it has some plausibility when the goods at stake are food, but hardly any when the goods are books, violins, canvas boards, offices, or honors. Different criteria are appropriate for different kinds of goods. Some things may reasonably be distributed in accordance with men's merits, others with men's abilities, still others with men's needs, without being open to the charge that the distribution has been unjust in principle.

To sum up: E.1 is so absurd that one can understand it only as a counsel of despair, a way of saying that no better system can be made to work. E.2 is also absurd if it is applied to *all* things that are to be distributed. To mention only one further objection to E.2: in that case no incentives would remain.

It is arguable that if food, lodging, and money were to be distributed in accordance with this plan, sufficient nonmaterial incentives would remain. Thus one can easily imagine a faculty on which all teachers received the same material benefits, while there were not only instructors, assistant professors, associate professors, and full professors but, say, eight ranks, and promotions would be based on a merit system. We have shown earlier how impossible it is to rank professors according to merit. This is not to deny, however, that rank can be a more powerful incentive than money; even now some young teachers, given the choice between a raise and a promotion, would choose the higher rank. It would not be too difficult to imbue a society with an ethos in which rank and honors would provide enough incentives for performance, while material goods were distributed relatively equally. Whether those publicly branded as inferior would be happier than those are whose salaries, which are not publicly known, have not had the benefit of any merit raises is another question. It is highly probable, I think, that nonmaterial inequalities in a highly merit-conscious society would be felt more deeply and would therefore make for more unhappiness than most material inequalities in our society.

Inequalities in the distribution of *some* goods, material or otherwise, is necessary as an incentive. Without it, some jobs will not get done, unless we abolish a great deal of personal freedom, empower a central authority to draft people to do whatever jobs are thought to be needed to be done, and then introduce some system of random selection. It might be held that such a society would be more just than any society in which exertion is rewarded, but anyone who abhorred the required loss of freedom would not be in the least likely to feel that it was more just, and he might argue—as I would—that *injustice meted out at random remains injustice.*

In sum, it is only in a situation in which, *ex hypothesi,* no conceivably relevant differences exist among the individuals concerned that any distribution could be reasonably called just. Dividing eight apples among eight children at the end of a party at which all have had plenty to eat might be a case in point. But the moment we suppose that some of them are much too full by now to eat the apple right away and will take it home to a house in which apples and other kinds of food are plentiful, while other children at the party are about to return to homes in which hungry brothers and sisters are plentiful, even this apparently so simple and trivial case may be seen to support the dictum that distributions can be unjust but hardly ever just.[12]

VIII

AT THIS POINT one might wish to fall back on *a formal conception of justice* and say that *justice consists in treating like cases alike.* Alas, no two cases are alike. No two students applying for admission are alike any more than two young men up for promotion or a raise in salary. It was one function of my chart, with all its detail about conceivably relevant considerations, to show this.

The man who wants to avoid being unjust must ignore *irrelevant* unlikenesses and base his decision on *relevant* likenesses and unlikenesses. But often it is exceedingly difficult to judge what is and what is not relevant. In some cases it is easy to say that the basis for a decision was blatantly irrelevant

---

12 The example of the children and the apples does not depend on some prior social injustice. All that is required is some relevant inequality; say, that some children need to eat more than others, or that some are allergic to apples, or that some are allergic to other foods but not to apples. I am indebted to Gilbert Harman for his comments on this paper, which have led me to clarify this point as well as several in section X below.

and that heinous injustice has been done, but our thesis still stands: It is hardly ever possible to claim that justice has been done. The point is not that we know what is just but lack the strength to do it. Rather, injustice is often palpable, but we could not say in most cases what would be just.

The obvious rejoinder, mentioned previously, is that we are just when we minimize injustice, and that a rule is just when it is not unjust. What does this mean in practice? The demand for justice is the demand to give reasons for unequal treatment—to show relevant inequalities, or, in other words, to be rational, or, in a legitimate sense of that word, honest.

What outrages us in cases of palpable injustice is usually rank dishonesty; for example, in the Scottsboro trial and in the techniques that have been used to keep Negroes from voting. Justice does not require that illiterate people should be allowed to vote. But the claims that have been made again and again in this connection, like the testimony accepted by the court in the Scottsboro trial, have been dishonest with a vengeance.

Still, it is possible to be honest but unjust. In such cases we confront either brutality (a lack of love) or low standards of honesty, or both. Honesty, in the sense germane here, should not be mistaken for the easy sincerity of those who have never bothered to develop their intellectual conscience. Men who sincerely claim what only a few minutes earlier they knew to be false, or what they would find to be false if they took even elementary pains to investigate the matter, have low standards of honesty. High standards of honesty involve scrupulous attention to evidence and to meanings, to pros and cons, and to alternatives. And what I mean by love is, above all, the habit, which can be cultivated, of thinking about how others feel and sharing their problems and sufferings.

Justice is not an irreducible principle that is required to guard against distributions that would outrage the moral sense of most philosophers who think we must rely on the

concept of justice. In *The Faith of a Heretic* (1961) I proposed four cardinal virtues (section 83) and then (84) tried
to show how various situations in which most philosophers
would invoke justice could be dealt with by relying on these
four. It would be tedious to quote or paraphrase at length
what has been published elsewhere, but since these pages may
be unfamiliar, it may after all be best, or the least evil, to
repeat here a single example, desegregation.

THE FIRST cardinal virtue, *humbition,* is a fusion of humility
and ambition. The man who acknowledges this ideal and
cultivates this habit would admit his ignorance of many
pertinent considerations without resigning himself to ignorance. He would neither assume at the outset that he was right
and his opponents wrong, nor would he take for granted that
those of his own color are superior to those of another. He
would engage in open-minded discussion and be willing to
learn.

The second virtue, *love,* involves seeing and sharing the
hurt and grief of other human beings and assuming some
responsibility and being willing to make sacrifices to help.
"Without believing all things and hoping all things, without
expecting the millennium from a piece of legislation and
without giving up because there will be no millennium, love
persists."

Thirdly, *"courage* does not shrink from danger, does not
hide from risks in sloth and resignation, even if they are
concealed behind the name of prudence. If lack of humbition, lack of love, and lack of courage do not fully account for
the injustice inflicted on the Negro, dishonesty remains."

Honesty is the fourth cardinal virtue, and any attempt to
show in detail how heavily racial prejudice and discrimination depend on its violation would extend this paper beyond
reason.

An analysis of several such examples would show that the

collapse of distributive justice does not entail the collapse of decency and humanity, and that the work that "justice" could not do can be done in other ways. This may be the best place to suggest one more example that shows how justice cannot do the job it is supposed to do.

Let us turn back to the view that "benevolence and justice are the two 'cardinal' moral virtues" and that "all other moral virtues can be derived from or shown to be forms of them."[13] In the first place, I do not see how humility and ambition, courage, and honesty can be derived from these two. In the second place, it is clear that justice, defined as the disposition to treat people equally, is invoked lest benevolence alone—that is, the disposition to maximize the balance of good over evil—should inspire distributions in which a slight excess of good over evil is purchased at the price of immense inequalities. But this attempt to work improvements on utilitarianism is open to several objections.

Suppose we could choose between two states. In one there would be only 100,000 people, all of them extremely happy, wise, and creative. The balance of good over evil—waiving for the moment the absurdity of all attempts to measure that—might be said to be, say, 100,000. In the other state there would be a billion people, none of them very happy, wise, or creative, but all of them a little more happy than unhappy. While in the first state, each man had achieved a balance of good over evil that amounted to one full point, in this state the balance for each came to, say, .01. Even so, the total balance in the first state would be only 100,000; but in the second one, ten million—a hundred times greater. Equality would be present in the second state, too; hence those who add justice to benevolence as a second cardinal virtue would be at one with the utilitarians in being com-

---

[13] Frankena, *op. cit.,* p. 50.

pelled to choose the second state. But I should opt for the first, and I trust you would, too.

What has gone wrong? Most of our moral philosophers fail to see that the most interesting moral questions are what sort of society we want and—we come to this as soon as we try to give reasons for our answer—what we would like to become of man. Our answers to these two questions are decisive when questions of justice arise in practice.

IX

LET US RETURN to the problem of selecting a few hundred students from thousands applying for admission. The counsel to admit those who deserve admission is empty if we do not know how to compute desert. The demand that we treat all applicants equally is equally unhelpful. Should we be guided solely by achievement so far? (What kinds of achievement? Scores in multiple choice tests? Examination essays? Course grades? Extracurricular achievements, and if so, which?) Or should we be guided more by promise? (Of what?) If it is our desire to maximize the impact of our limited resources and it is a fact that the rate of attrition among women students is so high that hardly any go on to obtain the doctorate and even fewer then go on into professional careers, is it "unjust," whatever else it may be, to give preference to men? And if we want to have more Negro leaders with a first-rate education and more Negro lawyers, surgeons, and professors, is it "unjust" to admit some Negro students who, but for their so-called race, would not have been admitted?

What *is* unjust is to announce one set of criteria for admission—or for fellowships, raises in salary, promotions, leaves of absence, and other rewards—and then to invoke different standards in practice. But such injustice comes down to dishonesty. If we announce our criteria and then do our best to stick with them in practice, can we still be said to be unjust? Can the *criteria* be unjust? They can be, in two ways. First, they may be arbitrary and irrelevant to our stated goals. In that case we may be convicted of low standards of honesty or a lack of love. Or our standards may be relevant and well designed to implement our social goals, but the society that we desire may be open to severe objections.

What sort of objections? The most telling criticism would be that the society did not promote humbition, courage, love, and high standards of honesty. In practice, those who call a society unjust often mean all or part of that. But it is neither necessary nor possible to summarize briefly near the end of this paper possible objections to societies. What is important is rather to insist that many questions about justice resolve into a dispute about different visions of man and society.

Our moral philosophers generally avoid such disputes and give—and probably have—the impression that at that point we are dealing with irrational preferences. But it is one of the most important tasks of philosophy to consider the pros and cons of different visions of man and society, weighing critically what can be said in favor of each, and to try to arrive at a reasoned conclusion.

X

In the end, let us relate this approach to justice to a very different one. Polemics have no place here, since space does not permit me to deal adequately with the views of those with whom I differ. My reason for nevertheless referring to the writings of some colleagues is to define my own position more clearly, and to indicate what seems to me to be at stake. While I am naturally making every effort to be fair, my central purpose here is not to refute anyone but to articulate my own doubts about justice.

There is a tradition in ethics that considers it the main problem of justice to neutralize what I shall call "grabbiness." Thus a recent writer on the subject says: "Questions of justice arise when conflicting claims are made upon the design of a practice and where it is taken for granted that each person will insist, as far as possible, on what he considers his rights. It is typical of cases of justice to involve persons who are pressing on one another their claims, between which a fair balance or equilibrium must be found."[14] But in the examples I have given—admissions, promotions, and raises—grabbiness may be totally out of the picture. Nobody need press any claim, each of the young men concerned may go out of his way to suggest his own unworthiness, and the decision may be up to senior professors who have nothing to gain whatever. The question before them may ultimately be a question of goals, of the kind of society to be desired.

The writer I have quoted says: "Amongst an association of saints . . . the disputes about justice could hardly occur; for they would all work selflessly together for one end, the glory of God as defined by their common religion . . ."[15] But selfless men can and often do disagree about the best distribution. The reference to the common religion is gratuitous; it introduces a point that has nothing to do with selflessness; and it ignores how much disagreement there has been among saints and, for that matter, among rabbis.

The crux of the view I reject is that justice consists in impartiality and transcends preferences. It is supposed to be a matter of rationality, which is associated with calculation and objective findings. Thus we are asked to imagine a society of rational men, and part of the very meaning of their being

---

14 John Rawls, "Justice as Fairness" (1958), revised version in *Justice and Social Policy*, ed. Frederick Olafson (1961), p. 87. For a critique of Hume's close association of justice with the restraint of selfishness see my article "The Origin of Justice," pp. 221–23.
15 *Ibid.*, p. 90 f.

rational is that "they know their own interests more or less accurately,"[16] as if one's own interests were always and entirely something knowable and not—as in fact they often are—matters of more or less informed and responsible choices.

THE MOST CRUCIAL QUESTION about distributive justice is whether *any* distribution, outside of simplistic cases, should be called just. I have given reasons for saying, No. The view I am now considering says: Yes, a distribution is just if it fulfills various conditions that can be enumerated. Among these conditions are at least two that are, I think, open to very serious objections. The first is that grabbiness is neutralized.[17] This does not strike me as so difficult to achieve, at least in a large number of interesting cases; but problems of justice persist even when grabbiness is out of the picture. The second condition is that "inequalities as defined by the institutional structure or fostered by it are arbitrary unless it is reasonable to expect that they will work out to everyone's advantage."[18] This I consider a utopian condition that crys-

---

16 *Ibid.*, p. 85.

17 To arrive at justice, the most important step is, in this view, to devise a situation in which "there is no way for anyone to win social advantages for himself" (*ibid.*, p. 87). In a more recent essay, "Distributive Justice," Rawls says similarly: "Consider the simplest problem of fair division. A number of men are to divide a cake: *assuming that a fair division is an equal one*, which procedure will give this outcome? The obvious solution is to have the man who divides the cake take the last piece. He will divide it equally, *since in this way he assures for himself as large a share as he can.* . . . We can design a procedure *guaranteed* to lead to [the outcome that is just]" (*Philosophy, Politics and Society: Third Series*, ed. Peter Laslett and W. G. Runciman, 1967, p. 77; all italics mine).
The italicized assumption is more problematic than meets the eye: see our example of the apples. Moreover, the "just" outcome is *not* guaranteed unless we assume that everybody is as grabby as the man dividing the cake is explicitly assumed to be. If he were not that grabby and assumed that other people weren't either, he might cut pieces of different sizes to accommodate different tastes and appetites; and if he *is* as grabby as the "since" clause suggests but knows that his friends are not, he may make one piece much bigger than all the rest, confident that it will be left to the last.

18 "Distributive Justice," p. 61. The same point is central in "Justice as Fairness."

tallizes the unwarranted faith that we need not make tragic choices.

Any attempt to keep the discussion of justice this side of preferences and choices seems hopeless to me. Even men who are, or try to be, rational and selfless are not alike. Even if the intelligent did not push the claims of intelligence, and the artistically gifted the importance of fostering artistic talent, some who are not themselves brilliant might urge us to weight intelligence, and others, though quite lacking in artistic genius, might argue that a society is ultimately to be judged by its accomplishments in art.

Indeed, right now the rules about college admissions and advancement of young college teachers are not designed or adopted by those who are most affected but by older men who have come through the system, and grabbiness is thus largely eliminated. But if this setup were changed and the rules were up to the people most affected, would *any* feasible arrangement be to the advantage of *all?* Surely not. This utopian notion is part of the false assumption that one system is rational and true without involving any choice or argument about goals.

In concrete cases, I would not necessarily differ with any of the writers I have singled out for criticism. This is not merely because I have selected only men who happen to be my friends, on the assumption—not biased, I hope—that they are among the very best living writers on the subject. Even as Protestants, Catholics, Jews, and unbelievers can work together for civil rights, philosophers who disagree about the best analysis of justice may agree in practical decisions. From this, however, it does not follow that nothing of practical importance is at stake, nor even that philosophy "leaves everything as it is."[19]

---

19 Ludwig Wittgenstein, *Philosophical Investigations*, Section 124.

Even when the decision about distribution is the same, it makes a difference whether we tell those who are affected by it—say, those who are not admitted or promoted—that our decisions and our rules are just, or rather that we realize that no such absolute claim is defensible. In the latter case, we might say: "These were our rules or criteria, which neither *are* perfect nor *could* be. We may yet be convinced to revise them. Meanwhile we have done our best to stick by them and not to be swayed by points whose relevance is tenuous. We know from experience that even at that level mistakes are made, but we did try hard to preclude them." To speak that way instead of invoking the chimaera of absolute justice is more honest and loving, more humane, and more mindful of the self-respect of those we disappoint.

We can point to examples of love and honesty, humbition and courage. We do not know in the same way what justice is, and we cannot point to examples of just distribution without becoming highly abstract and deliberately excluding a great deal of relevant data, as I have tried to show in the case of distributing apples among children after a party. Once we realize and admit this, and also that our rules and criteria are linked to our vision of a good society, we should become more humane, less sure of ourselves, and more inclined to argue the pros and cons of different visions of a good society. This would make philosophy more humane, too.

XI

PERHAPS MY ATTACK on distributive justice would seem more acceptable if I said—but I am not going to—that distributions, always excepting simplistic cases, can never be unjust any more than just. As it stands, my position may appear paradoxical.

It may help to note that the situation of distributive justice is not unique in this respect. Scientific theories, as well as interpretations of works of art and literature, can be proved false, but it is arguable that they can never be proved true. Many mutually incompatible theories may be tenable, but we should not call several mutually incompatible theories true. Yet there is no good reason why some untenable theories should not be called false.

The closest parallel to distributive justice is furnished by retributive justice. If a defendant is guilty and his punishment is neither cruel and unusual nor arbitrary, we still should not call it just or say that "justice has been done." Punishments never have the quality that Kant and other retributivists have associated with them, and that many retributivists still associate with capital punishment for murder. There is no one punishment that is the right one, any more than there is one distribution that is the right one. To call all tenable or defensible punishments or distributions just, bestowing this epithet on an indefinite number of mutually incompatible solutions, is sufficiently out of keeping with the traditional and still widely accepted meaning of justice to make it preferable and reasonable to suggest that neither punishments nor distributions should be called just. Yet both punishments and distributions often have the very qualities generally associated with injustice, and there is no good reason for never saying that an injustice has been done. If an innocent man is framed, or unequal punishments or shares are meted out for no relevant reason, we need not hesitate to call the punishment or distribution unjust.

Many distributions and punishments we should call neither just nor unjust. Anyone reluctant to accept this conclusion has three options. (1) He can call unjust all solutions except the one he considers the best, or (2) he can call just all tenable solutions, or (3) he can suggest that in fact only one punishment or distribution *is* just, although we are generally unable to tell which one is. All three alternatives seem to me to involve such significant departures from the usual meaning of "just" and "unjust" that my solution is better.

It is neither desirable nor possible to "use every man after his desert." However we treat men, we cannot claim, excepting simplistic cases, that they got what they deserved. But not all ways of treating men are equally undeserved. When unequal treatment is not based on relevant inequalities, or when one set of criteria has been announced and another is invoked in practice, we may say that an injustice has been done.

Thus men who do not agree on what would be best can still work together to minimize injustices, even as men with different theories may agree that *some* theories are demonstrably false. This is not paradoxical but glad tidings. While philosophers should argue more about rival visions of man and society, not all practical efforts and cooperation have to wait until they have come to agree.

It may seem that justice, unlike love, can be demanded. But this is wrong, as I have tried to show. What can be demanded is less injustice. If this should be demanded or offered as "simple justice," it may yet turn out to be tomorrow's "injustice."

Martin Luther realized that conscience can always ask whether we could not have done better. But because justice could not be found in the pursuit of good works, Luther concluded that man could be made just by faith alone—faith in Christ's redemptive sacrifice, faith that Christ had died for our sins. At that point Luther reverted to an archaic notion of justice: the magical sacrifice of the innocent scapegoat. Here our ways part.

After using their reason and examining the evidence, physicians and surgeons often do not know what is the best course. But if they therefore throw reason and evidence to the winds, they act irresponsibly. We expect them to use both in order to exclude a great many alternatives, even if in the end they cannot be sure that their course was the best.

Am I guilty of the old heresy that man knows the devil but not God? My heresy is worse. We know neither God nor the devil; we are beset by an endless number of devils—"No worst, there is none."[20] To fight evil without the illusion that it is the greatest ever, to choose the lesser evil without the faith that it is surely the least evil, to endure darkness without the boast that none could be blacker, and to create more light without the comfort of excessive hopes—that is humbition, courage, love, and honesty.[21]

---

[20] Gerard Manley Hopkins, poem #65. The question about the old heresy was raised by Abraham Edel in his prepared comments when I read this paper November 5, 1967, at Columbia University to the Conference on Jewish Philosophy.

[21] Some of the ideas in this paper are developed further in two articles: "Origins of Justice" in *Review of Metaphysics,* December 1969, and "Black and White" in *Survey: A Journal of Soviet and East European Studies,* Autumn 1969.

Law and Disorder: Some Reflections on the Political Philosophy of Edmond Cahn

DANIEL DAY WILLIAMS

THIS paper was first presented to a joint meeting of the faculties of the Jewish Theological Seminary and Union Theological Seminary. The occasion made it appropriate for me to begin by saying a personal word about one of the most cherished relationships I have had in New York City, my friendship with Edmond Cahn, professor of law in New York University and one of the distinguished interpreters of the philosophy of law in the American tradition. I was present at the dedication of the beautiful room which bears his name in the New York University School of Law and heard the tributes to him given by Chief Justice Earl Warren and many others. These statements, and that by Justice Hugo Black in the volume of his speeches and papers *Confronting Injustice,* superbly edited by Mrs. Edmond Cahn, are the informed and fitting praise of his colleagues in the law. As a layman I certainly cannot add to them at that level.

I can, however, testify to what the personal sharing of conversation about the law and about right and wrong meant for me in the brief years we had before Edmond Cahn's untimely death. A conversation with him was an event in which one plunged immediately and deeply into the moral problems in human behavior. While his field was jurisprudence, his moral sensitivity and humanity led him always to the central moral issues in legal theory and in the administration of law. For him the crucial problems of life were to be faced in open conversation between persons. Every person in a democracy is responsible for bringing his insight and feeling to bear on the issues which affect the common good.

This means that most legal questions are also moral questions. In dealing with them, Edmond Cahn moved with great learning and discernment through the tradition of the Hebrew Bible, the New Testament, and the broad ethical tradition of Western thought, and he saw the law in this context.

It will be a useful documentation of an event in the history of theological education to recall the course which he offered in the Jewish Theological Seminary on the relation of legal and moral theory. This course was destined to bring that Seminary and Union Seminary together in a significant common enterprise. It was, I believe, about 1960 that Edmond Cahn first offered the course for the students in the Jewish Theological Seminary. After a year or two in conversation with him we saw the possibility of bringing some Union Seminary students into the course. Some of our advanced students in ethics and a graduate student tutor joined the course, and I participated in it.

What Edmond Cahn did was to present to the students some actual case which opened up major ethical issues. It was usually a case which had already been before a court. He asked the students to analyze for themselves the moral questions involved and then to search everything they could find in the Bible, in Talmud, and in moral philosophy which might bear upon it. For example, one case was the suing of a cigarette company by someone who had contracted lung cancer and who was holding the company responsible not for what it had said, but for what it had not said in its advertising. The issue of truth-telling, of public responsibility on the part of those offering a product for sale, the ultimate issue of the responsibility of those with power to communicate the full truth were opened up. The discussion of the case was vigorous, productive and relevant.

This uniting of the lawyer's case method with religious ethical training for rabbinate and ministry was a creative move in theological education, and the establishment of such a course on an inter-faith basis was far-seeing in its promise for the future.

To know Edmond Cahn was to have one's ethical sensitivity and humane purpose challenged, reshaped and given a new toughness through facing issues of legal theory. I will never cease to be grateful for his life and spirit.

My purpose in this paper is to state from a lay point of view Edmond Cahn's central contribution to our understanding of the foundations of law, and then to continue my conversation with him by applying his insights to a pressing contemporary problem: the use of law to restrain strikes against the public as employer. This question has become increasingly urgent in very recent history. So far as I know, Edmond Cahn never wrote directly about it, and I never discussed it with him. What he did was to offer us, as Norman Redlich has said, a way of thinking about justice and the law which we can carry on as new problems emerge. It is in the spirit of his work to ask what light his view of law may throw upon this question.[1]

I

THE TWO FUNDAMENTAL CONCEPTS which Edmond Cahn projected in legal theory were first, *the sense of injustice,* and

---

[1] Norman Redlich, Introduction to *Confronting Injustice: The Edmond Cahn Reader,* edited by Lenore L. Cahn. Boston: Little, Brown, 1966.

second, the *consumer perspective.* I shall try to say what I understand to be his position on these two interrelated themes.

His first book was entitled *The Sense of Injustice* and it contains his central conviction. Cahn was a thoroughgoing moralist in his approach to law. He believed that public law, the codes, the statutes, and the constitutions were the result of a history of man's search for justice through a process of trial and error, a history in which new situations call for new responses. The basis of law is neither power, nor self-interest, nor ethical absolutes given in a tradition, but the sense of injustice. The perspective here is naturalistic, humanistic, and pragmatic. It is men who make law, and men who have to make moral and legal decisions. Cahn was continually seeking to uncover that factor in the human response to problems which moves life ahead to a higher order of freedom and fulfillment.

He defended his attention to the sense of injustice as a better way to understand the ethical meaning of justice by pointing out that we understand a concept when we sense its relevance to "the common earthly experience of individual human beings." When is a citizen of a democratic society disposed to invoke the name of justice? Cahn says:

> I believe he invokes it when personally or vicariously he experiences the impact of an act of injustice. It is not his custom to meditate in his study and search for self-evident juristic propositions or tidy utopian diagrams about abstract justice. If justice were only an ideal mode or state or condition, our response as human beings would be merely contemplative, and—as we all know—contemplation bakes no loaves. But the response with which men meet a real or imagined instance of injustice is entirely different; it is alive with warmth and movement

that courses through the human organism. How often when we are faced with a social problem and cannot determine which of many alternative solutions would be just, we find ourselves certain and unanimous that one particular solution would be utterly unjust.

Therefore, Cahn concludes, we cannot employ the term justice in a static sense, because as a fixed form or pattern it is hopelessly ambiguous. He continues:

> For us, justice will mean neither a static diagram on the one hand nor a mere quality of will on the other; it will mean the active process of remedying or preventing what would arouse the "sense of injustice." It will be taken not as a condition or a quality but as a species of human activity.[2]

He further held that beliefs must be ranked and graded according to the conceived cost that may follow from proceeding to act on them. A graded pragmatism is concerned with two main centers of cost: cost to the human subject of the conceived action, and cost to the human object. For example, people may believe sincerely in public education, but not at the cost of sending their own children to some public schools in New York City. "Judges may believe sincerely in the idea of speedy justice at the cost-level of opening court at ten o'clock, but not at the cost level of nine o'clock."[3]

Cahn is quite emphatic that the predisposition to resist injustice is not infallible. Like other natural capacities it is limited. All of us are tethered to our perspectives, but the tether is elastic, and Cahn rests on his conviction that there is at the heart of man a capacity for resisting injustice. His

---

2 *Ibid.*, pp. 10–11.
3 *Ibid.*, p. 12.

anthropology is an evolutionary and humanistic one, and for him there is no pure intuition in man which relieves him from struggling with the recalcitrant circumstances of his world and his own being.

> While the sense of injustice uses empathy, projection and emotion, it simultaneously summons perception, reasoning, intelligence, and judgment—all the capacities that make for understanding and the application of sense. In the experience of the sense of injustice, thinking and feeling suffuse each other reciprocally, reason and empathy blend together indissociably, and the rational directs the emotional while the emotional impels the rational . . . The combined process enables men to develop and communities to advance.[4]

Certainly this way into the meaning of justice leaves many questions open, both on the side of particular issues concerning the criterion of justice and on the side of the view of man and of what conditions his capacity to discover injustice and project a more adequate way for society.

THAT EDMOND CAHN felt the depth and complexity of the problem is clear in that his fourth book, on which he was working when he died in August 1964, was to be entitled *The Meaning of Justice*. It began characteristically with the case of Marie Bresnard, the French woman who was accused, unjustly as it turned out, of eleven murders, and who spent twelve years under the cloud of the accusations before being exonerated. In his notes for this book he had written that "justice is not a collection of principles or criteria. . . . Justice is the active process of preventing or repairing of injustice."[5]

---

[4] *Ibid.*, p. 14.
[5] *Ibid.*, p. 381.

There is indeed a fundamental issue raised with traditional religious perspectives in ethics by Cahn's treatment of justice. He might be interpreted as locating the meaning of justice solely in man as a biological, psychological organism developing in a natural process. Paul Ramsey, who has written sympathetically of Edmond Cahn's philosophy, judged that Cahn's view of law is "naturalistic" in a restricted sense and that he is no better off than other natural law theorists who try to find ultimate ethical obligation in the immanent processes of life. At least this is Ramsey's view of *The Sense of Injustice*. He thinks there is a different accent in *The Moral Decision* which stresses an ultimate righteous judgment in the biblical sense, but that Cahn imports this too directly into the realm of human law.[6]

Ramsey has pointed to a critical problem—from what vantage point do we get a criterion of justice which is not simply a description of what particular men think they want or desire? But I believe that he does not interpret Cahn's position rightly on two counts.

First, he does not do justice to the emphasis on process in Cahn's thought. Human life is a process in history, a discovery of the kinds of order that are possible and their consequences. Notice that the consequences are not simply immediate consequences but those which over the long road fulfill or frustrate man's powers of reason, feeling and creativity. There is a great difference between a naturalistic theory in which nature has a fixed structure, in which the determination of natural law is left to the discernment of given orders of value, and a view in which nature is seen as the whole concrete process of becoming, including the full realization of man's response to the evolutionary process and to his historical experience. It is justice for man which Cahn is seeking, and man is not finished; therefore justice is never

---

6 Paul, Ramsey, *Nine Modern Moralists*, Englewood Cliffs: Prentice-Hall, 1962, p. 226; cf. pp. 248–51.

finished. It is a process, and the determination of what is just can never be made apart from taking account of the concrete conditions and consequences of specific actions. In discussing natural law Cahn points out that its upholders have agreed on nothing about it except that it is discoverable by human reason. "Historically, natural law has been invoked to support every conceivable doctrine from anarchic freedom to feudal oligarchy, and from social utopianism to the ethics of the jungle."[7]

Now the difficult question must be raised: Is the criterion of justice solely within man's self-knowledge, or is it related to a source of right and good beyond himself? It is the question of God and moral law.

Edmond Cahn was a jurist, and for the most part he confined himself in his writing to modes of interpreting the source and nature of justice which can be appealed to within a democratic society and which make sense in relation to man's life, regardless of particular world-views or religious or special ways of understanding his existence. One must, therefore, look carefully at Edmond Cahn's writings in order not to fall into the erroneous conclusion that he meant to cut the search for justice off from any divine source of right and of ultimate law. In his essay "A Lawyer Looks at Religion" (1958) , he speaks clearly about this:

> Intelligent men realize that religion is one of the supreme factors in human affairs. Intelligent jurists know that religious influences—whether good or pernicious—have continually affected the history and growth of the law.[8]

After discussing the clergyman's misunderstanding of law and the lawyers misunderstanding of judicial process, Cahn says:

---

[7] *Confronting Injustice,* p. 391.
[8] *Ibid.,* p. 211.

We must develop a reciprocal understanding that divine law and human law are in constant process of growth, change and emergence. Religion and law will remain distant from each other, distrustful and alienated until men reach the point of knowing as thoroughly as they know their own physical existence, that both creation and revelation in the cosmos and in law are incomplete, ongoing and continuous.[9]

Here I believe is the key statement. When we get to the roots of man's life we discover that the process is not simply a human process, and that its meaning is not shut up within man alone; but that the full concreteness of his existence involves his response to the divine reality which is itself in the process, and that the structures of the divine working are not frozen forms but are related to the creativity in the ongoing interchange between God and man.

What Cahn protests against is not the introduction of the religious outlook into the search for justice; but the failure of the guardians of religious perspectives and values to overcome the inertia of institutional life and to achieve an authentic ethical protest against injustice. "Under pressure of society's daily needs, secular law is beginning to fill the ethical vacuum."[10] The proponents of "secular" theology will find in Edmond Cahn a powerful ally from the perspective of law; but in the end they will not find a restricted humanism. For him man's life was more than a lonely journey; it was a journey before God and with Him.

THE SECOND MAJOR THEME we must state is that of the consumer perspective. It is already implicit in the interpretation of justice; but it must be brought out as it came more and more to be the guiding theme of Edmond Cahn's reflections.

---

9 *Ibid.*, p. 215.
10 *Ibid.*, p. 219.

Most directly it means that the assessment of the authority, the weight and the usefulness of legal systems and procedures is to be judged not from an *a priori* set of principles but from the standpoint of those whom the law affects. Here the full personalism of Cahn's thinking appears as he continually brings problems of legal justice down to questions of the way in which they reach, modify, guide or obstruct the persons involved. This is why he criticizes with the intensity of a prophet attempts to justify legal systems by their "average" usefulness, or their performance "on the whole," allowing for certain failures. The use of the third degree in police methods, for example, is sometimes defended on the ground that it doesn't really affect many, it is useful in some cases, and there isn't very much of it anyhow. Against this Cahn hurled the full weight of the sense of injustice. He points out how differently we react to these considerations when we are the person involved.

There are at least three ways in which we, in a democracy, are consumers of law. We consume law, first, by being safeguarded and regulated from day to day, and in certain cases by becoming involved in law suits where rights or damages are assessed by the courts. Second, we consume justice and law as we influence the shape of policy and legislation, vote, and participate in the legal process. Finally, and here I quote his important words precisely,

> There is a third way to consume justice. It consists in the people's examining and assuming responsibility for what officials do in their name and by their authority—the unjust and evil acts as well as the beneficent and good.[11]

Here is the central point. The consumer of justice (or injustice) is himself a maker of it, and there is no authentic

---

11 *Ibid.,* p. 396.

way to a more just society which does not involve the transformation of men.

This is Cahn's theme in *The Predicament of Democratic Man*. In democracy man has created a society and a legal order which require him to participate, to make moral decisions, to give effect to his own sense of injustice. Hence he cannot opt out of the consequences of law in society. He cannot exempt himself from the effects of the acts of his representatives, his governors and jurists, for the democratic man is the consumer to whom all these acts are related and he is responsible for responding to them. Nothing outraged Edmond Cahn more than the easy tendency to blame the legislature or the "politicians," or "the power structure" for what is taking place. These institutions are finally shaped and controlled by the decisions which every one of us makes. This is not to say that our means of participation in decision-making are perfect. The point is that there is no one responsible for improving them but ourselves.

> Representative government has implicated us. It has made us participants—accomplices if you will—in the deeds that are done in our name and by our authority . . . *the true predicament of democratic man is his moral involvement in the misdeeds of government.*[12]

Cahn goes on to analyze the new modes of participation, and both individual and collective responsibility. He also discusses the quality of ethical judgment and analytically dissects it into the use of due process, the significance of compassion, and the grading of belief. His discussion of compassion is, I believe, one of the most important rational interpretations of compassion in relation to law. He shows that the

---

12 Edmond Cahn, *The Predicament of Democratic Man,* New York: Macmillan, 1961, p. 15. Italics in original.

quality of mercy in ethical judgments need not always be derived from a sphere other than the legal one. When we understand man in process we discover that there are conditions in the structure of human life which make compassion relevant to making a just judgment and that these can be rationally set forth. For example, there is the estimate of our own emotional bias, and the significance of the passage of time in its effect both on the person we judge and upon the goals we set for ourselves in judging. "What we need to develop in modern democracy is neither a judgment without compassion which is bound to be harsh, nor a compassion without judgment which is bound to be dangerous, but a continual application and intelligent use of compassion-in-judgment."[13] In this connection I remember Edmond Cahn's remarking one day when we were discussing the way in which our organic reactions enter into the sense of injustice, that when he wanted to resolve in his own mind some fundamental issue of human relationships and legal theory his favorite place to do so was in the subway.

Thus Edmond Cahn viewed the search for legal justice always in the context of man's growing, changing, organic response both to the demands of nature and life which force his adjustment, and to his inward sense of right and wrong which develops in history and is conditioned by many factors, but without which man is not fully human. Fallible as it is, man must assert and refine his sense of injustice if he is to affirm what gives worth to his life.

II

IT IS IN THE SPIRIT of Edmond Cahn's thought to move our discussion to a concrete issue of justice and law which we

---

13 *Ibid.*, p. 151.

presently face. It is an issue to which a good deal of thought is being given now, the question of legal penalties for strikes against the public as employer. I dare to tackle this question for two reasons. One is that it is of great importance to all of us who care about seeing our democratic society work; and the other is that it is a question about which the lawyers confess themselves as baffled as anyone else as to what can and should be done.

The background of the issue is simple enough. Public employees such as policemen, firemen, teachers, sanitation workers and public transportation employees are organized and negotiate the conditions of their employment with representatives of government. When the employees are dissatisfied they have to resort to more persuasion, or they can bring pressure to bear by the way they perform or fail to perform their duties. That is, they may engage in a job action or a strike. Governments of cities, states and the federal government have tried to prevent this by passing laws making strikes by public employees illegal and fixing penalties. At least two difficulties have arisen.

The first has to do with the penalties. They may be so severe that the community balks at enforcing them. In connection with this it may be recognized that the attempt to enforce them may cause a more widespread protest, the stoppage of public services, and therefore even greater damage. New York's Conlin-Wadlin law was unused for three years precisely for this reason. On the other hand the penalties may be so light that they do not act as a deterrent, and there is only a symbolic resistance to the stopping of essential services. A teacher's union representative is quoted as remarking that under New York's new Taylor Law the fines against the union amounted to about 20 cents per day per member.

The second major difficulty is that there is no way to bring the public as employer into the bargaining or judicial process the way a private employer participates in it. Courts can serve injunctions on unions but not on legislatures.

The legislature can pass a law requiring the transit authority to adopt certain safeguards for workers, and to pay a certain wage. But who is to compel the legislature to insure that a certain salary or working conditions shall be guaranteed—except the legislature itself? Hence bargainers for government are in the position of having to arrive at a settlement with the union and at the same time to assure themselves that the public bodies will provide funds necessary to support a settlement. Who is to compel the taxing bodies to do this? The same problem stands even in the case of compulsory arbitration; for arbitrators have no power to secure resources to comply with the decisions which they make.

THERE IS ONE ADDITIONAL FEATURE of the present mode of bringing pressure for a more generous settlement which complicates the issue still further. This is the creation of a critical situation for the public, not by striking, but by slowing down or otherwise altering the way in which work is done. Railroad unions have long known that they could create a drastic slow down in rail services by going by the rule book. Everything is done according to rule and at a pace which overlooks no requirement. As a result, the service bogs down. Firemen and policemen have adopted the same tactics, the former sometimes refusing to perform certain services. Policemen announce that they will complete reports, carry out inspections, perform their required duties to the point of slowing down the entire operation. No illegality is involved.

An interesting variant of this method was that initiated at Queens General Hospital on January 24, 1969, by doctors who were still waiting for salary increases negotiated the previous summer. The doctors instituted what they called a "heal-in," admitting patients who normally would be sent home and slowing the rate of discharge of patients. The goal to be achieved, said one doctor, "is to admit everyone they can and keep the beds in the hospital filled." And another doctor said, "The physicians decided to practice medicine to the full extent of grade A medical care." The goal apparently was to fill the hospital to the point that its services would bog down; and also to overload the hospital so that the unionized employees would protest to their unions and thus bring additional pressure on the city.[14]

But undoubtedly the most brilliant and exquisitely calculated method of protest in recent times was that adopted by the Long Island State Parkway police. Holding that they were not being given adequate contracts and protesting the slowness of negotiations, the policemen announced on November 13, 1968, through the president of their associa‑ tion, that on the next day they would start enforcing all the traffic laws. They would issue summonses to cars going 51 miles an hour in a 50 mile an hour zone. They would enforce the slow downs in areas where signs required slowing down to 35 miles an hour, signs to which American motorists habitually pay little attention. They would close all lanes at scenes of accidents, make spot checks of vehicles, refuse to operate unsafe police cars, and impound vehicles found to be mechanically defective or whose driver could not produce a license. This "speed-up" as the officers called it was put into effect and it began to snarl the Long Island traffic to the point of hopeless confusion. One irate motorist went into court to get an injunction against the police, charging that this enforcement of law constituted a harassment of the citizenry. The injunction was denied, but this appeal to the

---

[14] For these details and quotations I am relying on the *New York Post* for January 24, 1969.

court to stop the police from enforcing the law offers a nice problem in legal theory, and a dramatic documentation of Edmond Cahn's thesis that the law must be looked at from the standpoint of the "consumers" who, in this case, were the police, the motorists, and the community at large. The speed-up was apparently legal and came into no conflict with the New York Taylor Law which prohibits strikes or slow downs by public employees. An interesting side-light is that the accident and death rate on Long Island was sharply reduced during this period; but there is no question that such police vigilance would result in the immobilization of the society.

The issue is how the life of the community is to be pre-served amidst the disorder created by the discrepancy be-tween what the government offers, and the demands felt to be just on the part of groups in the community. There could be no clearer demonstration of Edmond Cahn's thesis that the search for justice goes on in the context of the human search for a viable way of life. Not only are abstract rules of justice of little help in resolving the issue, but the actual law of the state is seen to rest on an order and a set of temporary agreements and types of acceptance which have beneath them powerful forces which can erupt at any time and threaten the legal order.

The most critical problem of law and disorder in our democracy is not the problem of criminality, pressing as that is. It is the problem of how, in a highly technical, vulnerable community, every group can have freedom to assert its de-mands against the government and against other groups, while enough public order is preserved to enable the com-munity to survive. Of course one may say that this problem never really gets to the stage of desperation except in time of revolution; but that is not true. We were certainly very near a health crisis in New York City during the sanitation strike; and it would be foolish to assume that all groups are always so farsighted and finally responsible that they would never let the situation drift into chaos. Certainly, colleges and universities now face a similar problem.

One may say that armed force is available as a final resource. But this is precisely the difficulty. If we must rely on this for saving society from the consequences of negotiations with public employees we are no longer relying on laws, but on force. Furthermore, calling in the National Guard or Army creates its own social and political consequences. In a situation of violence we are all consumers.

To put it bluntly, the reality of this issue lies in whether legal and adjudicative procedures can be found to preserve both maximum freedom of bargaining with the state itself, and the minimal order of society.

No one has an answer to this question; but we may consider certain strands in Edmond Cahn's view of law which may point toward a possible solution.

THE FIRST OBSERVATION is that in the case of a strike which affects the public interest we are all consumers, not only in the general sense which he has demonstrated, but also in the most direct possible sense. We are consumers both because we are directly affected in health, safety and decency by what is taking place, and because the issues have to be decided between the government—which is ourselves—and a particular group among us involved in pressing its claims. If we are in the group making the demand we have direct interest in the outcome; but we are also members of the community, and its debacle would be ours also.

Now if we are all consumers in this sense, faced with the issue of a disagreement and resultant strike which affects the public interest, then according to Edmond Cahn's theory we cannot rely on statute alone to put people back to work or to invoke penalties which will be sufficiently deterring. On the most practical level we have discovered that the only law which has any chance of being enforced is one so drawn that the penalties it involves will not be serious enough to deter anyone. Further, the New York Taylor Law has a clause which permits a striking body the defense of "extreme provocation" which surely leaves a loop-hole for any court charged with enforcing the statute. The New York Legislature in its 1968–69 session increased the penalties of the Taylor Law, but it kept the "extreme provocation" clause. At this writing the effect of the increased penalties has yet to be tested.

The Taylor Law limits the fines imposed in any case, so that a union cannot be fined for each day of a strike more than the average dues it collects in a week. This means that a union can calculate with precision what its limit of liability will be. The revised law does impose penalties on individuals, but again it remains to be seen how this will stand up in a test case.

Beyond these difficulties looms a larger one. No matter what the law says, the grievance of a group can create an issue of sufficient magnitude to bring about the stoppage of essential services in the community, which is always the party of the second part. It can thus force the members of the community to make up their minds as to what the justice of the demand is.

The situation is dangerous because it seems to make the community vulnerable at the point where the greatest pressure is applied, or where the threat to the common welfare is the most acute. When one settlement is made it becomes a standard for others, and this raises the question of what the community is willing and able to afford. So we are back at questions of real justice or injustice. How should services performed be rewarded, by what standard and according to what view of the relationship of various needs, functions and values?

Now it is interesting that what would seem to be the concrete issues of justice involved in public contracts include such questions as, "What is a fair income for certain kinds of work demanding certain skills?" These questions are very little discussed publicly when the negotiations of public labor contracts are being carried out. We simply do not have a common body of tradition or criticism by which we can establish criteria for thinking about these issues. Here, of course, basic questions of social philosophy appear. Mr. Servan-Schreiber of France says there should be stringent limits placed on the gap between highest and lowest incomes. He points to Sweden where a first rate surgeon receives only four times the income of an average skilled worker. In the United States the disparity would be on the order of ten to thirty times.

It becomes clear that if the sense of injustice is to play any part in the settlement of such issues, statutory law will help only in so far as it rests upon the community's sense of a disciplined answer to the questions of standards of reward and conditions of work.

This leads to a second observation. If we in the community are consumers directly involved, then should not the consumer know much more about what is going on and what the issues are?

There is at least one thing the law could do which at present it does not. It could compel the state agency involved in a forthcoming negotiation to publish a clear, detailed analysis of the scale of reward, the conditions of work, the special problems involved in the area in which it is working. For example, how should we think of the relative claims of sanitation men and policemen? The community as a whole knows little of the actual points under dispute. I have known one or two cases where strikes were settled in a matter of hours when certain details of what was actually involved in the negotiations were made public. As consumers we have to be much more informed about the situation. Instead of brief news stories reviewing demands and offers in general terms, there should be a long period of widespread public education as to the issues involved. This could be compelled by law, and it might get the negotiations out of the sparring confrontation into a public discussion.

There is, further, the question of timing. As a citizen who knows little more than what he reads in the papers I am struck by the fact that with deadlines approaching when a whole city may lose its transportation or its hospital services, it remains one of the strategies of both sides to refuse to make an offer or to disclose specific demands until the deadline is almost reached. One variant is for unions to make exorbitant demands long ahead of the deadline, in such extreme form that everyone knows they have no chance of being accepted.

Why should not the law compel all agencies dealing with crucial public services to arrive at publicly stated positions two to six months before the contract deadline? Whatever one's judgment about some provisions of the Taft-Hartley Law, the cooling off period it provides has proved useful in critical situations. It is one way of requiring the parties to take enough time to reach an agreement.

Other devices such as fact-finding, mediation officers, and arbitration, compulsory or otherwise, are also useful. But the primary point here is that in the consumer perspective we see a relationship between the issues involved in public services and the informed judgment of the whole community which has not been sufficiently taken into account. We need much wider dissemination of facts and discussion of the principles involved. Newspaper advertisements by the contending parties do not as a rule meet this need. They are necessarily partisan, condensed and polemical. Why can we not use the resources of government to provide comprehensive and accurate information concerning the contracts government is negotiating?

A THIRD OBSERVATION is that the principle of government accountability must be affirmed. Indeed, there is a growing body of practice to give structure to this accountability. As Edmond Cahn says, "The principle of community enterprise has been making inroads on the obsolete belief that states are immune from being charged with wrong or being obliged to make reparation."[15] The road to the enactment of provisions permitting the sovereign to be a party to damage suits has been a long one. Late in 1961 only half of the states had such laws; Congress did not pass a similar law for the federal government until 1946.

It is far from clear as to how this principle applies to disputes between state employees and the state, but there seems good reason to hold that there could be a mode of redress of grievance by a group of public employees who believe they have been dealt with unjustly by some department or bureau. The central point is that the present laws aiming to prevent strikes put every group automatically in the wrong simply through the act of striking. There should be other processes for putting collective grievance before the whole community and asking for review and redress. The state is not infallible, and its servants certainly are not, including those who make the decisions affecting public employees. Striking for redress of grievance ought to be viewed as a last remedy not a first.

ONE FURTHER REFLECTION returns us to an issue which I discussed many times with Edmond Cahn. How is the moral weight of the community to be brought to bear on the

---

15 *The Predicament of Democratic Man*, p. 68.

judicial process? What we learn from the disorders of our system is that positive law functions only so far as it reflects and is sustained by the values, commitments and responsible action of the community in which it exists. That may seem too broad a statement, but each week of our present strife on campuses and in cities makes its truth more apparent. It is men who make the decisions which lead to chaos or order in community, college, nation and world. How then is the sense of injustice to be nourished which can enable a community to deal in a disciplined way with the extraordinary new forms of social protest and conflict?[16]

The issue here posed for ethical and legal theory is that of the sources of moral commitment. Here I believe we have to choose between a one-community theory of history and a two-community theory. We all recognize and live in one community, the company of men in history. This is itself a synthesis of many communities—family, state, business, profession, religious group. In this human community we confront one another as creatures on the same earth, men bearing the same human equipment of feelings and desires and hopes, having to live together, make terms with one another, and search together for a tolerable justice.

There is, however, another community which both Judaism and Christianity have asserted to be the most important seed-bed of moral commitment and the sharpener of the sense of injustice. It is the community which has as its basis for existence the faith that God has imposed a commitment upon it, summoned it to live as a people of God and honor its covenant with Him, and whose sole reason for existence is to serve God's will for His creation.

I would prefer to call this second community the "spiritual

---

[16] See the discussion of the national community and its morale in Edmond Cahn, *The Sense of Injustice*, New York: New York University Press, 1949, pp. 151–186.

community," to use Paul Tillich's term, because it cannot be
identified with any earthly community be it nation, or
people, or congregation, or church.[17] It is a community
which God establishes in His own way, using the empirical
communities of faith, but not bound exclusively to them. He
establishes it in His own time and its boundaries are not to
be drawn by any man.

Judaism and Christianity have understood the biblical
community as related in a peculiar way to the spiritual
community, adumbrating it, believing in it, seeking to realize
it. There is no "perfection" of the people of God on earth.
Even St. Augustine with his tendency to absolutize the City
of God was too realistic to endow it with perfection. We can
avoid any simple utopianism or romanticism about man in
any of his communities. Edmond Cahn knew the depth of sin
in man. No one could know the history of law as he did and
not have a realistic sense of the tragic evil of which man is
capable. What Edmond Cahn did believe in was the possibility of man's discovery of the way to justice in the give and
take of the human community. I agree with him.

What remains to be emphasized is that the vitality of the
moral tradition requires a community of people who live in
that tradition even when they are themselves most severely
judged by it. Edmond Cahn also affirmed this. He stood
within the biblical tradition, thought in its categories, found
guidance and strength within it. He fought all his life as a
lawyer to keep the freedom of the religious community and
of the state clear on both sides, not only for the sake of the
state, but also for the sake of the purity of witness of the
religious community.[18]

Edmond Cahn's own moral sensitivity was so profound and

---

17 Paul Tillich, *Systematic Theology*, Vol. III, Chicago: University of Chicago
Press, 1963.
18 See the essays in *Confronting Injustice*, chapter 4.

so richly informed both by law and by moral tradition that he sometimes wrote as if the issues of life were clearly there to be seen by anyone who would really look. He could say: "By merely seeking to ascertain what is righteous we can bring the quality into existence, where it persists until we learn, as we may, to form still more humane decisions."[19] My only comment is that agreeing with this we still have to acknowledge the difficulty of "really seeking to ascertain what is righteous." That is something we men find hard to do, and the religious traditions in their greatest prophets have stressed this. The biblical communities have had a glimpse of the holiness of God and the distance between His righteousness and the self-centered human heart. It is their task to keep before all men their profound capacities for justice and for injustice, and to communicate the faith in a divine mercy which can sustain commitment and hope in a tragic world.

IN EMPHASIZING the "two-community" theory I believe I am stating what was implicit in Edmond Cahn's thought. But let the last word here belong to the lawyers. A plea for moral insight and commitment given in general terms, which does not confront specific issues in the area of public life and disorder where the law operates and where lawyers work, is futile and irrelevant in our time. I know of no more pertinent and demanding area for discovering the significance of biblical faith today than the approach to justice which Edmond Cahn took through his profound involvement in the law, set in the context of an acceptance of public and human responsibility, and informed by the tradition which persistently asks: "What does the Lord require of thee, but to do justly, and to love mercy, and to walk humbly with God."

---

19 Edmond Cahn, *The Moral Decision,* Bloomington, Indiana: Indiana University Press, 1955, p. 315. But he could also say: "In moral decisions, if the truth comes at all, it does not come as a gift but as wages for strenuous digging"; *ibid.,* p. 256.

Ethics and Business

PHILIP SPORN

BUSINESS is the most important single activity in American society, whether judged by the number of people engaged in it, the total time devoted to it, or the resultant flow of product. Nor can there be any question that the American form of social organization, in which business plays such a vital role, has brought us a system of production and distribution of goods and services historically unparalleled in its abundance. This we could, with common consent, classify as socially good.

Yet the same society that has produced such great material abundance has also been accompanied by many phenomena and problems which are far from good. In years past it brought us massive unemployment. It has brought us a war which has alienated large segments of our population. It has brought us civil disorders which threaten to split this great nation into two societies, physically separated not only by color of skin but in a large measure geographically, with the cities increasingly occupied by our Negro population. It has brought to a large segment of our responsible population a deep sense of frustrated national purpose: We can—we should

—be a great nation, a guide and beacon to the rest of the world in every area of human activity, physical, moral and spiritual. And yet there is a feeling that somehow this role is escaping us for reasons that are difficult to grasp in concrete fashion. There seems to be an absence of leadership to point the way back to greatness.

Where does the trouble lie? In a *Wall Street Journal* review of *The Ethics of Business*[1] William H. Peterson wrote:

> The business system is inherently an ethical system. Without coercion, each participant—seller and buyer, employer and employee, shareholder and manager, and others—voluntarily gives in order to get, a *quid pro quo,* a mutually advantageous arrangement, a kind of social cooperation on a grand scale without the use of force.

Perhaps a critical analysis of Mr. Peterson's unreserved encomium, "The business system is inherently an ethical system," would provide an answer to our question.

In a stringent indictment of American business and the American businessman printed in *Fortune* in 1958,[2] Dr. Louis Finkelstein called attention to the fact that no institution will survive if it is dedicated only to self-preservation, and that in our almost universal adoption, in some degree, of the standards of our business society we have abandoned our ethical and religious traditions. This, it is apparent, is quite at odds with Mr. Peterson's view. It is important, therefore, to take a penetrating look at our social-business-economic environment for some evidence of either (or neither) view. This is particularly important if one is of the conviction that a salubrious environment is indispensable to the continued

---

[1] *The Ethics of Business: Corporate Behavior in the Market Place*, New York: Columbia Graduate School of Business, 1963.
[2] "The Businessman's Moral Failure," *Fortune,* September 1958.

soundness of our business society, and that its self-preservation is impossible without complete renewal and affirmation of its dedication to moral and ethical principles.

Let us take a look at some major areas of our American business scene, with a view of sampling the ecology of its moral and ethical environment.

THE PROBLEM OF AIR POLLUTION has by now become familiar throughout our country. The smog problem which at one time was considered a special piece of misfortune that had struck the residents of Los Angeles, is no longer so geographically selective, largely as a result of the ubiquitous use of the automobile in our society. But we must remember that economic or business factors, unmodified by other social considerations, have controlled the kind of automobiles that have been produced and the kind of fuel (gasoline) that has been made available to furnish their motive power.

Thus the Panel on Electrically Powered Vehicles stated:

> There has been inadequate incentive for an individual automotive manufacturer to apply pollution control technology to the automobile in advance of its competitors. . . . There has been inadequate incentive for an individual fuel producer to introduce products with improved pollution characteristics in advance of its competitors.[3]

It is not surprising therefore that the first and most important finding of this panel was:

> 1. Air pollution presents a serious threat of increasing significance to the health and welfare of this country and

---

3 "The Automobile and Air Pollution," report of the Panel on Electrically Powered Vehicles to the Commerce Technical Advisory Board, October 1967.

all industrialized areas of the world. Without prompt and effective action to control this contamination of the atmosphere, living conditions within and around the cities of the Nation will continue to deteriorate. Automotive vehicle emissions, namely carbon monoxide, hydrocarbons, oxides of nitrogen, and lead compounds, are principal contributors to this problem.

2. Emissions from automotive vehicles are largely responsible for the formation of photochemical smog in Los Angeles and some other areas, and vehicles are the principal source of carbon monoxide in the atmosphere. In addition to these known, specific effects, vehicle emissions combine with emissions from other sources, in ways and to an extent unknown, to contribute to general air pollution.

It is true that other areas of economic activity have contributed to the potentially critical pollution situation. Badly designed and badly located electric power plants have not helped. Both private and public incinerator plants have been serious offenders. But together these have posed only a minor threat in comparison with the automobile. The automobile and petroleum industries have done little or nothing to control automobile pollutants which create a serious threat to the health and comfort of the nation. It was not until the problem had deteriorated sufficiently to stimulate public activity that any positive efforts were undertaken. There would appear to have been a lack of social responsibility in the business sphere.

LET US LOOK AT ANOTHER AREA. In 1960 a series of antitrust violations by substantially all manufacturers of electric equipment came to light. Scores of indictments were handed down; many pleadings of guilty and *nolo contendere* resulted in heavy fines against most of the industry's members. As a result of subsequent civil suits, total damages estimated at $400 million were awarded by federal courts or paid in settlements.

These conspiratorial activities had extended over many years. Even more significant is the fact that the largest manufacturer in this group had been found guilty, had pleaded *nolo contendere*, or had agreed to consent decrees and the enjoining of further conspiratorial activities in approximately a dozen cases going back to 1911. The 1960 conspiratorial activities were merely the culmination of a long record of nonchalant disregard of previous criminal activities. One must assume that the moral effect of having treated the law with contempt over many decades did not act as a deterrent to the expansion of the antitrust violations, to the point that record-breaking damage payments were invoked. Nor was this violator deterred from continuing activities that led to even greater losses than the monetary fines—damage to his corporate image among customers, shareowners, employees, the government, the academic communities, and the public at large.

It would help to be able to cite government as having applied different criteria of ethics and morality. But while we have a *right* to expect that government would show business how to function without violation of any law, and also without doing violence to any generally accepted ethical principles—too often this is not the case. At their annual meeting at Washington in 1961, the Roman Catholic bishops of the United States officially stated that they did not find any difference in the ethical behavior of the various segments of our society. They did find that "The rosy deception is rated good if it succeeds in selling more products, in winning more votes, in convincing more taxpayers."

In recent years, two of our three largest coal companies

have been absorbed by large oil companies. By this step coal and oil, for many decades top competitors among our primary energy sources, became anti-competitive. Yet the anti-trust division of the United States Department of Justice apparently gave these mergers its blessing.

The situation is still worse. Within the past years nuclear power has been competing more and more extensively with coal, oil and natural gas in the country's electric power generating program. The exploitation of nuclear fuel depends on the progress made in the technological development of nuclear reactors—and the two leaders in the development of nuclear reactors have been the country's two largest electrical manufacturers. It is a truism that the public interest and public welfare are best served where coal and nuclear power *compete* in their main common market—the electric energy market. But what possible chance has this principle to prevail when the common tie between oil and coal discussed above carries over to important directorships in the production of electricity? Surely the morality of such relationships has either been inadequately considered or completely disregarded.

An even more flagrant lack of morality is exemplified by the Apollo story, from the project's inception, through its halcyon years of development, to the tragic fire of January 1967 and the incineration of astronauts Grissom, White and Chaffee.

This entire period was a grand tragedy compounded of amorality and breakdown of ethics on the part of government, business and the press, ending with the Gotterdammerung crash of January 1967. From the standpoint of the public interest, how justified was the *hasty* adoption of a program to put a man on the moon before 1970, at a cost stated to be minimally $22.7 billion? Were the demands on our finite resources—materials, men, scientific and technological skills—carefully evaluated? Were they ever put on public record for consideration or debate? What moral authority was invoked to reach the decision? Was the glib justification that we could not afford "to forfeit exploration of the solar system to Russia"[4] sufficient? What about the moral demands of our neglected cities, our polluted environment, our moribund educational institutions, and our underdeveloped health and welfare services?

The implementation of the Apollo project, which was turned over to business, was from the very beginning riddled with questions concerning the propriety of the major award and the abilities of the winning contractor. But, having entered the project with less than full approval, did the great business organization which was the beneficiary of this agreement resolve to perform with high competence and dedicated distinction? Far from it. In a report submitted by the Apollo program director almost two years before the 1967 tragedy, the contracting company was sharply criticized for its shoddy workmanship and its high accident record, and was chastized for not always showing "sufficient dedication to the job." The same director subsequently testified that he had considered taking part of the contract away from the original contractor.[5] Here again is a case where moral and ethical principles were given no more than lip service by both business and NASA, and with tragic results.

Perhaps the greatest moral failure should be ascribed to the press. Almost all the media and agencies that print and broadcast news abandoned their basic and historic functions of molding public opinion and acting as the public watchdog, and either played the role of a member of the team or, in the case of television, adopted the NASA program as a backdrop

---

4 *The New York Times*, August 4, 1962.
5 *Saturday Review*, March 4, 1967.

for projecting the space race, in an attempt to attract the viewing public, as reflected in Nielsen ratings.

Thus, with few exceptions, the communications media missed their opportunity in the early days to raise such questions as whether NASA was in the public interest, and whether the whole concept of the space race might need drastic revision. Later they did nothing to arouse public concern about the contractor's shoddy performance. It is true that this performance was later much improved, but at what a price!

PERHAPS WE HAVE BEEN FOCUSSING too sharply on narrow areas of our vastly extended and diversified society. But a quick cross-sectional look at the society as a whole is not too encouraging in the ethical image it projects. Thus a feature story in *The Wall Street Journal* is titled "Working for No. 1, Resourceful Employees Use Firms' Time, Tools for Personal Projects." If any further expansion of the headline were needed, the article furnishes it when it says: "In office and shop, an increasing number of workers are using company time—and often company materials—for their own projects. They may pursue profitable sidelines, using fellow workers as customers. Or they may work on their hobbies. . . . And executives, it seems, occasionally are more culpable than the hired hands."

Another story was headlined "Campus Shoplifters, University Bookstores Suffer Rising Losses from Student Thefts; Problem Serious at Wisconsin, Harvard, San Jose State; Poverty is Rarely Cause, Even Divinity Students Guilty." The body of the story is even more discouraging in its explanation that students are rebelling against the establishment when they steal. "Everyone feels oppressed by authority —the university administration, the draft boards and so on— and the 'Coop' is the dark side of authority." Moral scruples do not seem to enter the picture.

The recent resort to force by college students, frequently with the concurrence or encouragement of faculty, is an example of total confusion between the right of complaint and appeal, and the illegal, immoral and unethical disregard for the personal and property rights of others. But of course the universities themselves have in many cases been particularly remiss in their sensitivity to ethical conduct.

A great university finds the attraction of potential monetary gain so irresistible as to become allied with a cigarette filter firm—without even discussing the moral compatibility of such action with its own cancer research institute. Did this bad judgment (later retracted) on the part of the university contribute, even to a minor extent, to the breakdown in the moral behavior of members of its student body?

LET US MOVE FROM ACADEME to the money marketplace. A decision handed down in March 1968 by Federal Judge Edward C. McLean in the case of Escott vs. Bar-Chris Construction Company, stated that the underwriters, lawyers, auditors and directors of the firm all were to blame for any misinformation contained in a prospectus.

The judge found an important misrepresentation in the figure for the backlog of contracts, which the prospectus said totalled $6.9 million, but which was overstated by some $4.5 million (a small error of 190%). The lawyer's defense was that it is common practice to take the company's word on matters like that. "We'd get fired if we asked to see the backlog contracts," said one Wall Street lawyer.

The judicial decision, inescapable when considered from the moral viewpoint, stunned almost all the professional elements involved in the preparation and certification of the prospectus. *The Wall Street Journal* quoted a partner in a Wall Street firm as saying that the ruling "is a legal blockbuster that is standing the financial community on its ear."[6]

---

6 May 14, 1968.

A leading underwriter said that it was one of the most significant court decisions to affect investment banking in years. The American Institute of Certified Public Accountants called it a "landmark" ruling.

PROFESSOR ROBERT AUSTIN, writing in the *Harvard Business Review* of July–August 1965, pointed out that the crash of 1929 triggered the entrance of the federal government into the securities business. The resultant enactment of the Securities and Exchange Act and the creation of the Securities and Exchange Commission were direct results of the social change occasioned by the acceleration of communication, the need for equity capital, and much greater interest in the stock market. But the reaction of business leaders was to recognize neither the social impact of technological change nor the abuses possible in the light of such growth, and to resent the intrusion of government into these fields.

Today there is the same unwillingness on the part of business to face up to the social changes that have come about as a result of technological development, and to assume responsibility for the effects of its activities, whether required by law or not.

But all these examples of moral failure on the part of business are insignificant when compared with the greatest failure of all—our failure in integrating our citizens, in solving the problem of civil disunity.

A thorough study of this problem was made by Lt. Gen. James M. Gavin, USA (ret.), now a prominent management consultant, in his book *Crisis Now*. He sees an opportunity to invest funds now being used for the Vietnam war in new social organizations. But excellent as this study is in calling attention to the many physical problems that have to be solved, it does not quite focus on the problem in terms of the basic verities. For example, while pointing out that the 1960 census appears to have undercounted the American population by some 5,700,000 bodies, the vast majority being Negroes, Gavin does not stress the psychological damage that this population factor has caused to the Negro and white population. Great emphasis is given to the money that could become available to provide employment for twenty million people, if the struggle in Vietnam were brought to an end. But there is no ringing denunciation of the social injustice involved in the almost insuperable barriers to productive work erected by white citizens (craftsmen in particular) against the Negro.

The assassination of Martin Luther King may have highlighted our moral deficiencies on a national scale, but our real collective sin has been our long-drawn-out apathy toward our Negro citizens, an apathy which has produced a situation in which Dr. King's death became a possibility, and the burning of our cities a tragic realization.

Our society must become aware that the failure to recognize the moral and ethical errors in our behavior is at the heart of the problem of racial integration, perhaps the deepest and most far-reaching challenge confronting American society today. It would be superficial and specious to lay our current plight and shortcomings solely on the shoulders of business. At the same time, our increasing awareness of the remedial value of employment opportunities emphasizes how heavily the responsibility for the racial problem rests with the business community.

WHY HAS ONE OF THE MOST IMPORTANT ELEMENTS in American life failed in its responsibility to society by not giving proper consideration to ethical issues? The reason lies deep within the foundations of our modern corporate structure, which contains a disturbingly unhealthy degree of indifference to responsibility and self-deception regarding accountability. These traits are characteristic of the large, widely-owned public corporations that are central to this paper's analysis. Although only about 55% of the gross national product of the United States originates in non-financial corporations,[7] the small business sectors of our society have a relatively insignificant influence on the pattern of economic development, and the drive of our system comes mainly from the large-scale sector, now increasingly including the government as well as the large corporations.[8]

Although the corporate organization is ubiquitous today, it is well to bear in mind that only within the past century have general corporation laws come into being in the United States. While corporations have existed for many centuries, charters were originally granted only rarely, and generally only by special actions of king or legislature. American corporation laws made it possible for almost anyone to establish a corporation for almost any purpose, without having to seek special legislative action from a state legislature or from Congress.

Without question, the socio-economic invention of the corporation has been most important for the advancement of society. As a fictitious legal entity, distinct from its owners, which can sue and be sued in court, the corporation has a number of advantages. It solves the problem of human mortality by its right to have perpetual succession or existence; it can provide limited liability for its owners; and it furnishes an excellent mechanism for the raising of the large blocks of capital necessary in any dynamic modern business enterprise.

Because of its potential perpetual existence, the corporation also provides a mechanism for effecting social awareness in border areas where motivations of short-term profit and more socially oriented long-term gain overlap.

---

[7] Robert M. Solow, *The Public Interest*, No. 9, Fall 1967.
[8] Robin Marris, *ibid.*, No. 11, Spring 1968.

But the corporation has its problems and weaknesses, arising from the mechanisms of its control.

In theory, the mechanism for corporate control is based on a sequence of authority or legitimacy:

1. The corporation is owned by its stockholders.

2. The stockholders annually (in most cases) elect a board of directors to represent them, into whose hands they entrust the guidance of the affairs of the company.

3. The board elects the principal officers, and delegates to them responsibility for day-to-day operation and management. The management plans, builds, expands and operates the facilities of the company, buys its raw materials, hires its researchers, supervisors, workers and salesmen; management plans—or fails to plan—its future development and directs the research to bring it about.

4. Management invariably does something else. It selects new candidates for the board. These choices are subsequently formally approved by the directors and elected by the stockholders, but the process is almost invariably automatic; board members are in fact elected by management.

5. A subtle and legal shell game has been introduced between steps 3 and 4, in which management and the board of directors have exchanged positions by and large—there are always some exceptions. From then on, management controls the board instead of the board controlling management. Thus, policies which should be subject to the concern and decision of the board are brought to the board by a management which has cleared them in advance with an executive committee completely under its control. Very little room is left for the exercise of control by the board.

Management's gradual realization that *it* is in fact the corporation, that the board need be given no more than token consideration, and that the board's responsibility is what management decides it is, spreads like a virulent toxin throughout the corporate system. The results may range from corporate malaise all the way to complete corporate destruction.

Current practice leans to the view that corporate responsibility should not evolve from strong ethical motivation, but rather from legal requirements and marketplace considerations. The basic trusteeship responsibility, the morality of that responsibility, the "punctilio of an honor the most sensitive," to quote the late Justice Cardozo, disappear. It is this absence of morality in the basic business structure that can place the complete control of a modern corporation, with assets running into billions of dollars, into the hands of a small group of management. The power of self-succession through control of directorships permits management to exercise complete control of a business, regardless of whether it is in the interest of the owners, let alone of the social area in which it functions. In turn, management is limited solely by legalities, and its own sense, attenuated by the press of short-term operating problems, of moral and ethical constraints. In the absence of an ethical imperative, business is at best ethically neutral.

THIS ANALYSIS will be rejected by a good many apologists for the status quo—not surprisingly, since one of the characteristics of corporate enterprise is a natural propensity for the status quo—on the ground that it overlooks the ability of the stockholder to move in, exercise ownership rights and influence direction. This is, however, most unrealistic because one must rally a sufficient number of stockholders to join in unseating established and entrenched management—a most difficult undertaking. Proxy fights do occur occasionally, but they are generally successful only when the shareowners' trust has been grossly betrayed and the business effectiveness of the corporation seriously damaged.

It is argued that the large-scale institutional investor can be relied upon to assure more responsible control by management. In reality, however, the large-scale investor is often totally ignorant of corporation policy and activities, and sends in proxies with complete docility, thus proving wholly ineffective in exercising or even influencing control.

Theoretically, the time and place for asserting shareowner control is the annual meeting of stockholders where management is presumed to give a full account of its activities and the performance of the company. However, modern business is generally so technologically complicated that, with minor exceptions, not even the members of the board of directors are competent to pass judgment on the questions placed before them. Certainly, the shareholders cannot adequately evaluate the (public-relations-oriented) facts presented to them, and judge whether management has performed competently, whether what is proposed is in the best interests of the company, the public it serves, and the stockholders.

Theoretically, too, the management will be elected by the board which the stockholders elect at the annual meeting, but in fact the board has been picked by management which it later goes through the routine formality of electing!

Based on this description of the realities of corporate relationships, it is not too difficult to decide whether the board controls management, or management controls the board.

In *The New Industrial State,* John K. Galbraith calls the annual meeting of the large American corporation "our most elaborate exercise in popular illusion." It may be more descriptive to call it a statistical and graphic tour, so well organized and executed to completely support management that by comparison the famous Crimean tour of Catherine the Great, staged by her paramour Marshall Potemkin, becomes an exercise in stark realism.

WE ARE CURRENTLY EXPERIENCING various expressions of civic stress which cumulatively are potentially destructive to our nation. In an analysis of the causes leading to the slaying of Senator Kennedy, Joseph Kraft pointed out:

> . . . unless the underlying pressures of ghetto life can be relieved, it is predictable that the Negro community will continue to protest and picket and march and on occasions burn and loot. . . . [This outlook of the Negroes] is shared by a large number of the best young people in this country. Rightly or wrongly, they have the sense of living in a land that is deeply immoral, that wages war and wastes nature and gets goods and spends dollars without regard to the soul of man.[9]

Evidence has been accumulating for a long while that top students on many campuses are more and more disinclined to join business firms. Those who do go into business later find their ideals clashing sharply against business practices that seem low in principles and morality and high in expediency.

The development of a society that has brought its people an unmatched system of production and distribution of the world's goods, has also brought an accumulation of social evils. There is no question but that business must play a vital part in curing America's illnesses. Yet it hesitates to commit itself fully and unreservedly to the elimination of the nation's social ills, giving various reasons for holding back.

1. The problems involve both capital (business) and labor. What is labor going to do about them? But labor, it is apparent, is waiting to see what business will do. Our most forward looking labor leaders believe that labor is waiting to be challenged by business.

2. The problems are too big for business to handle. They belong essentially to government. But government has admitted that it needs help—the organization, management and drive that business provides.

---

[9] *International Herald-Tribune,* June 8–9, 1968.

3. The function of business is the satisfactory performance of our society's work in the economic arena. What does business know about social problems? The answer, of course, is that many of these problems have come about in connection with or as a result of technological-economic developments sponsored by business. If business recognizes its social responsibilities—and this is a matter of morality—it cannot ignore these problems. Moreover, from a practical viewpoint, if these problems are not solved, business itself will be a total loser.

4. A supposedly potent argument for the abstention of business from activities in the social sphere is legal in nature. According to its terms of reference, from owner to management via the board of directors, business is confined legally to the administration of the affairs of the corporation with the goal of maximizing the profit of the shareholders. But, of course, the valid answers here are:

    a. There is no specification in the terms of reference as to which profit, the long-range or the short-term, is to be given preference.

    b. Far more important than immediate profit is assurance of continuing (and profitable) existence.

    c. These new responsibilities are outgrowths of business activities in the past. They will either be assumed by business in the future (i.e. the present), or as a last resort will be assumed by the government. But then government will most likely pick up the business as well.

The failure of the business community to live up to its potential reveals a consistent flaw that threatens the integrity of its structure and its ability to survive under conditions of great or extraordinary stress. That flaw is its lack of concern for ethical conduct, its apparent acceptance of the cynical concept that business is merely another form of game "whose basic rules are set by the government, and that, as long as a company does not transgress the rules of the game set by law, it has the legal right to shape its strategy without reference to anything but its profits."[10]

It is almost a truism that no businessman is truly modern unless he is thoroughly versed in the principles of operations research and its application to decision-making. But I believe that true awareness of the principles of morality, and commitment to ethical principles as guides to every modern business decision, are more important than operations research in all its variants.

THE FREQUENT DISREGARD of morality in the business world can, in many respects, be significantly improved by law. (Conversely, some have held that both the American bar and the American bench have encouraged immorality and unethical behavior on the part of American citizens.)[11] Here are some specific legal steps that might be taken to achieve more ethical and responsible conduct of corporate business.

1. *Tight control on qualification and selection of directors; no special interest directors.* I realize that this goes contrary to the concept of cumulative voting much favored by progressive thinkers. But in a showdown, special interest groups seek to protect their own concerns, regardless of the effect on the corporation. *No dummies.* A Ph.D. degree does not preclude a man acting as a dummy on a board.

2. *Restriction on inside directors.* No one whose responsibility extends to the office of general or chief counsel should be permitted to serve as a member of the board; the possi-

---

[10] Albert Z. Carr, "Is Business Bluffing Ethical?" *Harvard Business Review,* January–February, 1968.
[11] Franklin D. Roosevelt to Charles C. Burlingham, May 27, 1937, *Roosevelt and Frankfurter,* Little, Brown, 1967.

bilities of conflict of interests are enormously increased where this is disregarded.

3. *Broad restriction on interlocking directorates.* Frequently they involve the holder of multiple directorships in conflicts of interest, and offer the strongest kind of temptation to overstep that poorly defined, but still existing, line of separation between legal and illegal (from an antitrust standpoint) communications between companies.

4. *Some fairly well-defined spelling out of the duties of directors.* Responsibility to do one's homework—study of statistics, analyses, reports relating to questions on the agenda, or registration statements in connection with the issuance of securities that his company will file. Attendance at meetings. Responsibility to be articulate, to speak one's mind and participate in discussions. Monologue addresses by the board chairman are not conducive to thorough consideration of a problem.

5. *A legal requirement that every corporation with an annual gross revenue above $250 million appoint one or more full-time directors of the company to study and plan for the future growth of the company.* One of the great advantages of the corporation, pointed out earlier, is that it has solved the problem of human mortality by creating a legal perpetual succession or existence. But the corporation has not solved the problem of its *own* mortality, as a result of socio-economic unawareness or inept planning of its future. Having been granted the right of perpetual succession or existence by society, it behooves the corporation's guardians, the directors, to provide for the future to a much greater extent than an individual is obliged to provide for himself.

The failure to provide for the future of the corporation occurs as a result of the assumption that in electing the chief executive and his fellow officers, the board of directors has fully discharged its legal, moral and ethical responsibilities.

The delegation of full-time directors to plan for the future growth of the company would underscore the inescapable sense of responsibility of the corporate management. These planning directors would have no operating responsibilities. They would have no responsibility to, and would be subject to no influence by, management. Their duties and responsibilities would be defined solely in terms of advising the board.

An innovative program of this nature was proposed by one of our highly progressive and imaginative electronic corporations, as part of its search for more responsible directorship and management.[12] In its 1968 Annual Report, dated February 28, 1969, it enthusiastically reports about the implementation of the program for the "restructuring of the Board as proposed at the annual shareowners' meeting in 1967", in the election of John B. Connally, the three-term former Governor of Texas, as the second "Director and Officer of the Board." The post of Director and Officer of the Board, rather than Director and Officer of the Corporation, is a bold pioneering step motivated, obviously, by a deep sense of ethical and moral corporate responsibility.

6. *The minutes of the executive committee and directors meetings should be reasonably comprehensive and informative.* Putting the judgments of the directors on the record in full (not in the meaningless general terms ". . . after full discussion, the motion was duly made and seconded . . .") would enormously increase the degree of consideration and care given a proposal.

BUT LAW CAN DO ONLY SO MUCH. It is not illegal to set up criteria for employment on the basis of physical health, education, skills, and evaluated most-likely-to-succeed perfor-

---

12 Report to the shareowners of Texas Instruments, Inc., at the annual shareowners meeting, April 19, 1967.

mance; it is not illegal but it will frequently deter acceptance of a Negro job applicant. Nor is it illegal for a great university which owns an applied science research laboratory with an established record of public and governmental service on a non-profit basis, to sell it for the highest price to a responsible private enterprise corporation. And it is not illegal for a United States Senator, member of an important committee dealing with banking and currency, to have his considerable private fortune invested entirely in U.S. Treasury Bonds (thus giving him a vested interest in deflation and depression). In fact, the last example is generally, but quite erroneously, considered exceptionally praiseworthy, since the Senator's complete divorce from potentially corrupting commercial influences is a guarantee of his integrity.

None of these examples is illegal; each is, however, morally and ethically tainted for reasons which become apparent as one digs beneath the surface. There is, to quote Paul Weiss, ". . . a world outside the law that can be governed by custom, by ethical ideals, by philosophical reflection, and by many other things. This shows that there are limits to the scope, applicability and meaning of the law and that it cannot be used to define ethics and morality.[13]

There is, of course, a widely held opinion that moral and ethical principles do not have to be taught, that they are absorbed naturally, almost with one's mother's milk, or that they are inbred in the circle of the home and in early religious training. But this too facile assumption does not stand up to critical analysis based on the facts of life. Childhood indoctrination does no harm, but all too often the results are cigarette-paper thin. Nor do the idealistic ethics of Plato or Kant absorbed in a scholastic framework later in life offer substantive guidance in the much tougher environment of

---

13 Paul Weiss and Jonathan Weiss, *Right and Wrong*, Basic Books, 1967.

business, of sales quotas, competitive position, profit, dynamic growth and personal advancement. Surely, rigorous training in ethics and morality at an advanced educational level should be given by people who live and work in the world of business, and who are aware of the humanizing potential of ethics in the development of a more civilized society.

Without practical ethical training, the modern businessman is only partially equipped to do a responsible job. As the late Clarence B. Randall wrote only a short time before his death:

> The difficulty is that the warning bell of their conscience does not ring as they make their decisions. They plunge into action without pausing to reflect upon the moral implications of the course to which they are committing themselves and their corporations. They have been carefully trained in engineering, cost-accounting, pricing, human relations, and other phases of management, but not in ethics.[14]

Perhaps programs of study based on the case history method will be found valuable for training in ethical awareness, as they have been for training in law and business techniques. Perhaps a court of ethics will have to be set up. Even if its functioning is limited to cases voluntarily submitted to it for advisory opinion or decision, it would perform a useful social function.

This is not the occasion to explore detailed suggestions. Prior and basic to any specific actions, business must determine that ethics and morality are indispensible for its historical goal of producing and distributing products which will

---

[14] *The Executive in Transition,* McGraw-Hill, 1967.

fill the physical needs and wants of man. Business must accept this philosophical assumption for its own good, in order for it and for society to survive and not be destroyed.[15]

In recent years we have heard a great deal about the death of God. This, I believe, is a shallow and grossly inaccurate description of the degradation and corruption of modern man and his social institutions. But unless these institutions—with business occupying a crucial place among them—are sensitive to the establishment of ethical priorities, it is not the death of God that the world will witness, but the death of civilized man.

---

[15] Research for this chapter which was originally intended as an article for a newly contemplated ethics journal, was completed early in 1968 and the final draft was written in July of that year. The delay in publishing the material forced a few minor modifications in the paper, but in the main it has been left in its original form.

Mission and Opportunity:
Religion in a Pluralistic Culture

REINHOLD NIEBUHR

ALL the free communities of the Western world are pluralistic in their culture; indeed, it may be the heterogeneity
within the community which gave birth to freedom. The
origin of Western pluralism lies in its history, in the disintegration of medieval culture occasioned by two forms of revolt:
the fourteenth century Renaissance, and the sixteenth century Protestant Reformation. These two revolts were contradictory in the sense that the Renaissance restored the
classical, rational component of the medieval Christian synthesis while, on the whole, the Reformation emphasized the
biblical component.

The disintegration of medieval Christian culture created
the three basic elements of modern cultural and religious
pluralism: empiricism, Catholicism and Protestantism. In
turn, the Protestant Christian church, bereft of the unifying
sovereignty of papal authority, became fragmented into
dozens of national churches. These ranged from orthodox
versions of Luther and Calvin, to a multitude of sectarian,
radical versions of the Protestant polity or faith.

The various Protestant bodies differed in their organiza-
tion of the community along congregational, presbyterian or
episcopal lines. They also differed in their credal interpretations of the common biblical faith, varying their emphasis on
Pauline conceptions of "grace." Some emphasized the
Pauline view of grace as forgiveness and were thus more
Augustine than Catholic theology, which usually was semi-
Pelagian. Some Protestant groups held views on "sanctification" which made them more perfectionist than medieval
Catholicism which had consistently interpreted the eschatological visions of perfect love as "counsels of perfection" to be
observed by monastics, but not by ordinary members of the
church.

The fact of Protestant pluralism reveals that the unity of
the religious community could not be preserved without a
sanctified supreme authority. It would appear, however, that
Protestant Christians, like Jews, have preferred liberty to
unity. This problem must be considered more fully when
dealing with the ecumenical issues on the American scene.
Provisionally, we shall regard both the Jewish and the Protes-
tant-Christian faith as two of three versions of a religious
tradition, and consider them as partners in the secular environment of modern culture.

We have pointed to the recovery in the Renaissance of
classical humanism and concepts of "reason," derived from
Plato, Aristotle and the Stoics. But ages of history were required before the nominalism of the pre-Reformation could
challenge Thomistic, i.e. Aristotelian, "realism" and develop
into modern inductive, empirical science. In time, however,
the growth of modern science led to Darwin's nineteenth
century climactic discovery that biological forms were subject
to incessant change. Thereafter, the method of acquiring all
knowledge, of both natural and historical phenomena, pre-
supposed "humility before the facts." Scientific progress, en-

couraged in free societies, increasingly refuted the legends in which all religious history abounds.

It is the contradiction between the legends of religion and the sobering historical realities discovered by an empirical science that introduces the primary problem of the relation of religion to modern secularism.

I

THIS PROBLEM finds a viable solution only as it returns to the beginning of Western culture with its creative compound of the religion of Israel and the philosophy of Greece, a compound created partly by pre-Christian hellenistic Judaism. The Greek element in the compound was the sense of form and structure in the world, which reason could analyze and know. The Jewish element was the religious sense of the transcendent, the faith in a Creator-God whose creative activity transcends all natural causation, who is involved in the mysteries of historical destiny, who called His chosen nation to have a messianic vocation in the destinies of nations, and who judges and redeems individuals and nations.

The main role of all religious communities in a pluralistic but increasingly secular culture which subjects all historical and natural events to empirical scrutiny, is to bear witness to the necessity of the realm of the transcendent, even if it must be interpreted symbolically. For it is in the sphere of the transcendent that the meaning of life is established, the integrity and unity and uniqueness of the individual soul is emphasized, and the mystery and meaning of the growth of human freedom over nature is appreciated. A culture without a penumbra of mystery surrounding its realm of meaning robs both man's history and man's individuality of meaning. The incoherences of life, the historical and natural evils, destroy man's basic trust in the meaning of his existence, particularly when a rational or "secular" world view tends to identify meaning with rational coherence.

But religious faith, according to the Jewish inheritance, makes it possible for the individual to understand the integrity of his person, through the freedom of his reason and spirit. Indeed, only in terms of Judaism is it possible to comprehend the unity of the person, despite the incongruity of his involvement in and transcendence over nature and history. And it is the ultra-rational idea of the "resurrection of the body" which is the ultimate symbol of this unity.

Finally, more than the cyclical conceptions of history developed in Greek metaphysics, and more than all the Oriental mystic faiths, Judaism made it possible to understand historical progress. The hopes of a Messianic Age in Hebrew prophetic writings guarded against all utopian illusions; the Messianic Age would arrive only if a transformed nature gave support to an ideal history. The vision of Isaiah, "The wolf shall dwell with the lamb, and the leopard shall lie down with the kid," suggested that unity of history would be possible only as the aggressiveness which men share with animals would be transformed in nature itself.

Judaism made it possible to appreciate that growing human freedom involves both creative and destructive possibilities. Our technological nuclear age, in which we enjoy a precarious peace based upon a "balance of terror," can be accepted without complete despair only if we accept this paradox.

Christian messianism, which presents Jesus as the crucified and not as the triumphant Messiah, may have provided an even more paradoxical symbol of the constant historical contradiction between human achievements and ultimate perfection. At their worst, Christian interpretations of history were transmuted into an otherworldliness in which a Platonic heaven of disembodied souls, i.e. minds, negated but did not fulfill or transform history. At its best, Christian eschatology provided a symbolic interpretation of the fulfillment of history in an event which anticipated the growth of human freedom, in both its creative and destructive aspects, within nature and history. We must postpone a further consideration of this difference until we analyze the relations and differences between the Christian and Jewish faiths.

The second mission of religious communities in a secular culture is a moral one. The non-mystical religions are each imbued with the sense of man's relation to all men. Hence, the moral responsibility for the welfare of one's neighbor, implied in the commandment "You shall love your neighbor as yourself," is the existential fruit not of the rational, but of the integral self, as biblical religion understands the human person.

The great virtue of biblical faith is that its sense of a divine mystery does not prevent it from affirming unambiguous moral principles. The Prophet Isaiah expressed the transcendent mystery in the words: "For the heavens are higher than the earth, so are My ways higher than your ways, and My thoughts than your thoughts." But this sense of religious mystery does not prevent a vigorous moral demand: "Cease to do evil, learn to do good. . . . Defend the fatherless, plead for the widow."

THE OPPORTUNITIES open to religious faith in a secular culture are also twofold. The rational and empirical disciplines which appear to anxious piety as perils, are themselves the means of criticizing and purifying religious faith. The empiric challenge of the symbolic truths of religion separates history from legend, and thus guards against the persistent danger of obscurantism, a danger which is revealed when religious faith regards the legendary embroidery of its history as actual history. Secular empiricism is also helpful in guiding moral imperatives, so that they embody responsibility toward ones neighbor through the relativities of historical contingencies.

In the area of morals, biblical religion always prompts a commitment to the law of love, because it is fully aware of the social substance of human life. The individual can never realize himself without including other selves in his fulfillment. Jesus' paradoxical statement that "Who ever seeks to gain his life will lose it; but who ever loses his life will preserve it" (Luke 17:33) may be interpreted to read: "A too consistent search after self-fulfillment is bound to be self-defeating. On the contrary, self-fulfillment requires that the self forget itself in its commitment to the social purposes of life."

But there is a serious lacuna in the Christian interpretation of love. Perfect, i.e. sacrificial, love is presented as the ultimate moral possibility. But the biblical doctrine of sin also interprets man's "corrupted" nature as tending towards unremitting self-regard. If both affirmations reveal undoubted dimensions of man's nature, it follows that all human communities must rely on norms of *discriminate justice* in order to achieve a tolerable harmony between egoistic individuals, and even more, between the collective self-regard of human communities. Even though the radical sense of justice—both in the thought of the Hebrew prophets, and in the theory of natural law of Catholicism which borrows from its classical inheritance—supplies these standards of discriminate justice, all morally committed religious faiths, and Protestant Christianity in particular, are in need of secular disciplines for the direction of moral imperatives, more particularly the duty of responsibility which the religious imperative "Love thy neighbor as thyself" enjoins.

In a world in which international relations become ever more complex, and domestic, technical and economic relations ever more intricate, it is important to be furnished not only with the regulative principles of justice—equality and liberty—but also to be directed by a host of empirical historical disciplines, which analyze as accurately as possible all the historical contingencies and which can help make true and relevant moral decisions on specific issues—the war in Vietnam, the struggle between Jews and Arabs in the Middle East, the problem of race relations and civil rights, the threat of unemployment in an era of automation.

Kant erred in regarding the *intelligible self* as the lawgiver, and the *sensible self* as the law-observer. It is the *integral self,* functioning in a moral environment, which is both the law-giver and the law-observer. But rational and logical or analytic processes always operate in directing moral imperatives to relevant and satisfactory ends.

Religion is the source of the moral imperative in the sense that the integral self, as understood by historic religions, is the source of moral sense of duty. But all religions have the problem of distinguishing between the ultimate and the contingent. In new situations they are all inclined to offer specific moral directives drawn from their sacred traditions— which are informed by all the contingent elements implied in those traditions.

Thus, for instance, Judaism has been relevant to the collective problems of an industrial society, because the Hebrew prophets affirmed a radical spirit of justice, and sought to redress the inequalities of nature and history, demanding that the devout "plead for the widow and succor the orphan." On the other hand, many of the precepts of Pentateuchal law have proved to be a source of moral confusion in the new partly-religious and partly-secular State of Israel.

Medieval Catholicism tried to solve all collective moral problems by the standards of its "natural law." But it was unconscious of the fact that the pressures of medieval feudalism had changed the allegedly immutable principle of the "natural law" from Stoic equality to Aristotelian justification of inequality. Thus the spirit of justice was defined as the disposition "to give each man his due"; but the substance of justice was "to treat unequal things unequally."

With the disintegration of a feudal economy, the rise of modern bourgeois or commercial cultures, and the protest of the industrial workers against the morality of "individual initiative" and "free enterprise" of the middle-classes, the Catholic Church began to champion the interests of workers, and again returned to the moral principle of equality. It made a difference when the industrial workers, rather than feudal lords, became the clients of the church!

Pope Leo XIII, in his encyclical *Rerum Novarum*, laid the foundation of a modern social ethic, and affirmed the right of workers to organize and bargain collectively. Catholicism thus affirmed its awareness of the social substance of man's existence. It also helped to create a new equilibrium of power between organized workers and organized management. This equilibrium created justice in the newly industrialized democratic nations of the West, and saved them from the Marxist rebellion occasioned by the impact of industry. The contribution of Catholicism to the solution of the problem of justice in modern industry was, significantly, a compound of the moral imperatives of biblical faith, plus the inherited traditions of historic Catholicism, plus adaptation to the new realities of industrial cultures.

The social ethics of Protestant Christianity were naturally colored by the history in which Protestantism developed, and therefore differed from those of Catholicism, though both had the same biblical origin. The Protestant rebellion against the medieval order was informed by bourgeois perspectives and influenced by middle-class interests. Max Weber, in his *Protestantism and the Spirit of Capitalism,* called attention to the Protestant emphasis on the individual "economic virtues" of "diligence, frugality and honesty" through which the complex standards of a commercial economy were inspired and ordered. But the Protestant faith, particularly in America, was generally tardy in coming to terms with the collective problems of modern industry. It was significant that the school of Protestant social theory usually defined as the "social gospel" sought to correct the bourgeois individualism of the reformed churches by the simple expedient of rediscovering the radical social ethics of the Hebrew prophets, particularly of Amos and Isaiah. In this case a biblical moral norm served to correct a modern one.

The political ethic of the early Reformation was consistently conservative. It did not conform to the democratic impulses of the bourgeois forces. Both Luther and Calvin placed exaggerated emphasis on the duty of obedience to the particular political authority. Luther defined it simply as "Obrigkeit," while Calvin assumed the absoluteness of the national state. This conservatism was partly due to a pessimistic estimate of man's self-regard. It was the duty of civil authority to be a "dike against sin." Luther made a minimal order, rather than justice, the norm in the "earthly realm"; this was clearly the "realm of Caesar," in which Christ's norm of "heavenly love" was not relevant.

Fortunately, the Calvinism of the seventeenth century was rescued from this political absolutism by the historical contingency of the battle against the Catholic princes in Scotland, France and Holland. This historic fact served to make "resistance to tyranny" not only a right but a duty for the "lower magistrates," i.e. all authorities below the level of royal sovereignty.

It is important for all devout believers, of whatever creed, to note the effect of contemporary history on religiously enshrined social doctrine. This will prevent them from placing undue emphasis on the ultimate authority of any historic, religiously-inspired social doctrine. It will teach them that all human doctrines are touched and tainted by historic interests and contingencies, and will thus help to abate the bigotry which is the universal temptation of religiously-inspired social doctrine.

ONE OF THE TENSIONS between religious faith and modern secularism derives from religion's use of myths and symbols to point to the realm of transcendence. In Judaism, for example, the chief mystery of transcendence is the fact of creation. The creation story in Genesis has on many occasions given rise to controversy between a pre-scientific religious culture and the scientific portrayals of the evolutionary process. Yet it may be suggested that religion may adapt itself to modern empirical culture by accepting the mythical and symbolic nature of all statements about the mystery of the transcendent. In the words of Erik Erikson, "Religion . . . elaborates on what feels profoundly true even though it is not demonstrable: it translates into significant words, images and codes the exceeding darkness which sorrows man's existence, and the light which pervades it beyond all desert or comprehension." Thus, myths and legends, whether the Hebrew story of creation or the garden of Eden, or the Christian stories of the birth and childhood of Jesus and the account of his physical and historic resurrection, should be understood as supporting faith in the dimension of transcendence. In time, however, the myth and the story which are the symbolic vehicles of truth tend to become identified with the truth. A secular, scientific culture must remind the faithful that the distinction between symbols and meaning is implicit in all religion. For man sees through a glass darkly, and although man may behold the glory of God, no man has seen God at any time.

It must be noted that biblical faith has outlasted the most imposing philosophies. Hegel's absolute idealism gave a too rational account both of the individual and his history. It was supplanted by Marx' dialectic materialism which created a heaven-on-earth—and proved to be a hell of tyranny. Herbert Spencer's liberal, scientific, evolutionary optimism was refuted by the contrast of good and evil in a nuclear age. Even Kant's critical idealism was inadequate because he reverted to the old Platonic dualism in his conception of two selves—the "intelligible" and the "sensible" self. The integral unity of the human person refuted this dualism; and Kant's vision of a peaceful community, governed by reason, was refuted by extensive contemporary evidence of irrational and non-rational forms of social cohesion and social conflict.

Thus, classical faith in a transcendent source of meaning has outlasted all the philosophies which had predicted its imminent demise from the seventeenth to the nineteenth centuries. Moreover, religious faith shorn of its absurdities and obscurantist scientific pretensions, has proved more vigorous than all primitive forms of faith for which the ethos of a scientific age rang a death knell.

The uneasy partnership between religious faith and empirical disciplines has persisted in the culture of the open societies of the West, and it is significant that these pluralistic societies have proved themselves more creative than either the monolithic religious medieval culture of Spain, or the communist culture of Russia which is rooted in a secular utopian illusion. This superior creativity expresses itself in religion, philosophy, the humanities and arts, technology, and in the moral and political tasks of creating tolerable human communities within the ever increasing complexities of a technological economy.

The superior vitality of pluralistic cultures which have retained the religious sense of mystery and meaning, thus lends basic security to fragile men who are exposed to the vicissitudes of life and its natural and historic evils. Simultaneously, pluralistic culture permits the expansion of every empirical discipline by which the earth is made productive, human ailments are alleviated, and men achieve more comfortable and artistically satisfying lives for their families.

II

AN ANALYSIS of the three religious communities which are components of the partly-secular and partly-religious cultural pluralism of the United States compels us to admit that their great potential for contributing to the moral and existential needs of the society does not guarantee that a moral quality will exist in their attitudes toward one another. In fact, their relationships are frequently marked by bigotry.

Critics of religion usually ascribe this bigotry to an inherent defect in religion itself, but a more careful study of the causes of religious bigotry indicates that it may derive from the fact that all symbols of mystery and meaning in religious faith have a twofold character. On the one hand they point to the ultimate source of meaning; on the other hand they are historically conditioned. The devotees of a particular faith are always tempted to ascribe ultimate significance, as they experience it, to the historically contingent symbols. These contingent elements are the cause of all religious bigotry as manifest in religious controversy. Our problem, as members of particular biblical faiths, is to mitigate bigotry by careful analysis of the relevance of both the ultimate and the contingent elements in all historic religions.

In this country, the three faiths with their common biblical root have achieved peculiar and frequently unique forms of creativity or weakness. We have been spared to a great extent some of the difficulties Catholicism and Protestantism experienced in Europe because of local or national history and religious politics. It is mainly because of our secular heritage that we have the doctrine of the separation of church and state—and a balanced ticket in politics.

One aspect of American religious pluralism is the multiplicity of Protestant denominations, but by and large the sectarian differences between them have been eroded in the American experience. Protestants are presented with a wide variety of choice, in which preferences about polity, liturgy and even creedal emphasis can be expressed. Simultaneously, however, the Councils of Churches speak for a united Protestant faith on local, state and national levels; and in the university-affiliated theological schools, denominational differences offer no obstacles to a common theological education.

One difference between the American and European experience deserves special mention—the Jewish component of the three biblical faiths is much larger and more influential in our culture than in any other modern pluralistic democracy. The influence is due less to religious strength, than to the power, position and talents of the Jewish minority in education, science, law, medicine, commerce, and most of all in public affairs.

The cultural prestige of the Jewish community and its capacity for civic virtue has prompted many Christians to soften their prejudices against a dissident religious minority, to inquire about the sources of its personal and civic virtue, to regret the century-old bigotry of the medieval period in which Jews were labelled "Christ-killers," and even to seek to understand the disposition of the Jews to cling to their faith and thus to "reject Christ." However reluctantly, the Christian community in America has been led to include the Jewish community in its now famous religious triad—Catholic, Protestant, Jew.

This relative concession meant that the Christian community found itself able, after centuries, to appreciate the Jewish religious community for itself, not only for the common heritage of piety as expressed in the Psalter, in prophetic theism, and in morally rigorous historical pronouncements. Indeed, this "common heritage" was more than common; it defined the Christian faith as derivative from the older faith and revealed, in the phrase of Pope Pius XII, that "Spiritually, we are all Semites."

The acknowledgement of the Christian legacy from the older Jewish religion also introduced the problem, now obvious in all ecumenical dialogue, that mutual respect between different faiths depends upon the recognition of non-negotiable differences in the symbols and instruments of faith. Thus, in relation to the Jews, Christians had to face the non-negotiable difference with regard to Christology. They were also forced to recognize that the difference between Protestant and Catholic versions of a common Christian faith involved an equally insurmountable non-negotiable principle: the supremacy of papal authority as an instrument of the unity of the church.

The difference between Christianity and Judaism is very great, because the non-negotiable principle is imbedded in the sacred scriptures of the two religions. In contrast, the Catholic acceptance of papal supremacy and the Protestant rejection of papal authority, is a difference created by history. Nevertheless, the two issues are similar because it is impossible to reach agreement on either even in the most friendly ecumenical dialogue. In fact, it is important in any ecumenical dialogue to begin with the assumption that individual participants in the discussion are not absolutely free to alter their opinions on these two issues, because each represents a watershed of history. The two mountain peaks dividing the faiths are, in the first instance, the organization of the Christian church, inspired by the drama of Jesus Christ's life, death and teachings; and in the second instance, the historical fact of the Protestant Reformation. Those who debate these issues are bound by a whole mesh of values which derive from historic cultures developed on either side of the watershed—Jewish or Christian, Catholic or Protestant. While opinions and decisions in the ultimate instance may be individual, they also involve collective preferences, as informed by the separate cultures. Understanding will be encouraged if both partners in dialogue know that decisions and preferences on these issues are informed by historical destinies.

III

THE LATE GREAT JEWISH PHILOSOPHER, Martin Buber, described the issue of Messianism which divides Jews and Christians in an address to Dutch clergymen: "To the Christian, the Jew is a stubborn fellow who, in an unredeemed world, is still waiting for the Messiah. To the Jew, the Christian is a heedless fellow who affirms, in an unredeemed world, that redemption has somehow or other taken place." Buber's astute description of the non-negotiable Christological issue derives, naturally, from a Jewish viewpoint.

A Christian might answer Buber in two ways. He might affirm that the vague "somehow or other" really describes the Christian belief, that there is a permanent contradiction between historical achievements and the divine perfection, and that the revelation of Christ merely discloses the ultimate relation of divine mercy over divine judgment. Thus a problem is solved which Hebraic Messianism holds to be a persistent mystery of the divine. The Christian might also retort with a question: "If you are still waiting for a Messiah, does this expectancy imply that you honestly believe in a Messianic Age in which the transformation of history is guaranteed by transformed nature? When are we to see lions and lambs lying down together?"

The issue between the Christian and Jewish faiths revolves about the centrality of Christ as the Messiah in Christianity, and the rejection of Christ by historic Judaism. Incidentally, this includes all sects of Judaism, from Orthodox and Conservative to Reform and Liberal elements of that faith who are, in Buber's words, "still waiting for the Messiah."

This issue may be analyzed on two levels: On the historical level, Christians rely on the drama of Christ's life, teachings, death and resurrection as summing up the faith of "the law and the prophets." An ultimate culmination of all the mystery of the divine, it is primarily the mystery of the relation of divine judgment to God's mercy. Christians also believe Christ's life to be the revelation of a "new law" of love, which is the fulfillment of the "old law" of the Torah. On this level the issue is primarily historical. The Christians accept the testimony of the four Gospels, which emphasize in various contexts that the life of Christ fulfilled the messianic prophecies of the prophets. For Jews, these claims of the Gospel are analyzed in terms which suggest that the Gospel records are less reliable history than ideological presentations which were calculated to elaborate the faith of the early church that a crucified Messiah, rather than a triumphant lord of a Messianic Age, was a fulfillment of messianic hopes.

This issue between Christians and Jews cannot be settled by an "objective" historical study of the events of history, for such a study must rest on two assumptions. One of these is that Jesus himself had co-opted the idea of a suffering servant for his interpretation of messianic hopes. This assumption would imply that passages such as Mark 8:31, "The son of man must suffer many things," report Jesus' own sayings; and that the suffering servant passage from Isaiah 53, "Surely he has borne our grief and carried our sorrows; . . . upon him was the chastisement that made us whole, and with his stripes we are healed," is a true reflection of the suffering and crucified Messiah.

Obviously, this conclusion rests upon an original presupposition of faith. In itself it does not compel any Jew to accept, rather than reject, the idea of a crucified Messiah.

The second assumption is that it was not Jesus, but the early church which merged the symbol of the suffering servant with the messianic hope. This view is held by many Christian scholars, as for instance by John Knox in his book *Christ the Lord*.

One cannot be certain whether one or the other assumption is valid. The second assumption is in agreement with the belief of many New Testament scholars that it is impossible to extract from the Gospel accounts, replete with all the pious presuppositions of the early church faith, a biography of "the Jesus of history." But one must also record that the assumption that the mystery of the "Christ of faith" is really the mystery of the spontaneous faith of the early church, has affected neither the Christ-centered piety of the theologians who projected this theory nor the quality of piety of Christian laymen. It certainly has not prompted them either to skepticism or to a transfer of religious loyalty.

THE SECOND PROBLEM of actual history and its interpretation by the two faiths is, of course, the problem of Christ's resurrection "on the third day." St. Paul gives us the oldest account of this "event," predating those of the Gospels. Significantly, it indicates that the resurrection experience was not so much a public event, as an internal spiritual awareness of the disciples. Paul writes:

> For I delivered to you, as of first importance what I also received, that Christ died for our sins . . . that he was buried, that he was raised on the third day in accordance

with the scriptures, and that he appeared to Cephas, then to the twelve. Then he appeared to more than five hundred brethren at one time, most of whom are still alive, though some have fallen asleep. Then he appeared to James, then to all the apostles. Last of all, as to one untimely born, he appeared also to me, for I am the least of the apostles, unfit to be called an apostle because I persecuted the church of God. But, by the grace of God, I am what I am (I Cor. 4:3–10a).

The fact that Paul interprets the experience as an *internal perception* is understood by his inclusion of his own experience. "As to one untimely born" has suggested to many New Testament scholars that the stories of the physical resurrection represent later versions, which undoubtedly were added to overcome the skepticism of the early church. It is certainly significant that the same apostle, Paul, could say: "If Christ has not been raised, then our preaching is in vain and your faith is in vain" (I Cor. 15:14).

It is significant that an eminent New Testament scholar, Rudolph Bultmann, who in his *Kerigma and Myth* was concerned to cleanse all biblical literature of pre-scientific myths without touching the mythical symbols which were embodied and expressed in the "Kerigma," nevertheless analyzed the various accounts of the resurrection, and acknowledged that the early records suggested that the resurrection was not a "public event" at all. He further concluded in his *Theology of the New Testament* that the Gospel accounts must be regarded as "postscripts" of the Crucifixion. This would suggest that the early church regarded the cross of Christ not as a defeat, but as a triumph in the Christian plan of salvation.

This leads us to another level of contrasting interpretations of the religious, symbolic significance of the entire

Christ drama. Here we have the vivid reminder that these contrasting interpretations reveal a "non-negotiable" article of faith between the older and the newer religion. The two principal themes are the attitudes toward the law, and toward the mystery of the relation of divine judgment to mercy. For the Jews, the Pauline anti-legalism is offensive; and for them the Christ drama reveals no insights not already contained in the prophets.

The Christian faith, however, is Christ-centered in the sense that the Christ drama revealed both a "new law," and divine mercy to all believers. The symbolic significance of the Christ drama is twofold and emphasizes, on the one hand, the ideal possibility in human nature, and on the other hand, the mystery of the relation of divine forgiveness to mortal men who know themselves to be guilty in the contradiction between their self-regarding impulses and this ideal possibility. This, probably, is the reason why the Christian faith has been consistently Christ-centered and why, since the early triumph of the new faith, it has regarded its devotion to Christ as non-negotiable, despite the refutation in modern culture of such primitive myths as virgin birth and physical resurrection.

It is important to emphasize the twofold significance of this drama if one wishes to understand why modern Unitarianism —reacting to the incredibility of the doctrine of the Trinity and presenting Christ as the ideal man—could not triumph over the older orthodoxies. It eliminated the old incredibilities signifying the mystery of the divine mercy, but it reduced the human story to an optimistic estimate of the human situation. Men were aware, even in the optimistic nineteenth and early twentieth centuries, that human life was characterized by a tragic contradiction in the very heart of man, and even the skeptical faith of modern man is inclined to accept a symbolic presentation of a divine answer to this human situation.

WE MUST ALSO CONSIDER the Christ drama in its relation to
Judaism, the older faith which forms the background or
furnishes and states some of the main themes of the new
faith.

The cross of Christ in a Christ-centered faith symbolically
represents two main themes. On the one hand, it symbolizes a
pinnacle of human virtue: the sacrifice of the self for others.
Paul states this theme in the words "And the life I now live
in the flesh I live by faith in the Son of God, who loved me
and gave Himself for me. I do not nullify the grace of God;
for if justification were through the law, the Christ died to no
purpose" (Gal. 2:20). The second theme is that Jesus' death
on the cross is an expiation for our sins, an exposition and
revelation of the mercy of God, a payment of the debt of sin
demanded by the divine justice.

The first theme of the pinnacle of human morality proved
insufficient in Christian history whenever the church was
confronted with the persistent self-regard of even those who
were in theory "new creatures in Christ." The second theme
of forgiveness and pardon emphasized that the mercy of God
is directed toward saints as well as sinners. This was the point
of Jesus' parable of the Publican and Pharisee. The sinner
who confessed his sin was "justified" or "accounted worthy"
more than the man who was conscious of his virtue. "For
every one who exalts himself will be humbled, but he who
humbles himself will be exalted" (Luke 18:14). This
emphasis represents a radical transformation of moral values.
It is, in a sense, the root of a permanent religious revolution.

In the ecumenical encounter with Judaism, Christians
must know that both these themes rooted in the Christian
story are important for the new gospel; but also that they
represent themes which the older Jewish faith previously had
projected.

The cross of Christ, for instance, was and is a vivid symbolic presentation of the theme that God was, in Christ, reconciling the world unto Himself. It was a revelation of the relation of divine mercy and forgiveness to divine judgment, a theme often explored in the Jewish religion.

If Christians can claim that the new faith universalized this mystery by making it relevant to individuals, the Jewish faith can point to the words of the Psalmist, "Enter not into judgment with Thy servant; for no man living is righteous before Thee" (Ps. 143:2). That prayer of the Psalmist, incidentally, may be used not only to point to the individual character of divine judgment, but also to the universality of the uneasy conscience among all sensitive spirits. It is a parallel to the Pauline "For there is no distinction; since all have sinned and fall short of the glory of God, and seek glory in His presence" (Romans 3:22, 23).

It is true, of course, that the prophets of Israel emphasized God's judgment and mercy toward the "chosen people," though the emphasis was not exclusively concerned with the nation. Christians therefore might claim that the Christ drama was the primary cause of universalizing a faith which hitherto had been confined to a nation.

The contrasting attitude of the Jewish and Christian faith toward the crucifixion of Christ as a "revelation" of the mystery of the relation of divine mercy toward divine judgment, reveals how difficult, or impossible, it is for two historic faiths to agree on their symbols. For the Jew, the whole drama of a divine father moderating his judgment of sinners by asking his son to take upon himself the "wages of sin" seems a ludicrous religious legend.

Christian theologians have given this drama various interpretations. The more orthodox Christian scholars regard the atoning death upon the cross as an objective precondition of divine mercy. This would seem to point to a difference in the divine character before and after the Christ drama. Most

Christian theologians, who regard all religious statements as symbols of some ultimate mystery, simply view the relation between father and son in the Christ drama as an indication, ultimately considered, of the paradoxical relation between judgment and mercy. They point to analogous, though not ultimate, mysteries in all parental discipline of children, which requires both moral rigor and merciful compassion for the erring child. This may impress Christians; but we cannot blame the Jews for remaining unimpressed.

WE MUST RETURN TO THE FIRST THEME of the Christ drama, which prompts Christians to affirm that in Christ law has been both abrogated and transcended. Paul, who is not a favorite figure for those of the Jewish faith because of his negative attitude toward the law, regards the pardon through Christ as being free of judgment. He writes: "There is therefore now no condemnation for those who are in Christ Jesus" (Rom. 8:1).

This motif includes not only freedom from the law because of the pledge of divine forgiveness, but also an eschatological dimension of a new ethic—the ethic of *Agape*, sacrificial and forgiving love. Bishop Nygren, in a learned study, argues that, of all theologians, only Luther understood this concept adequately, assigning it to the "heavenly realm" of personal relations, to be distinguished from the "earthly realm" of Caesar.

The new morality of love was occasioned by the Jewish messianic hope that in the Kingdom of God the law will be transcended. Since Christ had defined the law of love, including both love of God and love of one's neighbor, as the "greatest commandment," and since he revealed his love for all men on the cross where he prayed, "Father, forgive them; for they know not what they do," it was inevitable that the new Christian faith should define this ethic in terms going beyond the Mosaic law, as *Agape,* sacrificial, forgiving love.

This enterprise involved the early Christian Church in the heretical notion of an "interim-ethic" (A. Schweitzer). It certainly seems to justify Buber's critical remark that Christians are heedless in affirming "that in an unredeemed world, redemption has somehow or other taken place."

If we analyze Buber's challenge to the Christian faith in regard to one of the two themes of the Christian *Kerygma*, namely the new and more rigorous morality which Hebraic faith leaves undefined—merely expressing the hope that the decalogue will be transcended in the Messianic Age—we might well translate Buber's challenge in this way: "Christianity pretends that it has achieved a new and more rigorous selflessness in an unredeemed world in which a universal motive of self-regard must be taken for granted."

Buber also might point to the fact that Christian history has been embarrassed by this perfectionist motif in Christian ethics, particularly in the field of collective relations, in which collective self-regard must be taken for granted. Christianity finally had to come to terms with political and economic programs of justice after the early church's hope of the *Parousia* waned. Then it regulated all collective relations with norms of "natural law" borrowed from classical sources, and defined the eschatological ethic, particularly the norms derived from the Sermon on the Mount, as "counsels of perfection" to be observed only by monastics.

We have previously observed how Luther instituted a new dualism in which the radical ethical norms of Christianity were regarded as normative only for the "heavenly realm" of personal and individual relations. Subsequent experience proved that only in intimate family relations could *Agape* be regarded as relevant. Mothers, rather than mystics, might achieve this *Agape* of sacrifice and forgiveness—at least in high moments. Martyrs may have realized these radical norms, and thereby suggested that, even in a world of universal self-regard, there is place for the pinnacle of *Agape*. This pinnacle is relevant whenever individuals come to realize that standards of integrity may become desirable even if physical life must be sacrificed. "For what will it profit a man," Jesus observed, "if he gains the whole world and forfeits his life?" (Matt. 16:26). So saying, he put his finger on the moral ultimate which persists in a sinful world, and not only in the messianic age.

From the Jewish viewpoint, and perhaps from the sum of non-Christian points of view, the effort to spell out this ideal beyond the law was elaborated in too specific terms. One of the most distinguished New Testament scholars of our day, W. D. Davies, has scrutinized the problem in all of its ramifications in his massive volume *The Setting of the Sermon on the Mount* (Cambridge University Press, 1964). Dr. Davies points out that most of the norms of the so-called Sermon on the Mount were taken by Matthew from the Q source in an effort to spell out in detail this new eschatological ethic beyond the Law of Moses, thus presenting Christ as a more rigorous law-giver than Moses.

Professor Davies denies that the picture of Jesus as the author of a more rigorous law was consciously anti-Pauline and was intended to refute Paul's anti-legalism, particularly his insistence that Christ was the "end of the Law." He points to the fact that Paul's and Matthew's purposes were identical in the sense that both were concerned with pointing to the "Law beyond the Law." This calls attention to the similarity in their emphasis on *Agape,* on the radical norm of sacrificial and forgiving love. Professor Davies rightly, I think, observes:

> The Christian life as Paul understood it was lived in a formative ethical tradition. This tradition was not an isolated deposit, however, but part and parcel of what Paul understands by the Christian Dispensation, and

therefore seen, not in opposition to grace, but as a concomitant of it (*op. cit.,* p. 365) .

Though I am not competent to judge all the details of Dr. Davies' massive comparison of the ethical and religious doctrines of the Pauline epistles and the Gospel of Matthew, more particularly the material from the Q source which appears in the three Synoptic Gospels, I agree with the learned author that we must note a common early Christian moral tradition. It appears to have been intent upon specifying the radical eschatological norms about which the earlier prophets and later writers in Judaism had only commented in general terms, indicating that in the Messianic Age that Torah would be transcended.

This thesis is important for many reasons, but chiefly because it suggests that the new faith spelled out a "morality beyond morality" which Hebraic messianism left as a matter of hope. Thus the difference between the two faiths is not, as generally assumed, the difference between law and grace. It is a difference between the messianic *hopes* of the old Hebraic faith—and the claims of messianic *achievements* of the new Christian faith.

OBSERVERS OF THE COMPETITIVE ATTITUDES of organized religions will be conscious of the fact that despite the similarities between the two faiths, and the debt of Christianity to Judaism, differences between the organized religious communities exist and are more polemical than the scholarly analysis of the historical mutualities of the two related faiths would warrant. There is pathos in the fact that the gap between the polemical attitudes of Christianity and Judaism is, in fact, more pronounced than between entirely unrelated faiths.

These competitive attitudes represent a heavy burden of

debt and guilt for Christians, particularly because they have been the majority group. The Jewish minority has been subject to anti-Semitic prejudices, based more than a little on religious attitudes, though ethnic animosities contributed their share.

Christians must acknowledge their debt to the older faith, and the guilt of the majority toward the minority must be confessed and corrected far beyond contemporary proceedings of Catholic and Protestant councils with their negation of the vulgar epithet for the Jews as "Christ-killers" and their warning against the moral evils of religious prejudice. But perhaps it is too much to ask that communities confess their past and present sins, even if the communities pride themselves on being congregations of "forgiven sinners."

Perhaps it is even more important for the Christian majority to become conscious of the fact that its sacred books contain echoes of the sharp contrast between the Jewish synagogue and the early church. In the Fourth Gospel these echoes of the conflict were more pronounced, because the enemies of Jesus were simply defined as "the Jews." It may be significant that in the famous Oberammergau passion play, whose narrative was taken from the Johannine Gospel, anti-Semitism reached monstrous proportions. The Christian churches are bound, in the name of religious charity, to make known to their laymen the historical framework of this church-synagogue contest, as reflected in the Gospels, as they long have been analyzed by their own scholars. Further, they must also revise the educational textbooks for their children, a task which a committee of Catholic, Protestant and Jewish scholars is in the process of undertaking.

Any thoughtful analysis of the history of the messianic problem, whether by Jews or Christians, must convince even missionary-minded Christians that the two faiths have much in common, and that the Jews' rejection of the messianic claims for Christ is understandable. The inevitable conclusion is that Christians must understand Judaism as an authentic religion, rather than tolerate it in the hope of its ultimate absorption and extinction. The Vatican Council acknowledged this, by implication, by refraining from allusion to St. Paul's poignant confession: "My heart's desire and prayer to God for them [Israel] is that they may be saved" (Rom. 10:1). The greater authority of the Bible in Protestantism had interpreted these Pauline words as an injunction to convert the Jews in the inevitable and futile "Christian mission to the Jews."

The change from polemical competition to a creative ecumenical dialogue challenges Christians more than Jews, for reasons previously analyzed. But the Jewish minority must also make its contribution to this change. It is important for Jews to reexamine their convictions that the universality and persistence of a Christ-centered faith is merely the consequence of the influence of the legends which embroider the life, the birth and resurrection of Jesus; or that the dogmas about Christ's "two natures" and his exaltation to become the second person in the Trinitarian dogma is merely the way in which the orthodoxy of the Constantinian Christian establishment tried to explain the original messianism by means of the categories of Greek metaphysics. It is natural for Jews to be skeptical about both the legends and the Greek metaphysics. But they have to come to terms with the fact that a Christ-centered faith has persisted for centuries, in spite of skepticism about both the legends and the metaphysical integuments of the Christ drama.

Different schools of Christian theology may have different theories about the universality and power of the Christ drama in western history. Some would attribute it to the purity of his teachings and might therefore unite with some Reform Jews in counting him among the Hebrew prophets, or even hailing him as the greatest of the prophets.

In religious history, however, with the inevitable symbolic

pointers toward ultimate realities, this reduction of the Christ drama to the teachings of a brilliant *guru,* is inadequate. Whatever we may find wanting in the credibility of historic legends, modern Christians who have, in spite of skeptical overtones, a Christ-centered piety, are bound to the conviction that the Christ drama, particularly with its central symbol of the reconciliation between the divine and all human history, is the real reason for the universality and vitality of Christianity.

A nuclear age in particular would be conscious of the relevance of this drama of reconciliation between the divine and the whole human enterprise. For it reveals both that history is creative in the sense that human freedom increases enormously, and also that every advancement of freedom provides scope to the destructive corruption of freedom by the self-regarding motives of individuals and of human collectives. There has not been a "moral gain" in history which has not prompted sensitive spirits to devout recognition of the necessity of a grand reconciliation between God and man, and to heed the Pauline word "And kind to one another, tenderhearted, forgiving one another, as God in Christ forgave you" (Eph. 4:32) .

I V

IT IS SIGNIFICANT that Catholicism and Protestantism, which do not have to concern themselves with contrasting attitudes about Christ, since they both worship him as saviour, have their own non-negotiable issue, namely their contrasting beliefs about the nature of the church, and particularly about the authority of the Pope in the church. For Catholics, the Pope is regarded as the "Vicar of Christ." For Protestants this designation seems idolatrous. The Reformers were free to hurl epithets at the Pope—the most frequently used being "Anti-Christ."

The religious dimension of both terms, one inculcating reverent obedience and the other expressing hostile scorn, might suggest that ecumenical problems are as perplexing between these two versions of the Christian faith as between Judaism and Christianity.

In England, Tudor absolutism expressed the new national spirit by defying the Pope and creating an autonomous Anglican church in which Catholic and Protestant pieties could be satisfied. But this effort to merge old and new religious pieties and national patriotism could not prevent the persecution of Catholics under the Protestant minor heir of Henry VIII, King Edward VI; nor the persecution of Protestants under his Catholic heir, Queen Mary. Even the establishment of national unity in the golden reign of Queen Elizabeth did not last. Her Stuart successors could not prevent a civil war between the radical Protestant Puritans and the royal Anglican establishment.

In France, the Huguenot rebellion provoked the cruel repression of which the atrocities of St. Bartholemew's Day were a vivid symbol. The history of France indicates that coerced religious uniformity may lead to the erosion of piety. When Louis XIV revoked the Edict of Nantes in the beginning of the eighteenth century, the triumph of the old religion seemed to be complete. Nevertheless, the French Revolution broke out under his grandson; and Jacobin fanaticism took its revenge upon the *ancien régime,* including its religion, politics and economics.

The ecumenical issue between Catholics and Protestants in our own nation presents us with unique problems and opportunities. Before analyzing them, we must briefly review the history of religious hostilities unleashed by the Reformation in Europe. These hostilities reveal to us the virulence of religious bigotry between two religious communities, despite or because of their common base of scriptural faith, and teach us that the spirit of love, or *Agape,* which they share as a moral ideal, if not as a reality, stands in contradiction to their historical animosity.

The Wars of Religion, following the Reformation, disrupted the Western empire, for the princely electors were divided between the old and the new loyalty. The Treaty of Westphalia in 1648 finally achieved a momentary peace, on the basis of a formula which ordained that each prince should have the right and opportunity to enforce his own religion on his subjects. The formula reflected fear of the anarchy which different religious loyalties could create in an integral community.

Inevitably, this limited peace in the boundaries of the empire had but little effect on the life of the rising nations. They were all threatened by civil wars in which the devout of both the old and the new faiths would manifest an equal bigotry.

Our own nation seemed free of the religious bigotries of the Old World. It had been peopled by refugees from the religious and political persecutions of Europe. Before our birth as a nation, Roger Williams had anticipated the separation of church and state later expressed in the First Amendment of our Constitution. His protest against the Puritan theocracy of Massachusetts called attention to the peril inherent in the partnership of political power and religious pretension. The very pluralism of our Protestant culture made the First Amendment necessary—and also politically possible. We had cut the Gordian knot of religious bigotry, or so it seemed.

But the perennial forces of religious controversy were not so easily frustrated. The enormous immigration of the nineteenth century had brought Catholic immigrants from all European nations to man our burgeoning industry, and the old religious conflicts were thus unleashed among us. Catholics were a minority in a Protestant nation, but they were a highly disciplined and cohesive minority, and the church was the instrument of their union across ethnic boundaries. The Protestant majority felt itself threatened. The anti-Irish riots in our cities revealed how easily religion may serve as a veil for racial animosities.

Thus the nineteenth, rather than the sixteenth, century marked the beginning of religious hostilities in the United States, hostilities which our recently organized ecumenical enterprise must assuage and transmute into a creative dialogue between two partners of one Christian faith. Contacts, not to speak of dialogues, between Catholics and Protestants, have been minimal in our nation, in comparison with Europe —in Germany and Holland for instance—until the Second Vatican Council encouraged them.

As we have now made a hopeful beginning, it is well to remember that a creative exchange in friendly, rather than hostile, relations requires attention to, and discrimination between, two types of issues. One type consists of issues in which there can be a fruitful borrowing from the virtues of each version of the Christian faith. The other category of differences consists of those issues which are so basic to the long history of each version that charity must concede, and be promoted, by both partners, in the realization that there is little promise of either side persuading or "converting" the other. In our analysis of Jewish-Christian relations, we suggested that the issue of Christology was of this non-negotiable type. If our categories have any merit at all, it is suggested that the non-negotiable differences between Catholics and Protestants are the definitions of the nature of the church, and particularly of the authority and supremacy of the Pope as the instrument of its unity, order and discipline.

In the first category of issues, in which each ecumenical partner may creatively borrow from the virtues of the other, we find that both Protestantism and Catholicism can benefit equally by appropriating the moral achievements of the other.

In the field of social and industrial problems, it is particularly important for American Protestants to realize that Catholic encouragement of collective organization and bargaining is clearly preferable to the Protestant social attitude in which religious and bourgeois individualism have been compounded. Pope Leo XIII's encyclical, *Rerum Novarum,* was the first religiously inspired social document to anticipate the modern equilibrium of economic power, which enabled modern democracies to transmute exploitation into social welfare in the modern State.

On the other hand, in the realm of family relations, Catholicism's ethics of natural law are clearly too rigid. This is shown particularly in the stubbornness with which the Church clings to its prohibition of contraception in an era when the population explosion threatens the viability of undeveloped nations. Surely it must become evident that marriage should be sanctified, not by the procreative process itself, but by the spiritual purpose of enhancing the human qualities of the children and of the marriage partners themselves.

Indeed, some conclusions of the Second Vatican Council prompt the hope that Catholicism's expression of these larger and higher purposes of marriage has undermined its rigid position on birth control in such a way that the dogma of the Church on the prohibition of birth control is bound to be abandoned in the not too distant future. In this case, the Catholic Church has been influenced not only by the Protestant view that marriage is sanctified "for the comfort and continuance of mankind," but also by the moral consensus of an empirical culture including Protestants, Jews and secular humanists. This is but one more example of the effect of

contemporary history and social pressures on religiously enshrined social doctrine.

WE MUST CONCLUDE our analysis of the ecumenical problems
confronting Catholics and Protestants by briefly analyzing
that issue between them on which there is little opportunity
of their reaching a consensus. This issue may be defined
variously as dealing with the nature of the church, or with
the problem of freedom vs. order, but above all with the
authority of the Pope as an instrument of order and unity in
the only obviously universal Christian community.

On this issue, both partners will avoid undue resentment if
they realize that it is, on the one hand, impossible for Catholics to modify their obedience to the Pope, and on the other
hand, equally impossible for non-Roman Christians to sacrifice their liberty by this unconditional obedience. On this
issue collective history will have more authority than individual preferences. Protestants cannot but choose liberty at
the price of order, because their history prompts them to
regard this liberty as creative; while Catholics must point to
the anarchy prevailing in the realms of religion, international and social affairs, and label liberty as its ultimate cause.

The understanding of non-Catholics as to why Catholics
persist in their reverent obedience to the authority of the
Pope, might be hastened by recalling that the Church as a
disciplined community of faith has survived the disintegration of two civilizations; and in each case the Pope was the
chief instrument of its survival and continued relevance and
creativity in a new culture.

In the first instance, the fall of the Roman Empire gave
occasion for the pontiff to rescue the church from the decay-
ing Roman civilization and make it the nurse, teacher and
source of political unity for the European nations, still en-
meshed in barbarism. The Pope and the church were thus
the chief agents of a new European culture in which Roman

law and Christian faith were integrated. It was the Pope who created a new Western empire, crowning Charlemagne, the king of the Franks, as Emperor.

The empire was a ramshackle affair. For five centuries, from 800 to the Golden Age of the thirteenth century under Pope Innocent III, the Pope and the Church were clearly the ultimate source of European unity and order; and the Emperor and empire were clearly junior partners in the religio-political structures of European life in the Middle Ages. But this imposing religious, moral and political structure fell into decay in the next two centuries, through the philosophy of nominalism and the first stirrings of the Renaissance in Italy, until Luther, in the sixteenth century, "hurled the apple of discord" in the world.

The Church managed to survive this crisis too, and papal authority was a significant instrument of its survival. Shorn of its political power, it became a universal religious community, offering moral guidance and spiritual security in the pluralistic culture of the Western democracies and the new nations of Asia and Europe.

In the light of these two chapters, it is not a mystery that the Catholic Church should cherish obedience to the Pope as a sacred principle of order and unity. That is why the final keystone of papal monarchy, the doctrine of the Pope's "infallibility," was a post-Reformation achievement, proclaimed in the First Vatican Council in 1870. Even though heretics may find it idolatrous or a "convenient fiction," the doctrine of papal supremacy was bound to be a non-negotiable doctrine of faith, for the purpose of guarding the unity of a universal church which must speak with one voice across the barriers of national loyalties and comprehend at least two cultures, medieval and modern.

We must, of course, realize that the Second Vatican Council has changed the character of the dialogue between the two branches of the Church. It did so partly by empowering national synods to meet; these synods passed upon papal encyclicals, either approving, disapproving, or partly approving them. The second fact that has altered the situation is the Jesuit Order. This historic order began as a very paladin of papal power in the Post-Reformation era, and now has become the organ of criticism of papal doctrine, whenever or wherever it violates what the Society of Jesus regards as "Natural Law."

Despite these qualifications and modifications of papal authority, the fact of papal absolutism still remains. This was clearly demonstrated by the Pope's action with respect to the Dutch Church and the issue of celibacy. The Dutch Church, consistently rebellious, had voted 72 to 2 to make priestly celibacy voluntary. The Pope thereupon vetoed this expression of independence and simply ordained that celibacy did not belong to the realm of discussion.

The Second Vatican Council has also initiated many creative dialogues between the two versions of the Christian faith. The dialogues will proceed more hopefully if it is realized that these two versions are imbedded on either side of a watershed of history. Protestants, after all these years, cannot yield obedience to the Pope. But Catholics cannot afford to discard a voice and instrument of authority which guarantees their survival as a universal religious community.

JUST AS DIALOGUE between Christian faiths can be fruitful, a valuable two-way relationship exists between the religious communities and the pluralistic society, which can be extremely productive. The disciplines of secular culture and the cross-teachings of various historic religions act upon faith, criticizing and refining it. In turn, religious belief and commitment contributes to man's sense of moral responsibility toward his fellow man, and his relationship to the transcendent realm of God's mystery, without which both man and human history lack meaning.

Reflections on Over-Population

CHARLES MERRILL

My grandfather, who was physician and pharmacist of Green Cove Springs, Florida, used to say that the two greatest innovations for preserving children's lives were the flush toilet and the ice box. He dreaded the long Florida summers because the diarrhea from spoiled milk and the typhoid spread by flies that sped from privy to kitchen killed more children than small town doctors like himself could hope to save.

The flush toilet contributed statistically to our expectations of longevity, but it had three by-products my grandfather did not consider. First, by channeling Green Cove Springs' sewage (which used to seep slowly into the wells) into the St. John's River, it helped lead to the present general pollution of our water resources. Second, the added usage of six gallons of water each time a toilet is flushed has contributed to the steady drop in the sub-soil water table, and each year the new wells must go deeper than the old ones. And, third, the toilet has contributed to over-population by changing the traditional balance between a high birth rate and a high children's death rate.

A radical population rise, with its concomitants of pollution and the exhaustion of natural resources are problems which the last generation ignored and which our generation must face. Otherwise, they will be out of control for our children's generation.

I

No VISITOR who watches a mother with her first baby can be insensitive to the emotions she shares with mothers throughout the centuries—the mystery of having created life from out of her body, of nourishing it from her own breast. Her joy in the puckered little face, the fragile fingers of the warm, soft bundle she holds to her, is tempered by wonder at who her child will turn out to be and—if only at the very back of her mind—apprehension as to what life will offer him. The visitor listens to the mindless chat about digestion and whom baby takes after, but if he is cursed with a taste for statistical sociology the following figures go through his head.

All the centuries of man's life on earth were needed to produce a living population of approximately one billion people by 1850. The second billion took seventy years more, from 1850 to 1920, and only another forty were needed for the third billion. The fourth billion will be here by 1980. Unless drastic changes in birth or death rates occur, the increase between now and the year 2000 will be larger than the entire population of the earth in 1968.[1]

If Baby is American he was born when the national birth rate (17.4 per thousand in 1968) stood at its lowest point in history, lower than the 18.4 of the 1933–1936 depression years, totally different from the peak of 26.6 in 1947. Though the birth rate per thousand stays low, the large number of women born during the Truman years' baby boom are now

---

[1] These classic statistics come from *The Population Dilemma*, edited by Philip Hauser, Prentice-Hall, second edition, 1969.

at the age (20–29) of peak fertility. Despite Vietnam and Nixon increases in unemployment, American births have been increasing steadily since October 1968. If there were one hundred million Americans about fifty years ago, there are two hundred million now; there will probably be three hundred million in the year 2000 and perhaps four hundred million by 2020.

If the developed, industrialized and largely white part of the world (United States–Canada, Europe, Australia–New Zealand, Japan) follows American patterns and reaches the figure of only 1.3 billion by the year 2000, the remaining countries will reach about 5 billion. While in 1960, the United States–Canada and Latin America each had the same size population, by 2000 Latin America, the fastest growing region of the world, may have seven hundred fifty million people—the size of China today. Mexico City had 1.2 million inhabitants in 1930; it had seven million by 1969.

Population change is based on the interrelation of birth and death rates that vary with each country. The death rate of Sweden, a typical advanced Western country, began a steady drop over two hundred years ago, rising only with chance famines or the influenza epidemic of 1919. The birth rate began to fall in mid-nineteenth century, for various reasons. Falling child mortality rates obviated the necessity of having many babies in order to insure that a fair sized family would survive. The urbanization of the country meant that children no longer added to family upkeep by helping with farm chores, but rather added to family expenses by requiring education or an additional room in a city apartment. As living standards rose, a refrigerator or a car became more important to family happiness than a fourth baby.

In the thirties the depression lowered the birth rate further; the relief at the war's end caused it to rise. Today it is stabilizing at around 15 per thousand.

Ceylon, a typical backward Eastern country, has had a

fairly stable, high (38 per thousand) birth rate since statistics first began to be collected in 1900. The death rate was also high and constant enough to maintain a manageable relation between population and resources. A disastrously successful anti-malaria campaign in the ten years following World War II, however, cut this death rate in half, and the population, therefore, will double itself in thirty years.

Turkey is a country with both Western and Eastern patterns. The birth rate in Izmir, an industrialized, westernized city on the Aegean coast, is 27 per thousand, while in a village in central Anatolia it rises to 55, just about at human limits. Turkey, however, has an infant mortality rate of 160 per thousand (twice as high as Yugoslavia or Mexico). Ankara is ringed with shanty-towns of fugitives from the villages, but the population pressure is still manageable unless a public health campaign (certain to be encouraged and aided by the United States) cuts the terrible death rates of babies and their fourteen-year-old mothers before the 55 per thousand village birth rate is cut. Turkish leaders have an old fashioned pride that lots of babies mean lots of soldiers, and are deceived by the emptiness of their land, forgetting that the empty plateau would be ravaged by dust storms and eroded by gullies if it had to support any more men and sheep than it does. They say they are not worried. Even if they were, it is questionable how much village customs could be affected by state action. Perhaps only urbanization will give ex-peasants a personal motive to limit their families.

A certain amount of food is shared by one half of the world with the other. Canada and Australia sell wheat to China for gold. Freighters with wheat from our Midwestern states tie up at the Calcutta docks to keep a large part of India's population alive on a hand-to-mouth basis. But to maintain the American standard of living and the industrial plant that permits such generosity, America was using in 1954 about half the world's raw material resources consumed that year.

By 1980 the figure might go to over eighty per cent. Each year one American consumes (a statistic presented by Lincoln and Alice Day in *Too Many Americans*) the resources that will keep twenty-nine Indians alive. We feel that we do other nations a favor when we buy their natural resources—copper from Chile, oil from Arabia, bauxite from Ghana—but their citizens may not continue to agree.

IT IS POSSIBLE to measure the future with statistics or with images of Apocalypse. Unlike medieval painters, we don't have to invent the imagery; we know it already. We have seen photographs of the human rag bundles of Calcutta sleeping in the streets, photographs of its skull-faced children. Apocalypse could be closer to home—a city beach on an August Sunday, any expressway at rush hour—if we knew it would never end. The crowds grind against each other and produce other familiar images, whether a screaming street of rioters or the helmeted police that will try to check them. An officer signing an order to send a thousand persons to a concentration camp, a trembling young woman waiting vaguely in an emergency ward after an overdose of drugs: different images of Apocalypse—same cause.

Rodents can also have apocalyptic fates. Male rats jammed together in a pen become frenzied and tear and eat each other, turn homosexual, or withdraw in apathy and become paralyzed. Female rats miscarry and forget how to build their nests. They bear their offspring on the floor of the pen, forget to nurse them, forget whose young is theirs, wander away and leave their young to die. With wild rodents the population gluts and crashes are cyclic. Snowshoe hares swarm over the tundra and then die in convulsions, or die lethargically from brain and gland hemorrhages. Lemmings hurl themselves into the fjords, but they are already dying from injuries to their brains and adrenal glands before random frenzy topples them into the water.

The slaughter of half a million Chinese in Indonesia in 1966—even if the ostensible cause was Indonesian fear of a Communist take-over backed by the native Chinese—was a sort of population crash. So was the mutual slaughter of Hindus and Muslims during the exchange of peoples after Indian independence. In each case, the two groups had never trusted each other but they got along. When the pressure for existence worsened, any accident could set them at each other's throats. The American version of a population crash may be alienated adolescents so maimed by drugs, gonorrhea and hepatitis, police brutality and general misery that they just won't be a part of the family-raising culture. The usual war, paradoxically, is not such a population crash. The relation of natural and artificial resources to people per square mile, not the census totals by themselves, is the real measure of population balance. American bombing of Vietnam has been so destructive of forests, of farm land, of every conceivable factory and workshop, that the decimated nation will nonetheless emerge from the war more over-populated than ever.

The problem of limiting population growth must be recognized as *the* task of the coming decades. All other problems—avoiding war, preserving democracy, bringing justice to the poor and non-white—are by-products of this central one. As painful as efforts at population control may be, the costs of limitation *now* are nothing compared to the costs of an uncontrolled population rise later. The pressures of population and the pressures of trying to limit it will affect every facet of human life—our concepts of law, property, education, medicine, the family, every detail of human freedom. The issues of population control will be expressed in intense conflict between the individual and society.

American thinking on this issue has not been realistic. There is the popular myth of citizen and society as one—the smiling neighbors gathered around the barbecue pit. There is the liberal myth of heroic individual against mediocre society—Thoreau going to jail rather than pay taxes for the war against Mexico. But over the next few decades, society will intensify its demands upon the individual in every area, and the individual will have to obey. The hero will be Creon, who represents rational state authority, not Antigone, who would sacrifice her life to uphold her ideals. In a beleaguered fortress, Antigone and Thoreau are luxuries.

II

THE WORLD'S POPULATION is using up the water, the top soil, the forests, the ores. It is polluting every part of the earth it lives upon. The major clash between individual and society will come as the latter tries to safeguard the supply and cleanliness of the resources that support it.

Pollution can be a simple problem, like beer cans on a beach, or a subtle one, where the pesticides essential to high yield agriculture are washed from field to river to sea. There they are concentrated by one-celled diatoms which replenish the supply of atmospheric oxygen. If our pesticides limit or maim these diatoms, we inhibit our supply of new oxygen. Another example, the burning of fuels has caused the carbon dioxide content of the earth's atmosphere to rise fourteen per cent in the last century. More carbon dioxide causes the atmosphere to become warmer. A warmer atmosphere may cause the Antarctic ice cap to start melting, which in turn will raise sea levels and threaten the inundation of coastal areas.[2]

The automobile, at least in our country, provides a total

---

2 This paragraph's material comes from an excellent article on over-population, "The Human Race has, Maybe, Thirty-five Years Left," by David Lyle, in the November, 1967 *Esquire* Magazine.

expression of the problems of pollution. There is the pollution of exhaust fumes which go a long way to make New York and Los Angeles (barometer cities for social stress, as Negroes and young people are barometer groups) unlivable. The pollution of noise, the pollution of disposal and the pollution of congestion are results of the automobile culture. A car built to go a hundred goes five miles an hour at five P.M. Two-thirds of downtown Los Angeles is paved streets or parking lots, alternately clogged or empty. There are rational means for limiting automobile pollution—and every one of them will be opposed. Electric motors may be practical in the city where drivers go short distances and can readily recharge their batteries; horn-blowing can be outlawed; fines can be imposed for noisy mufflers. Dead cars can be dropped into the sea to make artificial reefs for fish. By law rather than taste, cars can be made smaller, to save metals, fuel—and parking space. Whole sections of cities can be closed to traffic; people can employ novel forms of public transportation. They can walk.

These changes will cause trouble. Vice-presidents like limousines. Young men like noise. Negroes like to park their cars in front of their houses and ignore white sociologists who say they shouldn't. America considers the number of cars manufactured per year in Detroit as the prime index of national economic health. But if it considers the problem urgent enough, society can do what it wants.

III

HOUSING WILL BE THE FIELD where population pressure will cause the most trouble. Every city in every country in the world has a housing crisis. In America the situation is worse because our cities are becoming black ghettos walled by white suburbs. Again, what are the priorities? After a while, if slum dwellers don't get better housing, they burn the city down.

The challenge to society may be met by Federal support for the construction of housing rented below cost to the poor, or by recognition of the tenant strike as a legitimate weapon against landlords who violate housing codes. Another approach is city condemnation and seizure of buildings whose landlords make no concession to tenant demands, as well as seizure of vacant land and buildings.

American law has traditionally been prejudiced against the poor, but the pressures of over-population will inevitably lead to city governments becoming more radical in their response to the growing political power of poverty groups (whether through organized voting or through their readiness to tear the streets apart). The change in police approach was reflected during the rioting in Washington, D.C. following Martin Luther King's murder. Armed police stood by while looters ran in and out of television and liquor stores. If the looters had been checked they would have turned violent; the shops were expendable.

Similar "prudent" radicalism may appear in the field of housing, perhaps placing limitations on the space that a wealthy widow can occupy, or restricting luxury construction —the whole heavy-handed Spartanism of post-war Europe.

A discussion of housing under the pressures of population brings up the question of *privacy*. How important is it for a man to be alone? Does my need for privacy justify your being crowded? A wealthy man can *buy* privacy. What can the poor man do? Sometimes a church provides a place to enter, sit alone and in silence. A mosque has a shadowy emptiness when one enters it from the ant heap streets of Istanbul. An English commuter, even in a crowded train, has the discipline to make a private world for himself behind his newspaper.

Traditional Japan might be worth study as a civilization of

privacy. The people are crushed upon each other, but the dwarf trees, the flowers, the raked pebbles of the garden supply a world spacious enough that one does not look over the neighbor's fence. The tiny house of unpainted wooden walls and sliding paper panels seems spacious because people squat on the floor instead of sitting on chairs. If a person is trained to find beauty in a single vase, there is less need to crowd the house with furniture. The house is silent because discipline puts restraints upon how people speak to each other. Ceremony limits the friction of personality.

But this culture of discipline was bought dearly. Its silence was the subjection of the woman to the man, of the young to the old. The only serious protest of the individual was suicide. Its beauty was static, and when the traditions were cracked by Western taste, there were no skills for judging good from bad, so the houses filled up with over-stuffed armchairs. Its privacy meant callousness to a neighbor's sufferings; to help him was to expose oneself to unnecessary involvement, further demand upon the tense courtesies that restricted life. And in a situation where the rules of behavior did not apply, such as the conquest of a foreign city or the administration of a prison camp, the Japanese ran amok.

In 1945 when the Japanese saw themselves smashed by the war, stripped of their empire, with ten million people crowded upon a mountainous archipelago of only one-seventh of an acre of cultivable land per head, they met this crisis problem with the crisis solution of abortion. By 1953 the number of abortions, reported and unreported, was perhaps higher than the number of live births, and the birth rate had declined to 21.5 per thousand from 32.8 in 1949.

It is also possible to move in the opposite direction. In addition to privacy, man needs an improvement in the pleasures of crowd life. If the English middle-class commuter is private man, the English working-class family on a holiday is crowd man: the slow-moving, good-natured crowd—Mum and Dad and George and 'Arriet, munching from their bags of fish and chips, chatting with the family next to them in the tea queue.

Among my students, adolescents from small, well-educated families that stress individuality and reserve, I see the positive impact made by a summer at a Quaker work camp. There is the group work of repairing the roof and digging the foundations, the ease of sharing group property, the experience of group analysis, group mysticism. The Woodstock rock festival in 1969, with four hundred thousand young people jammed together in noise, drugs and dirt, would seem like Dante's Hell to most adults. The adolescents who crowded to it saw the experience as a mystical expression of solidarity and "love," of strengthening themselves against the outside.

IV

EDUCATION IS THE INSTITUTION that suffers most from overpopulation. The pressures of crowded society are felt most painfully by the young, who lack the adult's armor of habit and position, no matter how unsatisfactory those may be.

The first skirmishes of race war are fought in the halls and lunchrooms. The alienation of young people from society becomes a school problem. In higher education, student demonstrations against the Vietnam war and the military establishment turn into attacks against the universities, as the nearest representatives of organized society—and the most vulnerable.

The much discussed alienation of youth calls forth, in turn, an alienation *against* youth. Societies that send for the riot police as a response to student rhetoric pay a high price for a cynical, brutalized student population. And in the process, education can be wrecked.

The maintenance of quality in mass education is also

complicated by over-population. What does quality mean? Academic quality is maintained by admitting only those whom one can educate well. If one out of three applicants is chosen this means higher standards. How about one out of ten, or thirty? This leads to cheating, to grovelling, to irrationality as the deans of admission use ever more random criteria. And will those who are chosen grind ruthlessly to beat the competition, or will they loaf because they know how élite they are?

Traditional education was designed for young people with money or intellect. Mass education serves the student with neither. The large number of second-rate schools, the American contribution to educational history, help ordinary youngsters climb from rung D to rung C in the social ladder. They also establish the educational equivalent of the custodial society. People are sent to school because there's nothing better to do with them. They don't work very hard. They don't have much respect for themselves or their institutions. They are kept amused, and if they have any ingenuity at all they enjoy more sexual freedom than at any other time of their lives.

I see some serious tasks, however, for higher education in an over-populated society. In the seventies computerized technology will destroy the job opportunities of ordinary college graduates as it did in the sixties for high school dropouts; but an institutionalized society will need a huge staff of people educated to make its machinery work effectively and humanly. For example, if large police forces are going to be indispensable for keeping our cities from exploding, what sort of a cop do we look for? How can his uniformed authority become a source of stability—a man who knows his neighborhood, who recognizes the symptoms of trouble and can act responsibly before the situation blows up. We will need more and better clerks and guardians for our social agencies, and we will need better men to check their actions—the ombudsman who supports the widow against the pension bureau, the inspector who investigates how the inmates are treated in our lockups.

V

I HAVE TRIED TO SKETCH some problems of an over-populated life. Can the rise in population be limited? If we are willing to pay the price, man can do anything he wants. The price of some desires, however, may be higher than he is willing to pay.

For a number of reasons the 1968 birth rate was the lowest in American history. Catholic opinion had begun to change its attitude on birth control. Some states relaxed their laws against abortion, permitting a woman to obtain a legal abortion for reasons of physical or psychological ill health. The marriage age, which had dropped steadily since 1940, began to rise as a result of adolescent use of better contraceptives, which in turn reduces the need for forced marriage, and permits sexual pleasure without the need for marriage. Perhaps adolescents have seen enough unhappy marriages among their older friends to be soured on its mystique.

Densely populated England has gone much further than our country in the serious discussion of population size. With a courage no American politician would risk, the parliamentary leader of the Labour Party, Douglas Houghton, raised the question in the British House of Commons whether a large family should not now be considered a form of social delinquency. Why shouldn't society be involved when a couple produces six children and expects that housing, schooling, medical care and jobs will be provided automatically?

New techniques are being developed that will have a long-range effect on fertility. For example, a capsule can be placed under a woman's skin that will leak chemicals into her system to cause infertility for three to six months. The techniques will be improved; a woman's entire reproductive life could be blocked from the age of fifteen on.[3] But what is now voluntary can be made compulsory—and there's the rub.

Even if population growth becomes a political issue as in England (perhaps permeated with an ugly flavor of racism, as in the debates on restricting non-white Commonwealth immigration), it allows man a sense of being able to control his own destiny, to weigh the priorities of need and cost. There isn't the dismay that followed the callous archaism of Pope Paul's prohibition of all artificial forms of contraception. What will be the effects of this edict? Less chance for wretched Latin America to put its house in order; a new rise in its abortion rates;[4] greater guilt or greater alienation from their church on the part of "progressive" Catholics.

In the United States the problem is compounded, as usual, when race becomes involved with population control. Should women on relief be offered contraceptive information, or should they be pressured to use it? California has attempted to do the latter, by limiting payments for illegitimate children. However, since American employment and relief practices have cooperated to destroy the Negro family (a family cannot ask for relief with a man under the roof), many children born to dependent Negro women are illegitimate.

The social worker is white; the woman on relief is black. The words, spoken or unspoken, of the two have nothing in common.

---

[3] It is still a man's world. Most doctors are men. They take for granted that experiments in physiological alteration, even of the most radical sort, are made on women. Only primitive countries like India (where a transistor radio is sometimes awarded the man who accepts the operation), Pakistan and Puerto Rico have widely employed male sterilization.

[4] The low 1.3 per cent annual growth of population in Uruguay, where contraceptives are not available, comes from an abortion rate estimated at three abortions for every live birth.

1. A woman should not bear children that society must support.

No—whites have created this society with the suffering of the woman and the purposelessness of the man. Let them change its basic ills and not nag at the symptoms.

2. A limited family allows the parents to build toward a higher standard of living and pay more attention to the education of their children.

No—this is honky talk. The good life is not necessarily white-type life. The large black family, warm, noisy, full of life and mutual helpfulness, is an expression of "soul" values.

3. The rise in population swamps the city's ability to serve its people properly.

No—the schools and services blacks get aren't worth anything anyway. Talk about population just covers up fear of *black* population. No one lectured Robert Kennedy about *his* ten children. No matter how it is rephrased, family planning is just a variant of honky genocide, another effort to castrate the Negro male and keep Us under Their control.

Thoughtful analysts of population, like Dr. Rene Dubos,[5] agree that the problem is not that of finding the perfect gimmick—the cheap, foolproof contraceptive—but of creating a climate which will accept the small family group as desirable. The Puerto Rican sees children as a proof of manliness. The Indian in Calcutta sees children as his only security when he is too old to work. Children are one of the few pleasures of a wretched life; their smiles and embraces make the day bearable. It is not poverty, as Malthus claimed, that limits population. Poverty *breeds* population. The woman on relief has illegitimate children because she is so demoralized by poverty that she has lost all hope of controlling her life. Middle-class rules that stop payments for her fatherless babies will reduce her to prostitution and her children to

---

5 *Man Adapting*, Yale University Press, 1961.

starvation. They will not stop her making new babies. It is only when comparative affluence gives a man some confidence in his future, some sense of control over his own life, that he will rely upon fewer sons and daughters.

SUPPOSE WE GET WHAT WE WANT—the universal family of 2.2 children—will it be worth having? Should every couple that wants children see this desire tinged with guilt? Perhaps some families should have lots of children and others none at all.

If we are to avoid a joyless society of rationed children, perhaps we can buy a little freedom by reversing our trends and raising the death rate wherever we can. Perhaps Western society has made a serious error in assuming that there is nothing worse than death.

Shall we begin by changing our stand on keeping alive babies born with serious defects? Until now the argument has been that it is better that a hundred hopeless children should live, than one potentially redeemable child should die. We may not be able to afford this. Better that one redeemable child should die than a hundred defectives should live. This is not more callous than the way defective children are actually treated in the custodial society. And the future will bring us more, not fewer, defectives, from the drugs we dose ourselves with (thalidomide, L.S.D., marijuana, the bag of housewives' tranquillizers) and the pollutants (insecticides, preservatives, additives) that spoil our food and drink.

Shall we reverse our assumption that capital punishment is always evil? It is wrong when those usually executed have been Negroes and the poor who are unable to pay for a good lawyer. But the earth is crowded. Why should we burden it with those who have harmed society?

Within the larger picture of numbers growth, I doubt the value of bravura medicine. 1968 was the year of the heart transplant—with exciting publicity, tremendous cost and doubtful value. An elderly invalid has been kept alive a few more years. Is cancer or senile decay preferable? Maybe it was time for him to go. Aged people should be permitted to hold on to their dignity. It is tragic to see the vulgarity of their treatment when they finally come to the hospital. Whether a former President or a forgotten ex-bookkeeper who has outlived all her insurance policies—every body orifice is stuck with some sort of a tube to keep the cell structure ticking. It isn't as if we had unlimited medical resources. The society that pays $25,000 for a heart transplant will not pay for clean and quiet hospitals, for nurses to have a little time for kindness, for some one to hold the hand of a dying man and reassure him that his life was not a waste and that he isn't alone.

The changes I have suggested are dangerous. Catholics have condemned mechanical methods of contraception as breaking nature's link between sexual pleasure and the creation of life. If life is stopped at conception, then it is only a matter of degree before society continues on to abortion, infanticide, euthenasia, genocide. The Catholics are right. Hitler gave us a case study of rational killing. At the war's beginning he ordered the elimination of the senile and insane. Then he got rid of the Jews and Gypsies. When the war ended, as he liked to sketch during his dinner table monologue, he'd kill off half the Czechs and Poles to provide more room for Germans. Also people with heart disease and tuberculosis. By now Negroes are even more sensitive to the ambiguities of social pruning than Catholics or Jews. If anyone is going to be cut back in America they know who the victim will be.

It is not a matter of "selling" Death with a crash program of spot commercials, but that a man's death—*how* and *when*—must be seen as part of his whole life. The death of its members must become part of the way society looks at itself. And two points are worth stressing. (1) We have already interfered with the natural balance of nature by introducing smallpox vaccine and flush toilets. (2) The alternative to population control is a rat pen society of chaos, callousness and despair. We don't have an unlimited range of options.

VI

WHAT SORT OF A SOCIETY will emerge? One may forecast either a society of violence as resentments and frustrations seek an outlet; or a society of passivity. We may see the creation of what I call the "anodyne society"—keep people amused, don't let them think, dull their pain, exhaust their energies with imitations of real living. To use an ugly image, we may create a society based on infinite varieties of masturbation.

The universal acceptance of television makes it the example of anodyne culture. We all share in a little bit of art, a little bit of citizenship, a little cruelty, a little sex, without leaving the sofa except to open another beer. Other examples of the anodyne society are stamp collecting, strip tease bars, meetings of college trustees, psychoanalysis, sociologists' questionnaires, fashion shows, political rallies. Those with more energy indulge in motorcycle racing or throwing rocks at the police. Those with more money build space rockets or collect art. Anodyne activism: the student scrawling "Pig go home" on the dormitory wall, heart pounding with pride at the blow he has struck for freedom.

What sort of men will survive in this world of overpopulation? The obedient who don't ask for much and won't get much; the aggressive who will grab the best that is available.

The grimness of the forecast may force men to face these problems more honestly. Perhaps the super-abundance of life will force men to become more sensitive to death, and in turn more sensitive to the question that underlies both life and death: What is man that Thou art mindful of him.

Ethical Issues in Psychotherapy

NATHAN W. ACKERMAN

ONE of the strangest paradoxes of modern dynamic psychotherapy is its avoidance of the issue of ethical values. In the day-by-day practice of psychotherapy, problems of ethical conflict pop up repeatedly like a jack-in-the-box; they cannot, in fact, be held down. Yet, oddly enough, until now systematic discussion of the question within the folds of the profession has been conspicuously scarce. If one searches the literature of psychoanalysis, one must look hard and long for anything pertaining to values—sexual values, yes; ethical values, no! The indexes of classical psychoanalytic publications and psychiatric textbooks simply do not list these words. This is not an accident of history. Psychotherapy, according to formal doctrine, is not in the "morals business." Morals, ethics, values are not taken to be the responsibility of this profession. In the main, they are judged as irrelevant and are excluded. This is the official posture of psychoanalysis and it has been widely adopted by the various versions of modern psychotherapeutic practice.

The power and tenacity of this trend is all the more remarkable when we consider how far its validity is contra-

dicted by the sheer facts of life. Insofar as the psychotherapeutic encounter reenacts a piece of life, the human struggle
with values and ethical choice enters the very heart of the
experience. As Anant says: "The real world of man is society
and the plasma of society is morality." Thus to continue to
assert that psychotherapy is not in the "morals business"
becomes a hardly tenable position. This is also Erich
Fromm's stand. Says Fromm: "Mental sickness cannot be
understood apart from moral problems. The psychoanalyst
is the physician of the soul." Yet, curiously enough, it was
Freud himself who excluded values from psychoanalytic procedure; from this strange historical contradiction emerges an
odd predicament for the patient, the psychotherapist and the
social community as well.

Clearly, the taboo on psychotherapeutic dealing with ethical values is an extension of the heritage of classical psychoanalysis. Freud laid down a powerful tradition; his value of
"no values" established the rule. The analyst's values must
play no part in the treatment process. He must confine his
work to analysis; he must not attempt psychosynthesis. His
prime responsibility is "freeing the id," "making the unconscious conscious."[1]

"Man's power to control the id cannot be increased beyond
certain limits. If one asks more of people, one produces revolt
or neurosis."[2]   "Genital man needs to express his aggressive
instincts in order to experience his potency and be happy."
(Note the equation: potency and happiness.) It is this drive
that "must inevitably bring him into conflict with the welfare of society."[3]

In this orientation there is, in fact, an implicit value: the

---

[1] The writer refers here to an unpublished Ph.D. thesis by Beatrice Goodwin
Adkins, *Guides to Conduct in Reconstructive Psychotherapy*, Columbia University, 1960.
[2] Freud, Sigmund, *Civilization and Its Discontents*, London: Hogarth Press,
p. 140.
[3] *Ibid.*, p. 79.

support of individual assertion against the authority symbols of family, society, and religion. Nonetheless, as we shall see later, Freud, with his uncanny penchant for perceiving the polarities of human experience, partly contradicts this stand.

Influenced by his dedication to science and the theory of evolution, Freud adopted a biological model for mental illness and assumed a stance of technical objectivity and detachment. In so doing, he felt impelled to divorce the psychoanalytic treatment process from any concern with philosophy, morality and religion.

For the role of the analyst, he espoused the couch technique. The analyst sits behind, anonymous, faceless, a "blank screen." As the patient projects his fantasies, conflicts and fears, the analyst remains strictly "non-judgmental." He guards jealously the purity of the therapeutic process and permits no contamination of the field of transference. He withholds all cues regarding questions of "right and wrong." The patient's attempts to seduce the analyst into taking a stand are viewed as resistance, and countered accordingly. Problems pertaining to values and ethical choice remain exclusively the patient's domain, not the concern of the analyst. This is Freud's prescription for the psychoanalyst as a technician.

The rationale for this role rests on two main considerations: the principle of *Habeas Mentum,* the right of each man to his own mind, and the central concern with the oppressive force of the infantile superego. According to standard theory, parental authority imposes the threat of castration; from this comes "the tyranny of the should." The infantile superego is imprisoning; it is anachronistic; it strangles the individual. The goal is to free the person from this oppressive force. But, what of the conscience of the mature person? This, in fact, is rarely discussed.

When we turn from Freud the technician to Freud the man, the picture is different. Freud's concept of the mature man, potent, able to love and work and to enjoy "object relations," implied an ethical ideal, an optimal human being cultivating optimal human relationships with a deep, earnest concern for others as well as for the self. Freud was committed to the basic human value of each person's right to his own mind. He upheld the ideal of freedom of individual expression. While he diagnosed all religion as neurosis, he nonetheless gave explicit recognition to its ethical values. "He who knows nothing of these religious values is ignorant indeed and he who has assimilated them may consider himself enriched."[4] Freud, the self-styled "Godless Jew," knew how to respect spiritual values. Almost as a lone fighter he waged a life-long battle against the scourges of mankind—madness, prejudice and cruelty.[5]

In one aspect, Freud supported the principle of psychic determinism; he assumed a fatalistic view of the imperfectability of man, of the primacy and universality of man's instinct for aggression. Concerning the possibility of eradicating man's inhumanity to man, he was a severe pessimist. On the other hand, he was the author of that hallowed statement "where id is, there ego shall be." He yearned to believe that man, with expanded insight, could become dominant over his instincts and (within limits) achieve mastery over his own destiny.

Here we have it; the enigma of Freud, the subtlety and complexity of his ideas, the ambivalence inherent in his polarization of love and destruction, the ambiguity of his value of "no values" for the practice of psychoanalytic healing.

The tendency of many of Freud's followers was to interpret literally his interdiction of values in the psychoanalytic treatment process. They limited their responsibility to their pa-

---

[4] Earl A. Grollman, *Judaism in Sigmund Freud's World*, Bloch Publishing Co., 1965, Introduction.
[5] *Ibid.*, Foreword by Nathan W. Ackerman, p. 1.

tients to the task of helping them to release their instinctually bound energies from the strictures of superego (parent and community), regardless of the consequences in social behavior. They disassociated the technique of cure from the whole sphere of ethical development. They adopted the stance that the cultivation of a valid system of ethical values is simply outside the realm of their therapeutic work.[6]

Here are a few representative comments: "a doctor has to cure his patient whether he is good or bad"—"a doctor has no specific value"—"the patient must discover the ability to gratify his instincts within certain limits" (what limits?) — "depression and self-castigation are symptoms, unscrupulousness is not" (note here the echo of Freud's emphasis on potency and aggression) —"it isn't the primary purpose of therapy to have the patient become a participating member of a group instead of a world unto himself."[7]

To be sure, this represented the extreme position and it has been moderated by the more flexible segment of the profession. Nonetheless, the locking out of ethical concern continued as a powerful tradition. The patient-analyst relationship became isolated from the ethos and moral fabric of family and community. It is the rigidity of this classical taboo on ethical concern that has evoked in certain quarters a sharp critical reaction. There is a real and present danger, say some critics, that the denial of ethical responsibility in psychoanalysis produces a generation of psychopaths. Freudian theory, so the argument goes, contributes to the disintegration of the moral fabric of western society. It encourages the doctrine of instinct gratification. It gives license to the sex-seekers. It supports the trend of ruthless aggression; it nourishes a pervasive permissiveness, a trend toward self-indulgence and the quest for fun. It cultivates laxity in social and moral

---

6 See, for example, Nunberg, Herman, *Principles of Psychoanalysis,* Int. Univ. Press, 1955.
7 Adkins, Beatrice Goodwin, *op. cit.*

rules. It relieves the individual of his anxieties and inhibitions and turns him toward sociopathic behavior. When, however, the pursuit of fun gives out, when its intrinsic shallowness and emptiness emerge, say these critics, there is nothing left but disillusionment and despair.[8]

FROM OTHER QUARTERS comes a different cry of alarm. Does psychoanalysis spawn a generation of stereotyped, conformist characters committed solely to the goal of competitive power and material acquisition? Does it produce people who keep busy chasing "success" while they turn spiritually bankrupt? Does psychoanalysis foster a breed of isolated, alienated persons, cut off from all sense of family and community?

The Freudian "establishment" tends either to ignore these assaults or offers a rejoinder somewhat as follows: We are misunderstood! Such criticisms are a naive, faulty interpretation of the psychoanalyst's function. Psychoanalytic therapy is designed to protect the confidence of the patient, to safeguard the integrity and purity of the treatment process. It is dedicated to the principle of non-interference with the emotional growth of the patient. Above all else, it holds sacred the principle of free expression for the individual.

A crucial factor still inadequately understood is the role of radical social change in modifying the theory and practice of psychoanalysis.[9] The controversy continues; it is in no sense resolved. For further clarification of the issue, I shall here spell out anecdotally some relevant experiences from my own practice.

A man and wife, the parents of three children, came for

---

[8] Anant, S. S., "Psychotherapy and Morality," *Psychiatric Opinion*, Vol. 4, No. 4, August 1967; McNeill, J. T., *History of the Cure of Souls,* New York: Harper, 1951, pp. 319–324; Tiebout, H. M., *Philosophy and Psychoanalysis*, Columbia University Press, p. 210.

[9] See Ackerman, Nathan W., "Cultural Factor in Psychoanalytic Therapy," *The Psychoanalytic Bulletin*, Vol. VII, No. 4, December 1951; Freud, Anna, 18th Annual Sigmund Freud Lecture, *New York Times*, April 17, 1968.

consultation regarding a marital crisis. A quick survey of the situation disclosed four distinct components of disorder: marital conflict, parent-child conflict, personality disorders in both parents, and disturbances in all three children. The question arose as to where to begin—with the family or with its separate members? Should the whole family be treated? Should each parent be analyzed separately? The wife blurted out: "The crisis in our marriage won't wait. By the time my husband and I are psychoanalyzed, our family will be completely destroyed."

Another woman, the mother of four young children, was repeatedly admonished by her analyst for her preoccupation with problems concerning her relations with her husband and children. Her analyst told her: "Don't bother with them; concentrate on yourself." Within a short time this patient abandoned her analytic treatment. On consulting me she exclaimed: "This is the most ridiculous thing I ever heard. What shall I say to my husband and children? 'Excuse me, I'm busy with my analyst. I'll be back three years from now!' "

A man of 55 came for treatment of his depression. As he lay down on the couch, he quipped, "At these prices I can't afford not to be honest! I will tell you everything you want to know except two things, my women and my money." This was a man obsessed with the goal of material success. In his private aspect, he was isolated, suspicious, aggressive and competitive. "If I don't do my share of killing every day in business, I just don't feel good. I get frightened and depressed. I lose my sense of power. I begin to feel paralyzed. To stay on top, I've got to go on killing. Otherwise I am finished."

This man's way of life affords a classical example of contradiction in ethical values. In his public aspect, he was a "pillar of society," a business executive, a devoted family man, an officer of his church, a highminded contributor to philanthropy. There was in his personality makeup a remarkable dissonance, a dramatic split between his inner and outer self. On the outside, a conscientious family person and a leader in his community; on the inside, a secret sense of triumph in getting away with murder. As a young man having his first work experience, he stole gold from his employer. Later in life he experienced a special relish in spending "the dirty money" he was able to steal from his business. He lay awake nights secretly scheming how to get the best of his business partners, who were his own brothers. From other men, he stole both dollars and women. He sneered at and victimized his women with flattering attentions but was secretly contemptuous of them. They were useful for only one thing, to bow down and perform fellatio. This was his disguised psychic device for sharpening his "gun" for the next day's battle with his business rivals, for new killings of old enemies.

Now let us take a glimpse at the 19-year-old son of a success-minded gentleman. He was referred to me as a college dropout. Having flunked all of his courses, he was immediately subject to the military draft. His attitude toward entering the armed services was one of blatant cynicism. Let the boys of the working class go to Vietnam. They had little to lose; he was intent on holding his position of social advantage. In place of a responsible application to his studies he dissipated his daytime hours playing golf. At night, craving "easy money," he gambled. In his social life he bumped his way from girl to girl; he buried himself in these "toilet holes" in order not to think or feel. He had no genuine feeling toward them. They were useful only to gorge himself and to drown out his fear of being shot at in Vietnam. He had no real life goals, no plan for the future except to slide into his father's business. This is a typical, over-indulged, middle-class "cop out."

Another critical value problem emerges from the psychoanalytic tradition of refusing contact with relatives. An intelligent executive surveying the family scene surrounding him in his comfortable suburb quipped: "If you want a divorce, send your wife to a Freudian analyst." Many of the neighboring families were severely troubled with marital conflict, loss of parental control, disturbed children. Often, these families had separate psychoanalysts for two, three and four members of the family. Among these neighbors he detected a strong tendency for husband and wife to grow apart, for parents and children to become alienated. Under his very eyes these families seemed to disintegrate. His friends in the country club were holding drinking parties by the pool, "skinny dipping," and sometimes even swapping sex partners. In the meantime the adolescent members of the family went their parents one better with huge sprees, sex parties, drinking and turning on with "pot." For his own troubles, he preferred family therapy. By dint of sheer determination he managed to hold his family together, even as those about him seemed to be cracking up.

Following a lecture I gave in another city, an obviously intelligent but disturbed man came up to me to express a bitter lament. His daughter had undergone psychoanalytic therapy. One crisis followed after another. No matter how hard he tried, her analyst refused to grant him an interview. Nevertheless, month after month this worried father continued to pay the doctor's bills. "What else could I do?" The story ends in tragedy; the daughter finally committed suicide. The father reacted to the ritual of the sacrosanct privacy of the psychoanalytic relationship with bewilderment, pain and anger. Tormented beyond words, he told me he was prepared to dedicate his entire fortune to a movement to break the whole tradition of treating troubled individuals in isolation from parents and family.

The hallowed tradition of the secrecy and separateness of the psychoanalytic relationship from family carried over into the field of child guidance. The custom of "separate treatment" of child and mother prevailed for many years. Melanie Klein, the famous child analyst, did not permit mothers of her child patients to wait in the ante-room. The awareness of the mother's physical nearness during the child's treatment session might contaminate the child's transference. When I asked a well-known child analyst if she interviewed mothers, she retorted, "Oh, good heavens, no!" It is against the background of this type of practice that child analysts have sometimes facetiously been called "mother killers." Save the child and kill the mother.

The most violent case of scoptophiliac guilt and anxiety I ever encountered was a gifted young lady who consulted me together with her recently acquired husband. She introduced herself as the daughter of four analysts. Her biological parents were divorced; each then married another analyst. She therefore had two analytic parents and two analytic step-parents. She and her husband, a young college instructor, came for consultation with a critical sexual disturbance.

They were unable to make it; sexual union, though attempted, was invariably aborted. At the slightest approach, this young lady suffered a fit of guilt, shame and anxiety. For her, the merest body contact was an indescribably dirty, degrading, frightening experience. She responded with panic to her fantasies of sexual peeking and masturbation.

The background for this acute phobia was readily ferreted out. In her childhood she was conditioned to a special way of life in the Viennese apartment in which her parents practiced psychoanalysis, her father at one end of the home, her mother at the other. All day long, strangers came and went. They stealthily entered one door, exited another. No one was allowed to see anyone else. What went on behind the closed office doors of her two parents, one at each end of the apartment, was a dead secret. No one ever uttered a word concerning these strange, private activities. Everything was dread silence. There was, however, a regular evening ritual. The patient was permitted to see her parents at the dinner table, but the taboo against mention of the comings and goings of strange persons was rigid and absolute. The patient was prohibited from exhibiting the slightest curiosity. With these shadowy visitors, God only knows what bad things went on from dawn to dusk behind the closed doors of her parents' offices.

IT IS APPROPRIATE at this juncture to pinpoint some important areas of value conflict within the framework of the psychotherapeutic process.

1. *Secrecy and shame vs. openness and sharing.*

The classical psychoanalytic procedure set a high premium on the secrecy and privacy of the patient-analyst relationship. Not only was the analyst hidden and faceless behind the couch, but each of the patients was faceless to every other. This was the setting for confession on the couch, a physical arrangement and an atmosphere that seemed implicitly to affirm the need for hiding and shame. Is this a cultural hangover from the Victorian prejudice toward sex that prevailed in Freud's Vienna some 60 years ago? In all likelihood, yes. In the contemporary world, however, it is an anachronism.

Surely, much has changed since 1910–1930. Across the years both psychoanalytic procedure and the attitudes toward sex have come out of hiding. In fact, the pendulum now swings too far in the opposite direction. In place of the original secrecy and hiding, patients tend to exhibit their personal analysts. The shift from viewing analysis as a private affair to a public one creates a whole new set of complications.

With today's greater understanding we are able to distinguish between valid and invalid forms of privacy. We can separate true secrets from pseudo-secrets. Most importantly, we can discriminate between those secrets that are on the side of health and those others that are on the side of sickness.

2. *The problem of guilt.*

The perspective toward the dissolution of guilt feeling is vital to the entire process of treatment. As the conception of the human guilt response is better understood and redefined, three large questions emerge: the relations between the conscience of childhood and the conscience of mature life; the distinction between ritual guilt and true guilt; the special problem of excessive guilt or too little guilt.

The history of the psychoanalytic orientation toward guilt highlights an imbalance: a one-sided concern with lifting an excessive burden of childhood guilt and a relative neglect of the challenge of establishing an appropriate type of adult conscience. With a lifting of the "tyranny of the should," there is still the responsibility of recognizing a valid guilt in adult life for mistreatment of both self and other persons. In the ritualized expression of guilt feelings often the purpose is to neutralize disapproval and a threat of punishment so as to enable the individual to confess, to win forgiveness and thus to be free once again to commit the same offense. By contrast, true guilt is a genuine emotion of remorse for actual wrong doing; it is both appropriate and necessary.

In our time we detect a trend toward shallow, impersonal relationships and together with this, a thin, weak guilt response. Many believe that our new technologically oriented society has changed character structure, has led to a shift from an inner-directed to an outer-directed man. The result is a trend away from a strong conscience to a weak, fickle and inadequate conscience. Today people suffer more from a lack of conscience than from an over-burdened one. Only too often it is felt that anything goes as long as you are not caught. A response of genuine remorse for inflicting hurt is supplanted by a facade, a show of false guilt, which functions simply as a special form of defense enabling one to continue a manipulative, destructive attitude toward people.

3. *The role of aggression.*

Classical Freudian analysis placed value on aggressive, competitive self-assertion as the road to strength, maturity and health. The goal of therapy was to relieve the anxiety which inhibits aggressive rivalry of son with father, daughter with mother. The path of success in life called for triumph and conquest, the acquisition of a rewarding power position.

In contrast, the trend of the Neo-Freudians reflects a shift of emphasis from an egocentrically oriented competitiveness and quest for dominance to recognition of the value of the common bond, the sharing of satisfactions, and a higher level of cooperation.

4. *Sex and/or tenderness.*

In classical Freudian theory, the sex drive and the binding force of tenderness were mainly viewed as emerging in separate paths. The first emphasis was on the achievement of potency and mastery. The tender caring and concern for the love object was relegated to a secondary position. Only in the later stages of psychosexual maturation was there a fusion of sex drives and tender sentiments. The sexual instincts evolved, stage by stage, in a relatively impersonal way. Egocentric drives held priority over the expression of altruistic concern for others.

In the Neo-Freudian modifications, sex and tenderness are joined. Object relations are given primary importance. The affectional bond is seen as the prime force of socialization. Sexual expression takes its appropriate place within the framework of evolving love relationships. A caring for others as well as the self becomes a main goal.

5. *Fantasy vs. reality.*

In classical psychoanalytic theory the liberation of the patient's fantasy life is central. What the patient feels and perceives inwardly is all important, while the reality of social experience is accorded a position of peripheral significance. The vicissitudes of external reality are played down and are not permitted to invade the analytic process. Pathogenic feelings and fantasies, surging up from the depths, hold first place. This point of view is epitomized in the comment of one classical analyst: "If an analyst permits himself to become interested in social reality, he is instantly in jeopardy; he may lose his ear for the unconscious."[10]

In this context, the projections of transference, the elaboration of transference neurosis, represent the core of psychoanalytic process, and reality testing is postponed to the later stages.

In the contemporary applications of psychodynamic theory, reality testing is given a greater weight. The therapeutic value of juxtaposing the pathogenic fantasy against a consensual definition of the existing interpersonal realities receives increasing recognition.

6. *Competition vs. cooperation.*

The tradition of psychoanalytic therapy tended to underscore the importance of competitive assertion of the aggressive drives. In contrast, the modified modern variations of psychotherapy give greater support to the principle of mutuality and cooperation.

7. *Isolation vs. union in the relations of the individual with the family and community.*

Classical Freudian theory seemed in the main to highlight the essential isolation of the individual psyche.[11] It empha-

---

[10] Bak, Robert, *A Personal Communication*, 1950.
[11] Waelder, Robert, in discussion at annual meeting of the American Psychoanalytic Association, 1952.

sized the struggle to overcome separation anxiety, the drive for strength, independence and self-sufficiency. It is against this background that psychoanalysts followed Freud's dictum in refusing contact with relatives. They took the side of the patient against family and community. In effect, the trend was toward a secret alliance of patient and analyst against the outside world. The consequence of this was a tendency in individuals undergoing psychoanalytic treatment to grow apart from the family. In Neo-Freudian forms of psychotherapy, the importance of emotional union and intimacy is reasserted.

8. *True values vs. pathogenic values as defense.*

In the psychotherapeutic process a clear distinction between true and false values is of central importance. Pseudo-values are all too often exploited for the entrenchment of pathogenic defenses. For example, a show of aggression and power, sometimes viewed as a positive value, is in fact a false value serving the purposes of pathogenic defense: the substitution of aggression for anxiety. The object is to arouse fright in other persons while denying one's own fright, the familiar device of building oneself up by tearing down someone else. It is the age-old mechanism of intimidation and scapegoating of an innocent victim.

Another example is the assertion of a claim of moral superiority through a righteous preoccupation with blame and guilt. The grand gesture of beating one's breast, *mea culpa,* is a way of pointing the finger of accusation and blame at another. The person who wallows in blame of self and/or others is precisely the person who fails to assume a true and mature responsibility.

Still another illustration is the pseudo-value of a show of pity for others. Frequently, this is not a true empathy or sympathy. It is rather an over-dramatized exhibition of pity, which is, in fact, a disguised expression of arrogance and contempt.

In the psychotherapeutic process, patient and therapist are involved in a joined struggle to discriminate between healthy and pathogenic defenses. The question is: which of the expressed values are authentic, and organically related to personal and group identity? Which others represent a set of pretended values that serve expedient or manipulative purposes, or are exploited as personal defense. In the exploration of these problems, it is to be borne in mind that family and social community exert a continuous influence, selectively reinforcing or suppressing one or another set of values and defense operations.

THE PROBLEM OF THE ROLE of values, morals and ethics in psychotherapy is largely unsolved. There is no single standard that prevails for all groups of practitioners. Each school of psychotherapy seems to hold its own special bias. While Freud's value of "no values" for psychoanalytic therapy persists, its unreal, anachronistic quality becomes ever more apparent. By now, except for a kind of Maginot Line tenaciously defended by a core group of classical Freudians, it is a tradition that is mostly honored in the breach. With the shift in focus across the years from symptom analysis to character analysis, from id to ego and ego ideal, from exclusive concern with intrapsychic conflict to a broader interest in the relations of inner and outer conflict, with the recognition of the role of environment, and the greater openness and lessened isolation of the psychotherapeutic relationship from family and community, the issue of ethical choice in psychotherapy becomes an inescapable responsibility.

The confrontation of value choice in psychotherapeutic process need not, however, be interpreted as an arbitrary imposition of the therapist's values. It is rather a question of a shared struggle, a process of emotional "working-through" of the personal and societal implications of commitment to one set of values or another.

What is involved is a kind of continuum along which the various systems of psychotherapy define their orientation to the relations of mind, body, society, and the cosmos. Some focus on mind and body, while excluding society and the cosmos. Others expand their concern to the social community. Still others establish an explicit link between psychology and philosophy and make room for the spirit of man and the meaning of his relation to the universe.

It seems possible to conceptualize the biases of different schools of psychotherapy, according to their allegiance to a particular theoretical model of personality development and interpersonal relations. Within this framework there are perhaps five main models:

1. The biological model: Man as an organismic energy system. Behavior is organized in a hierarchical pattern of instinctual drives.

2. The psychosocial or adaptational model: Man as a system of emerging relationships, with behavior patterned by these relationships.

3. The societal model: Man as the product of his social organization. Behavior is conditioned within a particular social-political system.

4. The spiritual-philosophic model: Man as a spiritual being. Behavior is shaped by man's oneness with God and the meaning of his relation to the universe.

5. The familial-transactional model: Man as a familial being. Behavior is determined in depth by the individual's integration into the emotional life of his family group.[12]

---

12 See Appendix.

In a general way, it seems possible to trace a correlation between the value perspectives of the various schools of psychotherapy and their respective views of human nature. Each system of psychotherapy evolves a particular orientation to the relations of the individual with the family and social community. Within this context a theory of behavior and of mental illness emerges together with a related theory of psychotherapy and a particular stance toward the issues of ethical conflict.

The classical psychoanalytic school of psychotherapy adopts a mainly biological model of behavior. The individual asserts himself against the restrictive forces of culture. In this model, there is no clearly defined position on the relations of man and society. The instinctual drives of sex and aggression, with their roots in the unconscious, are the area of prime concern. The past holds priority over the present. The person's relations with self and his own body are the center of the stage. Mind and body are one.

The relationship of patient and therapist is essentially nonsocial. Healing is a technique. The relationship is private; communication is privileged. The patient is treated in isolation. The ego ideal and social reality are minimized. Interest in social organization is peripheral. The healing process tends paradoxically to separate patient from family and community. The theory of therapy is divorced from societal, spiritual and philosophic questions. Within this framework the denial of the relevancy of ethical values is rendered plausible.

The adaptational or psychosocial school of psychotherapy emphasizes a view of man's behavior as molded within a nexus of relationships. Prime interest centers on processes of socialization, the link of sex and tenderness, and object relations. Inevitably, there is a broader interest in ego adaptation and character structure. Issues of ethical choice enter the psychotherapeutic process in a selective and limited way in relation to the functional value of one or another set of personality operations. The culture-personality school of psychotherapy exhibits a more explicit interest in value questions.

In the societal model it is the social organization that shapes values and adaptation to environment. An example is the Marxian view of personality. Psychotherapy is active, authoritarian; the process leans heavily on reeducation. It structures the social values of the patient.

The spiritual-philosophic model is exemplified in those forms of psychotherapy which place a first emphasis on moral questions and on the search for the meaning of life. They are represented in several versions: pastoral psychotherapy, the aim of which is "the cure of the soul"; Frankl's existential psychotherapy which undertakes frankly and explicitly to explore in the treatment process the philosophic problems of meaning and morality; also, Mowrer's integrity therapy which focuses specifically on problems of morality and responsible living. In essence, the cause of neurosis is viewed as a deficiency of conscience. The goal of therapy is, therefore, an honest confrontation of this moral weakness and the building of a more mature and responsible conscience. "The right feelings come from the right actions." Erich Fromm's modified type of psychoanalysis relates character to humanistic values and moral growth: "The psychoanalyst is the physician of the soul."

The familial-transactional model interrelates the way of life of the family, its identity, standards and values, to the emotional destiny of its members. The first four of these theoretical models involve a one-to-one psychotherapeutic relationship. Family psychotherapy joins the emotional destiny of the individual member to the psycho-social health and growth of the family as a whole. It deals with the interplay of inner and outer conflict, within and between family members and between family and community. Within this framework, it is essential to confront explicitly and work through issues relating to personal, familial and societal values.

THUS, ACROSS THE SPECTRUM of this range of psychotherapeutic methods, the orientation to problems of ethical choice varies. The more specialized the given form of therapy, the more focused on symptom-relief, the greater the concern with individual assertion, the easier it is to sidestep a systematic confrontation of ethics and values. As soon as the area of therapeutic responsibility expands to the relations of individual and group, and evinces greater concern for the "here and now," the more necessary does it become to face the value question.

Of special importance is the impact of the new world on the role of ethical standards in psychotherapeutic process. Two considerations are relevant here: the effects of revolutionary change on the development of new principles and practices in psychotherapy; the effects of social change on the orientation to the role of values in psychotherapeutic process.

The pace of change in the new world is revolutionary. Halbert Dunn puts it well: "It is a smaller world due to advances in communication; a more crowded world due to overpopulation; an older world due to the longer lifespan; and finally, a world of mounting social and political tensions."

The radical transformation of the human relations pattern in the new world exerts a profound influence on the development of social character. Many forces contribute to this change: the centralization of power and bureaucratic control; the loss of community; the decline of the importance of family and the discontinuity of the generations; atomization of relationships, inducing alienation and dehumanization; the lessened power of family tradition and the dramatic increase in the socializing power of the peer culture; and the decline of religious and moral values.

From these forces emerges what is sometimes called "the mass man." The changes in character structure are multiple: an increased orientation to power, to manipulation of relationships, to the treatment of people as things; a lessened capacity to feel for people; more "acting out" and a greater tolerance of violence; in general, a trend toward depersonalization and a weakening of moral fibre. The quality of the shift is toward "sociopathic" adaptation. Fifty years ago, the problem was too much conscience; today it is not enough conscience.

In this new world which changes people, families and whole communities, can the traditional forms of psychotherapy, such as psychoanalysis, continue to be effective? Will they survive? In Soviet Russia psychoanalytic therapy never gained a foothold. In Nazi Germany it was discovered that psychoanalytic therapy no longer worked. The United States, today, seems to move toward an industrial-military hegemony, with increasing features of a quasi-police state. Does this social-political change threaten the extinction of psychoanalytic and related forms of one-to-one psychotherapy?

The recent developments in psychotherapy do not isolate the patient-therapist relationship from family and community; they join them. The emergence of family psychotherapy more sharply delineates the role of ethical values in the psychotherapeutic process. Its explicit emphasis on sharing the value struggle, in contrast to the classic psychoanalytical tradition of excluding values from the healing process, points up the current ethical predicament in psychotherapy.

For the better part of a half century, the psychotherapeutic profession assumed a strange, ambiguous posture toward the problem of values and ethical choice. Only now is the profession beginning to face up to this challenge.

APPENDIX: ETHICAL ISSUES IN PSYCHOTHERAPY

Value Orientation	Biological Model: Freudian Psychoanalysis	Psychosocial Model: Interpersonal Psychotherapy	Societal Model: "Active" Psychotherapy	Spiritual-Philosophic Model: Ethical or Moral Psychotherapy	Family Transactional Model: Family Psychotherapy
1. Exclusion or confrontation of values and ethical choice	Exclusion	Confrontation, partial and selective	Training in values	Values and ethical choice the central concern	A shared struggle with values oriented to relations of individual, family and society
2. Love vs. hate	Hate, a basic instinct; love neutralizes hate	Love dominant; relates to respect and intimacy	Love dominant; relates to interdependence and cooperation	Love dominant; relates to faith in God and man	Love dominant, relates to mutual need and esteem
3. Creativeness v. destructiveness	Creativity is sublimation of destructive drives	Creativity, a primary drive and value	Creativity equated to the collective good	Creativity, divine inspiration	Creativity, the product of family closeness and interaction
4. Cooperation vs. competition	Competition, a primary drive for potency and mastery	Cooperation dominant; competition leads to higher cooperation	Cooperation essential to collective welfare; competition prohibited	Cooperation and compassion, a moral value, the meaning of God	Cooperation, mutual support and loyalty essential to continuity and growth
5. Freedom vs. conformity	Personal freedom first	Personal freedom and social responsibility complementary	Social conformity necessary for collective good	Freedom enriches the spirit; it is responsibility to and conformity with moral law	Freedom derives from responsibility and growth within family

Value Orientation	Biological Model: Freudian Psychoanalysis	Psychosocial Model: Interpersonal Psychotherapy	Societal Model: "Active" Psychotherapy	Spiritual-Philosophic Model: Ethical or Moral Psychotherapy	Family Transactional Model: Family Psychotherapy
6. Respect for the human vs. the human as object or thing	Respect rests on attainment of potency and "object love"	Respect for human rests on interdependency and mutual esteem	Respect derives from contribution to collective good	Respect rests on spiritual worth and on the "golden rule"	Respect relates to interpersonal esteem of family members
7. Inner reality vs. outer reality	Inner reality dominant	Inner reality matched against interpersonal reality	Inner reality shaped by social training	Inner reality is oneness with God and moral law	Inner reality molded by emotional life of family
8. Spiritual enrichment vs. material acquisition	"Success" and acquisition come with insight and mastery	"Success" and acquisition come with interpersonal competence	"Success" is effective integration into society	Spiritual enrichment the prime goal	Spiritual enrichment a product of good family life; "success" comes with devotion
9. Secrecy and shame vs. openness and sharing	Privacy and secrecy protected	Openness and sharing dominant	Sharing, a prime goal; privacy limited	Inner serenity comes with sharing and confession	Openness and sharing dominant
10. Guilt: true vs. false; too much vs. too little	Guilt excessive; goal to relieve guilt; lessen parental authority	False guilt and too little guilt are a main problem	Guilt relates to social conscience	Guilt is wrong-doing in the eyes of God	Guilt is self-seeking and injury to other family members
11. Aggression: free vs. curbed	Goal of freeing aggression is primary	Aggression modulated to fit interpersonal needs	Aggression curbed for social good	Aggression is evil	Aggression controlled for family unity and love

Value Orientation	Biological Model: Freudian Psychoanalysis	Psychosocial Model: Interpersonal Psychotherapy	Societal Model: "Active" Psychotherapy	Spiritual-Philosophic Model: Ethical or Moral Psychotherapy	Family Transactional Model: Family Psychotherapy
12. Sex vs. tenderness	Sex primary, tenderness secondary	Tenderness primary, sex secondary	Tenderness and loyalty extend to society; sex fitted to social aims	Tenderness and compassion dominant	Tenderness, respect, consideration primary; sex shaped to family need
13. Fantasy vs. reality	Fantasy dominant	Fantasy and reality inseparable; one matched against the other	Reality dominant	Inner spiritual reality dominant	Fantasy and reality matched against one another
14. Isolation vs. union and relatedness	Isolation of individual psyche	Union and relatedness dominant	Union and relatedness dominant	Union and relatedness dominant	Union and individuation parallel forces
15. Social responsibility vs. self-indulgence	Free expression of the individual comes first	Self-expression and social responsibility balanced	Social responsibility dominant	Moral responsibility to man and God	Family and social responsibility balanced with self-expression

Drama: A Mirror of Conflict;
A Prophecy for the Future

ESTHER M. JACKSON

THE history of Western civilization would seem to indicate that major human crises are reflected first and, perhaps, most accurately in the arts. The arts not only record major crises in history; they identify cause and effect. Sigmund Freud[1] described the arts as seismographic indices of culture; that is, as both tracings of the consciousness of individual artists and profiles of those modes of common understanding which the later theorist, Carl Gustav Jung, was to describe as "collective."[2] Freudian psychology identified the arts as mirrors of individual and collective crises; that is, as records of collisions between instinctual and cultural impulses in human history. Jungian psychology was to emphasize the arts as creative func-

---

[1] Freudian theories about the nature and function of the arts are diffused through a number of works, including *Interpretation of Dreams*, Vol. V (1953), in *Complete Works*, ed. James Strachey (23 vols., London, 1953–66); *Psychopathic Characters on the Stage*, Vol. VII (1953), pp. 305–310; and *The Future of an Illusion* and *Civilization and Its Discontents*, Vol. XXI (1961).
[2] See Carl G. Jung, *Psychological Types*, trans. H. Godwin Baynes, New York, 1923, pp. 207–336. Jung's theory of consciousness is an elaboration of Freudian structure. His esthetic theories are, perhaps, more highly developed than those of Freud.

255

tions of consciousness; not only as indices of received knowledges, but as collective responses, directed to the problem of ameliorating grave societal conflicts. Jungian esthetics was to interpret the primary function of the arts as the reconciliation of instinct and culture, at individual and societal levels. In Jungian theory, mature art does more than imitate reality; it reconstitutes experience through the use of reconciling symbols which serve to unify consciousness, at individual, societal, and—ultimately—universal levels of meaning. Both Jung and Freud followed Hegel in suggesting that human history is, among other things, the image of cultural process. If Freud, as rationalist, sought to impose reason over the disorder of the historical process, Jung assigned to the arts the creative role in human experience. It is, in Jungian theory, the esthetic principle which serves to shape history, mediating between the vitality of instinctual drives and the stability of cultural forms.

Both Jung and Freud agreed that history is a reflection of the ways in which societies have responded to destructive instinctual impulses. From this point of view, Western history is the record of a series of critical challenges to cultural forms by instinctual energies. The transcendence of historical crises thus would seem to be dependent on the capacities of cultures to produce new, enriching, and satisfying symbolisms, linking the vital and the traditional in meaningful ways. Jung cites Goethe's *Faust* as an example of the critical relationship between history and the arts.[3] In *Faust,* Goethe reflected the stresses of a world in which industrialization had begun its conquest of human activity. Faust, as symbol, subsumed within his person the crisis of the transition from medievalism to secularism. As such, he recapitulated the history of Renaissance man. But he also foretold the future of

---

3 Jung, p. 158.

the nineteenth-century man of science and, in significant detail, that of the twentieth-century man of technology. In *Faust,* Goethe posed the questions which would dominate the history of the nineteenth and twentieth centuries. What are the implications of a secular universe? What is the meaning of a world in which man is master? In which everything is—or seems—possible? Although *Faust* did not answer these questions, it may be claimed that Goethe's symbol nonetheless fulfilled an important function. For not only did this drama mirror a continuing challenge to mankind, it set the problem of secularism in the context of the entire human situation. In *Faust,* Goethe suggested—if barely—possibilities for the reconciliation of the religious past and the secular future. The continuing influence of the Faustian symbolism on the perception of reality in our time would seem to support Jung's claim that the arts are indeed the critical indices of history.

If the popular arts are direct transcriptions of human responses to crisis into tentative forms, the serious arts are concerned with the interpretation, evaluation, and reconstitution of reality in ways which link present, past and future. Society is, in a significant way, dependent on the arts to reveal what is happening beneath the surface of reality. Perhaps the most comprehensive of the forms providing such trans-historical insights into reality is the drama. The great philosopher of the Enlightenment, Immanuel Kant, suggested that consciousness itself is controlled by a dramatistic principle; that is, that reality appears as the evidence of creative process.[4] Drama, alone among the forms of knowledge, seeks to reconstruct the totality of consciousness; that is, to project images of experience, in all their

---

[4] Kant's primary discussions of esthetic theories appear in *The Critique of Judgment.* However, the philosopher uses the arts as metaphors for perceptions of reality in other contexts. In *The Critique of Pure Reason,* he describes consciousness as "transcendental." See *Kant,* ed. Theodore Meyer Greene, New York, 1929, pp. 43–66.

uncertainty and complexity, against a symbolic universe as complete as human understanding can make it. The history of the theatre, like that of societies, would seem to support the claim that drama is the record of human crises of enduring meaning. If Greek tragedy recorded ancient man's attempts to overcome the tyranny of religious superstitions, Shakespearean drama marked the advance of European man from feudalism to the concept of nationhood. If Aeschylus's *Oresteia* traced the development of legal codes seeking to submit destructive instinctual impulses to socialization, Shakespearean histories celebrated the movement of the idea of government out of the narrow context of familial obligation. Since the eighteenth century, Western drama and history alike have been concerned with interpretations of crises deriving from the continuing collision of the archaic instinctual with new social impulses.

I I

CRISIS IS THE ACCELERATION of historical process, the confrontation of the instinctual and the cultural for very high societal stakes. *Orestes, Antigone, Oedipus the King, Hamlet, Tartuffe, Oresteia Phèdre, Faust, Peer Gynt, Miss Julie* and *Death of a Salesman* are indices of human consciousness of such crises. Each is not only an image of events in human history, but also the substance of a collective response to a critical conflict of values. The greatness of the drama and the vigor of the social order appear, in this way, related. The collapse of societies has been foretold by forms of drama whose symbolisms were insufficient, irrelevant, incongruent, disunified, and lacking in communal satisfaction. The Roman theatre, moving between the decadence of the Circus Maximus and the sterile forms of Seneca, is one of the most revealing illustrations of the negative relationship between drama and history. But other instructive examples may be found in the history of Western theatre. The violence of Jacobean drama, the rigidity of French seventeenth-century classicism, the emotional excesses of Wagnerian theatre, the inertia of Chekhovian form, and the nihilism of German expressionist drama of the late nineteenth and early twentieth centuries were all portentous. Each was a seismographic indication of volcanic disturbances beneath the flow of history. Significant to this discussion is the fact that none of these dramatic forms offered a symbolism—neither a symbolic protagonist nor a symbolic resolution—capable of reconciling the historic crises which they foretold.

The twentieth century has seen an acceleration of human energies unparalleled in tempo. Intellectual historians such as Jacques Barzun,[5] Alfred Kazin,[6] and Lewis Mumford[7] have written of the impact of such an acceleration of human process on cultural forms. Three related developments have converged in this quickening tempo. The first of these may be described as *physical*. The development of highly sophisticated instruments of exploration, transportation, and communication has served to accelerate life processes; in effect, to alter space-time relationships and, thereby, the consciousness of reality. A related factor is *material* in nature. The speeding up of the processes of production and distribution has created new political, economic, social, cultural, psychological, and physical tensions throughout the contemporary world. But by far the most significant of the processes altering reality in the twentieth century is that which may be called *human*. The acceleration of the process of democratization—with the United States as its focal point—is, perhaps, the most

---

[5] See, for example, Jacques Barzun, *Classic, Romantic, and Modern,* second revised edition, Boston, 1961, pp. 115–31.
[6] Alfred Kazin, *On Native Grounds,* New York, 1942, pp. 3–50.
[7] Lewis Mumford, *Technics and Civilization,* New York, 1934, pp. 321–63.

significant development of the century. Efforts to create an open order capable of administering justice to all members of the human community without regard to race, color, sex, station, or previous condition of servitude may be regarded as a comprehensive attempt to accelerate the moral evolution of mankind.[8]

The American poet, Walt Whitman, traced the idea of democracy from its early development in ancient Greece.[9] The poet observed that democracy gained substantial support in the medieval period from the Judaeo-Christian tradition, especially from the absorption of the moral imperatives of universal dignity and equality in the sight of a just, responsible, and intelligent God. In the late eighteenth century, near the time of Goethe's creation of *Faust,* this system seeking to render freedom, justice, and dignity equally available to all men was tentatively established in the United States. In the early twentieth century, a second system, also claiming as its goal the democratization of justice, found a base in Eastern Europe. Both constitutional democracy and socialism have, in our time, claimed a common objective: the acceleration of benevolent socio-political process. Both have sought, if in different ways, to realign cultural forms in order to achieve societal goals. The American system, however, has differed from socialism in its reliance on the individual, rather than on institutions, as the primary instrument of history.[10] Constitutional democracy has aspired to reconcile freedom and form in a variety of patterns, linking individual aspirations to the achievement of collective goals in an environment characterized by personal liberty.

It seems correct to describe democracy not only as a new

---

[8] See Henri Bergson, *The Two Sources of Morality and Religion,* trans. R. Ashley Audra, Cloudesley Brereton, and W. H. Carter, New York, 1954.

[9] Walt Whitman, *Democratic Vistas,* in *Prose Works,* Vol. II, ed. Floyd Stovall, New York, 1964.

[10] See John Gassner, *The Theatre in Our Times,* New York, 1954, pp. 342–54.

stage in historical process, but as a new level of human consciousness.[11] Walt Whitman observed that the democratic idea subsumed the totality of Western history. It sought to join the usable past to a creative future; that is, to administer justice with equality, in a context of personal freedom. Whitman, writing in the 1870's of "Democratic Vistas," declared that this splendid but difficult ideal of a democratic humanity would be realized only when an enriching symbolism—linking all men in a common consciousness of the meaning of the democratic enterprise—had emerged. Whitman, as poet, saw history as created form. He regarded America as the concretion of a New World spirit; that is, as the symbol of a new concept of humanity. The New World emerged, in his poetic imagination, as the dramatic environment of an exceptional protagonist, a man whom Whitman named "common." But if Whitman's common man was to be ordinary, in terms of his inherited stature, he would be, in all other senses, most uncommon. For he would embody the finest attributes of the remembered past. At the same time, he would represent an open order, unrestricted by birth, wealth, position, class, sex, or race. The new protagonist—as he was to emerge—would be a symbol of the democratic transcendence of historical process; that is, a mode of reconciliation far more complex than any seen in earlier history. This new protagonist—democratic man—would, in his person, reconcile quantity and quality, freedom and form, reason and passion, tradition and originality, past and present, materiality and spirituality, idea and experience—*form* and *content*. The New World, Whitman wrote, would, like Nature herself, demonstrate unity in contrariety. It would provide those conditions which would allow for the rise of a new and unifying world spirit –democracy.

---

11 See Robert Brustein on consciousness in the drama of Eugene O'Neill, in *The Theatre of Revolt*, Boston, 1964, pp. 321–59.

Like Jung, Whitman thought the emergence of the idea of the democratic in history to be dependent on an appropriate symbolism. Ralph Waldo Emerson had posited such forms, immanent in the universe.[12] Whitman believed, however, that the concretization of democratic forms in America represented a major moral challenge. He called for the formulation of a metaphysics congruent with the democratic idea; that is, a language appropriate to the development of an ethic differentiating the prerogatives, privileges, and responsibilities of democratic liberty from the moralities embodied within older cultural forms. Moreover, Whitman envisioned a new historic protagonist appropriate to the comprehensive imperatives of democratic character. Whitman thus anticipated Jung in the suggestion that ideas require translation into symbolic forms if they are to serve a constructive purpose in ameliorating crises within society. Although, as poet, he contributed to epic and lyric interpretations of the idea of the democratic, he did not achieve the synthesis of that comprehensive dramatic form necessary for the interpretation of moral crises of decisive meaning.

III

THE ADVENT OF EUGENE O'NEILL, in the early years of the twentieth century, marked the first stage in the evolution of a dramatic form appropriate to the exploration of moral issues in a democratic environment. O'Neill's plays sought to define the condition of *technological man;* that is, to set Goethe's secular protagonist in the social, psychological, and moral environment of the twentieth century. His works offered an overview of problems which would command the attention of later playwrights in America and in Europe. *The Hairy Ape* foretold the urban crisis of the sixties and seventies—the

---

12 Ralph Waldo Emerson, "The Over-Soul," in *Essays,* first series, Boston, 1885, pp. 251–78.

progressive alienation of the working man from the sense of community which he had in his Old World home. *Dynamo* explored the theological implications of technological advances. *The Emperor Jones* and *All God's Chillun Got Wings* were early studies of racial conflict. *Strange Interlude* and *The Iceman Cometh* foretold that disintegration of cultural traditions which would accelerate in modern industrial societies. But if O'Neill identified the crises of democratic man in the twentieth century, he did not succeed in creating that reconciling symbolism of which Jung wrote. Rather, his lyric form exposed modern man in his anguish. For O'Neill, modern society was only the background for new explorations of the romantic agony.

The dramatists of the thirties and forties sought to correct the angle of distortion in O'Neill's lyric view of historical process. The plays of Maxwell Anderson, Elmer Rice, Paul Green, Clifford Odets, William Saroyan, Robert Sherwood, Lillian Hellman, and Thornton Wilder were to be concerned with new relationships between the individual and society. Plays such as *Awake and Sing!* studied the social conditions of the urban North. Paul Green's *Hymn to the Rising Sun* examined the problems of the rural South. William Saroyan was, perhaps, the first dramatist of "underground" America. *The Time of Your Life* predated the avant-garde theatre of the sixties by almost thirty years. Dramatists such as Elmer Rice and Clifford Odets were to be concerned not only about the socio-political structures of American life, but also about the ideas implicit in social forms. Maxwell Anderson, Robert Sherwood, and Lillian Hellman predated Arthur Miller in their common interest in the meaning of democratic history. *Key Largo, The Petrified Forest, Abe Lincoln in Illinois,* and *The Little Foxes* are representative of such attempts to measure the American experience against democratic goals.

The problem of developing a symbolism appropriate to

the interpretation of contemporary reality was to prove a major challenge to American dramatists of the thirties and forties. One of the most significant of these attempts to create a democratic symbolism may be seen in the plays of Thornton Wilder. Wilder remains, perhaps, one of the most history-minded of the major American dramatists. In the introduction to his *Collected Plays,* the dramatist has described his primary interest as the interpretation of the "idea of the middle class" in American history.[13] If *Our Town* was indeed written about middle-class Americans, it was interpreted from the perspective of a patrician. For Wilder was able to bring to bear upon his interpretation of historical process that sense of equilibrium which derives from the esthetic distance which is a function of patrician consciousness and a profound knowledge of the historic past. *The Skin of Our Teeth,* a war play, seemed to reflect less certainty about the destiny of the middle classes in the New World than did the earlier work. This play—an exceedingly important work, from the point of view of this discussion—dramatized that conflict between cultural and instinctual impulses which exploded in World War II. In *The Skin of Our Teeth,* Wilder, as humanist, suggested that the answer to the potential destructiveness of the instinctual lies in culture, the legacy of civilization. As humanist, he attempted to shape culture-bearing symbols capable of penetrating and reconciling crises.

Insofar as this discussion is concerned, there are two problems with *The Skin of Our Teeth* as democratic symbolism. One relates to its intellectual exclusivity; that is, to the prerequisite, for the spectator, of a comprehensive knowledge of history—both that of events and that of ideas.[14] A second

---

13 Thornton Wilder, Preface to *Three Plays,* New York, 1957, pp. vii–xiv.
14 Some critics, notably Joseph Campbell and Henry Morton Robinson, have been disturbed about Wilder's use of ideas, concepts, and languages drawn

and related problem involves Wilder's limitation of reality—both of events and of consciousness—to the experience of "Middle America," his virtual exclusion of racial, social, and cultural minorities from his democratic environment. In the sixties, it would seem questionable whether the symbolism for crisis projected by Wilder is fully congruent with present realities. For the historical issues he interprets involve groups which are excluded from his linguistic frame—as, indeed, from the primary structure of American culture.

Attempts to extend this democratic symbolism may be seen in the works of Arthur Miller and Tennessee Williams. If *Death of a Salesman* extends the ethical frame of *Our Town*, *Camino Real* is a variation on the imagistic interpretation of culture offered in *The Skin of Our Teeth*. Both Miller and Williams have been concerned with the synthesis of popular contents and traditional forms. In his essay *Tragedy and the Common Man*, Miller has written that he has aspired to shape a drama which will stand in the same relationship to the American experience as did Greek tragedy to life in its age; that is, to create "a high drama of the democratic."[15] In this important essay, the playwright has suggested that tragic knowledge must be democratized, that every man has not only the right to freedom, but also the obligation to tragic commitment. In the late forties and fifties, both Arthur Miller and Tennessee Williams were concerned with the use of the drama as an instrument for the acceleration of the evolution of a democratic morality. Miller defined such a moral progression in terms of the evolution of new cultural forms, while Williams interpreted such a development in terms of the estheticizing of instinctual drives. If Williams, like

from literary history. See Malcolm Goldstein, *The Art of Thornton Wilder*, Lincoln, Nebraska, 1965, pp. 128–29.
15 See Miller, "Tragedy and the Common Man," in the critical edition of *Death of a Salesman*, ed. Gerald Weales, New York, 1967, pp. 143–47.

Goethe, aspired to refine the instinctual, Miller, like Schiller, sought to reform the cultural. Miller's *Death of a Salesman* and *The Crucible* may represent, to date, the highest level of progress toward the creation of a comprehensive democratic symbolism. It is significant that the creation of these works coincided with an epoch of prosperity, influence, and relative tranquility for American society.

IV

WITH THE BEGINNING OF THE SIXTIES, a new period of crisis in art, as in society, became evident. New processes, both external and internal to the society, had been set in motion by the history of the post-war era. Ancient causes, such as racial animosity, were to interact with new developments. Perhaps the most dramatic of the new processes to become evident in the fifties were related to the acceleration of technological advances, particularly to those developments affecting communication and travel. The establishment of new relationships between man and space was to have an unsettling influence on the common consciousness. Because America was the focal point of a complex pattern of economic, political, and technological developments, it became, in an important sense, the center of the world of the sixties. Critics of culture such as Marshall McLuhan have commented on the effect of massive technological advances upon social forms.[16] McLuhan has suggested that the psychic forces generated by life in the "Space Age" in effect have overwhelmed the symbolisms of democratic societies; that the burgeoning energies of the collective consciousness have exploded traditional cultural frames. This explosion has resulted in an altered consciousness in America, as in the world; in a dis-

---

[16] See, for example, Herbert Marshall McLuhan, *Understanding Media*, New York, 1964, pp. 7-21.

integration of primary perceptions of reality affecting institutions, ideas, customs, behaviors, beliefs, aspirations, anxieties, and the very nature of human character.[17]

The societal problems which emerged in the sixties reflected a profound conflict of values based on interpretations of reality which differed markedly from those of the past. The racial crisis, environmental pollution, drug addiction, the question of law enforcement, generational conflict, the changing patterns of family relationships, the increasing evidence of sophisticated and legalized crime, and, most of all, the war in Vietnam, raised questions, especially among the young, about the relevance of cultural forms to experience. The sixties may be described not only in terms of a crisis of consciousness, but also in terms of a comprehensive conflict of democratic form and content. For there existed, in contemporary America, no symbolism appropriate to the interpretation of the major events of this critical decade. No mature symbolic structure served to reconcile ideas and events within the common consciousness. Some reconciling functions were served by the plastic arts, spectator sports, films, new styles of politics, popular music, and the dramatization of space travel. But such forms proved, finally, too limited to contain the volatile energies of the age. The results were that experience—like consciousness—exploded in the awesome and costly theatre of "real life."

The playwrights of the sixties attempted to record aspects of the explosion taking place below the surface of consciousness. Indeed, among the first indications of the crises within the common consciousness were the plays of Edward Albee. Today it would appear that Albee correctly foretold the developments of the sixties. *The Zoo Story* (1959) offered a startling but accurate projection of the psychology

---

[17] See Erich Kahler, *The Disintegration of Form in the Arts,* Braziller, 1968, pp. 73–109.

of urban violence. *The Death of Bessie Smith* (1961) anatomized racial hatred, including the crisis of the middle-class consciousness within the black community. *The Sandbox* (1960) and *The American Dream* (1961) projected the disintegration of the American family. It was, however, in his longer works that the accuracy of Albee's vision of the condition of modern man at mid-century would be proven. *Who's Afraid of Virginia Woolf?* (1962), *Tiny Alice* (1964), and *A Delicate Balance* (1966) examined the lives of men and women released from the problems which had concerned social dramatists of the past—poverty, illness, social rejection, and frustration of ambition.

Albee defined the condition of a humanity conscious that it had been cut adrift from cultural traditions. It may be claimed that his diagnosis of the condition of man was theological, for he was concerned with a society in which "God was dead." But if God was indeed dead, in the Albeean universe, so was scientific humanism. The world Albee projected was characterized by that which Freud termed "demoniacal possession." It was a symbolic universe in which Satan had become in effect the "father substitute."[18] In the pattern of his writing, Albee traced the influence of the destructive instinctual on both individual and institutional life. *The Zoo Story* was a study in dehumanization. *The Death of Bessie Smith* charted the decline of moral consciousness. *Who's Afraid of Virginia Woolf?* studied both the perversion of academic life and the degradation of the erotic. Perhaps the climax of the Albeean vision of transgression appeared in *Tiny Alice*, where the playwright projected the collusion of the Church temporal with representatives of international finance in the ultimate degradation of man—the selling of souls. Despite its bitterness, Albee's vision was

---

[18] Freud, *The Devil as a Father Substitute*, in "A Seventeenth-Century Demonological Neurosis," *Collected Works*, Vol. XIX (1961), pp. 83–92.

profoundly theological, for the playwright affirmed the presence of a principle—albeit a negative one—not only in history, but in the universe itself. Although Albee has suggested the need for a healing symbolism, he has not yet formulated a mode of reconciliation. He was to trace a tentative solution to human crisis in *A Delicate Balance*—a parable about the nature of fear in the modern world. But his work in creating a symbolism capable of healing the conditions he has described seems barely to have begun.

It can be claimed that some element of responsibility for the failure of American dramatists to develop forms capable of reconciling the conflict within the common consciousness can be attributed to those institutions traditionally charged with the preservation of culture—to organized theology, philosophy, education, and the arts. The disclaimers offered by these cultural institutions in the sixties were various. Theology remained so limited in its chosen sphere of influence that it was challenged by political activists, as well as by artists such as Albee, on grounds of meaning, relevance, and intent. American philosophers had, for some time, sought to withdraw from questions of value and meaning, in order to speculate about problems of language—about propositions often so abstract in nature and limited in scope as to seem sophistical. Education, at all levels, persisted in a class orientation, encouraging critically different patterns of understanding within the society. The culture-bearing forms of art—painting, sculpture, architecture, dance, literature, and drama—were virtually inaccessible to the majority of Americans.

It can be claimed that as a result of these failures to assume responsibility for the evolution of new and appropriate symbolisms, democratic culture in the mid-twentieth century has been usurped by the scientific imagination, a tradition whose culture-bearing limitations have been acknowledged by virtu-

ally all major thinkers of the twentieth century, including
Albert Einstein.[19] Such failures of cultural institutions to encourage the development of life-affirming symbolisms appropriate to the needs of a complex democratic society have resulted in the acceleration of divisive energies. In the sixties
there emerged two increasingly antagonistic segments of
American society—a tradition-oriented élite and a technology-
oriented majority. The seventies are witnessing the prolifera-
tion of yet other dissident sub-cultures, designated by race,
sex, age, and class.

V

IF THE AMERICAN DRAMA of the sixties did not evolve an
appropriate symbolism, it did succeed in recording some of
the shocks experienced by the culture as it was bombarded by
energies released in the collective consciousness. In terms of
symbol-making, two directions emerged. The radical theatre
of the sixties reflected an approach to imitation which had its
roots in European expressionism, particularly, in surrealism
and Dadaism. The idea supporting the symbol making of
groups such as the Living Theatre was post-romantic in kind.
It suggested that the corrupting influence in human experience is ever society itself, that only natural man lives in a
state of innocence, and that critical conflicts cannot be
ameliorated until men and women have rediscovered a common natural identity. Plays such as *Frankenstein* sought to reform reality by stripping away societal masks and rediscovering the essential structures of the collective psyche.

A second development involved the emergence of a drama
of philosophical significance. Writers such as the poet-
playwright LeRoi Jones sought to reform reality by linguistic

---

19 See Albert Einstein, *Essays in Science*, New York, 1934, pp. 112–114.

means. Like the Living Theatre, the Black Theatre of the sixties attempted to establish a reality of extrasocietal or suprasocietal definition. In the Black Theatre of Jones and others, the way in to the human condition was to be primarily linguistic; the reconstitution of reality was to be equated with the reconstruction of language. If the Living Theatre sought to recover a lost world of naive meaning, black writers undertook to redeem history through symbol. Plays such as *Slave Ship* sought to expunge from the collective memory the degrading language of the recent past, in effect, to create a new history by linguistic reform. Like the early plays of O'Neill, however, the new drama was directed to relatively small segments of the national population. Moreover, it was essentially subjective in focus. Rather than seeking to align ideas and emotions in the collective consciousness, the radical theatre was primarily concerned with lyric purpose, with expanding the role of the instinctual in society. As a result of its subjective emphasis, the new drama tended to exacerbate crisis, heightening consciousness without accelerating true enlightenment.

VI

THE EMERGENCE of mature dramatic forms in the theatre of the seventies, like the emergence of a just and peaceful society, would seem dependent upon the evolution of a collective symbolism capable of (1) rendering the conditions of crisis transparent; (2) illuminating collective meanings; (3) analyzing critical societal problems; and (4) suggesting social, moral, psychological, and esthetic alternatives for thought and action. The need for such a drama would appear to suggest the recovery of an ancient theological function. The claims of young dissidents that institutionalized religion supports racism, narcotic addiction, economic exploitation, brutality, and other societal ills appear, in some senses, justified. Such support is, however, indirect; it arises principally from the failure of religion to heighten that individual and collective consciousness which Arthur Miller has called "moral relatedness."[20] If the examples of history have meaning, the evolution of such consciousness cannot be spontaneous. Miller has suggested that the theatre can and ought to be an instrument of its development. The playwright has observed that the creation of a drama for a democratic humanity requires not only the lyric outpouring of anger about society's injustices, but also objective interpretations of the common destiny of all members of the body politic. Such interpretations of the condition of democratic man clearly require the reconsideration of problems of theological meaning.

Perhaps it is appropriate to suggest that a new phase of the ecumenical movement involving all faiths—including those which may be described as "secular religions"—be initiated in order to examine the contributions which theology can make to the arts, which the arts can make to contemporary theology, and which both can make to the healing of modern societies. Perhaps one solution to the problem of an appropriate symbolism in the American theatre might involve religious sponsorship of a new, distinctive, and challenging program for playwrights, whose goals would differ from existing programs in significant ways:

It would be committed to the penetration of the common consciousness; that is, to the interpretation of common problems, the revelation of a common destiny, and the exploration of solutions involving all races, religions, classes, ages, and groups within the structure of a modern democratic society.

It would be devoted to the definition, analysis, and

---

[20] Arthur Miller, Introduction to *Collected Plays*, New York, 1957, pp. 18–20.

interpretation of those critical issues which divide humanity in the modern world, to the end that solutions may be reached which are beneficial to all members of the human community.

It would seek to affirm the dignity, equality, and responsibility of all men within the democratic structure.

It would urge upon young artists a disciplined consideration of ideas, techniques, and human interests which can support formulations of appropriate, satisfying, and meaningful symbolisms.

It would undertake to extend the benefits of the arts to economic, ethnic, social, political, and intellectual majorities, as well as to minorities, to the end that democratic theatre may be brought into an appropriate relationship with reality.

It would seek to help young writers, technicians, artists, and spectators to rediscover the joy of creation, the pleasure of disciplined activity, and that personal and societal equilibrium which derives from self-respect and compassion for one's fellowman.

It would be devoted to acceleration of the development of a comprehensive symbolism which is truthful, functional, meaningful, life-enhancing, inspiring, enriching, and supportive of the ideals of democracy.

If the drama today mirrors the "broken world" of Hart Crane's poetic description, perhaps it is yet the potential instrument of reconciliation, not only between man and man, but also between man and his environment, and ultimately between man and himself.[21] It would seem evident that the contemporary world challenges both drama and theology to seek the evolution of symbolisms capable of reconciling profound and divisive conflicts. For it is the function of drama

---

[21] Hart Crane, "The Broken Tower," in *Collected Poems*, New York, 1933, pp. 135–36.

and theology alike not only to reveal to humanity the causes of its failures, but also to test those alternatives which can lead toward the achievement of universal solutions in a climate of justice, peace, and liberty. The evolution of mature dramatic symbolisms in America holds promise not only for the theatre, but also for the society and, perhaps, for the idea of democracy in human history.

Toward A New Cultural Federalism

EARL WARREN

THE world is in ferment and the word "revolution," which was one associated largely with warfare, has now become commonplace in connection with almost every phase of human activity—science, technology, medicine, education, gerontology, community organization and family life. The word "revolution" has become almost synonymous with the word "change," but still there are those who will acknowledge these revolutions only as the terminal product of change which, in their opinion, must soon end and, therefore, no longer be a matter of serious concern to us.

In this connection, I am reminded of the Annual Report of Henry L. Ellsworth, our first Patent Commissioner, to the Congress on January 31, 1844. In it, he speaks of the discovery of the electro-magnetic telegraph which he predicts "is destined to exercise a great and it is believed happy effect, in the transmission of intelligence from one section of the country to another," and also reports that "The experiment of illuminating the streets of Paris by means of the electric spark has, as communicated in the late scientific journals, been also most successful; and further developments of this application of electricity may be expected."

Ellsworth then sums up these startling revelations with the conclusion that "The advancement of the arts, from year to year, taxes our credulity, and seems to presage the arrival of that period when human improvement must end."

When I try to envision the future of our youth and the advances that will be made in the remainder of this century and the first half of the next, I can only believe that what has happened since Commissioner Ellsworth made his tranquilizing statement 125 years ago affords but a quick glimpse into the possibilities of what lies ahead. The complexities and magnitude of the results which will flow from exploring the unknown are beyond imagination. And the youth of today will be the ones to make those explorations and to live with the results. If their discoveries are to be for the benefit of mankind, youth must itself make the necessary adaptations to the far-reaching changes in our society. Those adjustments will, of necessity, be revolutionary in character. Indeed, youth, sensing the future changes and observing our failures to adjust to the changes which have come about in recent years, are already in revolution throughout the world.

Of all the revolutions which have marked the course of this century, perhaps the most fundamental and most enduring in its effects may turn out to be the emancipation of youth. From the earliest time almost until our own, it has been a truism that wisdom resides in advanced years. Only in the Book of Job do we hear a faint protest against this doctrine. Elihu, the youngest of Job's friends, sits silently by while his elders debate the meaning of evil. Finally, he feels compelled to speak. He remarks: "I said, 'Days should speak, and multitude of years should teach wisdom.' But it is a spirit in man, and the breath of the Almighty that giveth understanding. It is not the great that are wise, nor the aged that discern judgment."

In our time, youth refuses to be silent, and insists on taking its place in the councils of the nation and the world. This problem is not limited to particular universities or to particular countries. The demand of youth to be heard and to be reckoned with resounds all the way from California to Tokyo. It has become a world-shaking revolution.

We have, of course, long been aware of the tension between generations in the family. There was a time when families were run in an authoritarian manner; and when indeed even quite grown-up children who disagreed with their parents or displeased them were actually beaten into submission. I am told that in some European schools this custom has not yet disappeared. Samuel Johnson used to praise the teacher who beat him when he made a mistake in a Latin case-ending, saying something to the effect that "without him I would have achieved nothing." Visiting a family where he met a bevy of particularly well-behaved daughters, he simply assumed that they had been beaten into proper conduct, and remarked, "I thank thee, *Rod,* for this thy work."

Those days are fortunately far behind us. On the contrary, we are living in an age of great permissiveness in the family, where even young children make up their own minds about what is to be done, and consult their parents only when they feel it necessary. It is almost as if the familiar proverb were to be reversed, so as to read, "Parents should be seen and not heard." Perhaps the pendulum has swung too far; and we may discover that over-permissiveness is as dangerous to children's well being, as over-authoritarianism. It is said by some writers that children have to rebel, as a butterfly has to break out of its cocoon. It is said, too, that if anyone tries to break the cocoon as the butterfly emerges, he will hurt it; for the struggles and agonies through which the butterfly passes in the change from the caterpillar stage help develop the wings it needs to fly.

But the tensions within the family have now become tensions on the world scene. And the tensions are not only those between the generations, but within what would, until our time, have been called the same generation. The post-graduate student with a teaching fellowship has as much trouble as an aged professor in understanding undergraduates who are only four or five years younger; for a generation is now about five years.

This is a result, in part, of the rapidity of technological change, and the increasingly rapid development of knowledge in science and some fields of scholarship. A sixteen year old boy may be an expert in computers, and people many years older may have to be his disciples in that field. A precocious mathematician age twenty may afford enlightenment to the whole field. Einstein was no more than twenty-four years old when he revolutionized not only physics, but our whole approach to the universe. Einsteins are indeed rare, but minor figures with brilliant insights are common; and even more common are minor figures who think they have brilliant insights, and insist on being reckoned with.

Yet experience is still important. A person may make a brilliant scientific discovery in his late teens or early twenties, but the philosophical grasp needed to weave a texture of life out of a variety of insights still requires years of reflection. A young man may, like Swinburne, flash across the skies like a meteor; but to become an Aristotle or a Plato or a Maimonides with the power of offering guidance to the contemporary world and later generations requires decades of study, observation, and creative thought. This is as true in our time as it has been in the past.

In a rapidly changing world, however, a modern Aristotle would need to be reinterpreted as soon as he had completed his work. His examples drawn from scientific observations would, in the rapid progress of modern science, be obsolete by the time he had published his works. His concepts might still be valid; but their validity would be obscured because he would be speaking a language already obsolete and addressing himself to problems no longer relevant.

The revolt of youth has had a profound effect on all the tensions which beset mankind. The race problem in the United States in the early nineteen fifties related primarily to the legal systems prevailing in southern states. Now the race problem has moved far from Selma and Birmingham, and is centered in all our large cities. Vast numbers of youth are claiming their share of the national wealth and of national opportunities. And with youthful enthusiasm and vigor, they tend to present their case and insist on their rights in a manner quite alien to that of their parents.

The problem of unemployment or threatened unemployment is of concern to an entire generation of youth; it is not limited only to those who have traditionally suffered disadvantage in our country. It is now possible, through automation, for six people to do the work which only a decade ago required six hundred workers. All previous theories of unemployment seem irrelevant in the computer age, when literally tens of thousands of our citizens will have to be retrained if they are to be productive and to feel that their lives are useful.

The revolt of youth is not contained within national boundaries. Fashions of conduct and behavior spread from country to country with the utmost ease. The development of television, the speed with which newspapers report events in the most distant countries, have made the world a single neighborhood. New expectations are on the rise everywhere, as the inhabitants of the poorer countries of the world become acquainted with the life-style and vast opportunities available in the lands of opulence. Young people in less developed countries covet these opportunities.

A more serious point of contention between the generations is the difference in their outlook. Youth is idealistic, contemptuous of difficulties, impatient, and unconcerned about the risks of change. Maturity tends to be over-cautious in considering the difficulties to be encountered by initiating new approaches to life. The older generation has had the habit of sweeping its problems under the rug—with catastrophic results.

How is one to find a way to let youth, with its idealism, its new knowledge, its at-homeness in a constantly changing world, try its wings and yet not destroy that which it is trying to improve, and can improve? It is clear that the problem of the generation gap is with us to stay. The pace of technological change will speed up in the future, so that present progress will look sluggish. Breakthroughs in the biological sciences will provide new understanding of the nature of the unit of life, the cell, and with it will come discoveries regarding the nature of life, of man's being, of his prospects as a species. The possibility looms of artificially increasing man's reasoning powers, so that brilliant young men and women will ever more vigorously challenge not only the older generation but all of our past tradition.

It seems clear that some new institution is needed through which rapidly increasing knowledge can be transmuted into the type of wisdom which the foremost philosophers once created in the course of a long life. It should be an institution in which the vision, the dream, the innovation, the daring of youth is brought into contact with the mellow practicality, the concern for possible danger, the weighing of unnecessary risk characteristic of maturity.

At the moment, we are permitting the contact between generations to be one of combat and hostility rather than creative confrontation. The student revolt on the college campuses is hardly a way to achieve wisdom, although it may prove effective in shaking the establishment out of complacency and smugness.

In an attempt to make the institutions of their time responsive to the needs of society, and in face of conflicting outlooks, our forefathers, in 1787, embodied in our Constitution the principle of federalism, thus protecting the Union while at the same time guaranteeing the autonomy of the States of which it was composed. It seems to me that our situation today calls for a new type of cultural federalism that will enable us to consider the rapidly expanding differences in our basic approaches to life.

The problems of how to achieve peace among people, how to overcome hostility to those who are different, how to turn enemies into friends, how to educate those who have been deprived of the education children normally and naturally should receive in their early childhood, how to introduce reason into the affairs of mankind, are confronting mankind today with an urgency greater than ever before in human history. These problems will loom ever larger in the world in which today's youth will have to live out their lives.

Can we not bring the ablest of various groups together in an effort to create what Erich Fromm calls "the sane society"? Can we not move the struggle between the generations away from the streets and the college campuses, to a forum of free interchange of ideas? It seems to me that this can be done— and it must be done if we are to continue to grow as a nation and as a civilization.

The Jewish Theological Seminary which has pioneered in so many efforts to bring diverse groups together in common understanding; which, indeed, is often credited with creating the idea of ecumenism as it is now understood; has unique qualifications for formulating and launching such a new cultural federalism. Its tradition of profound scholarship and academic excellence, and its respect for all considered opinions and for the people who hold them, make it an ideal agency to bring together people of different age groups and backgrounds, not to debate or argue, and certainly not to struggle, but to think together constructively about the future of man and of our civilization.

It is curious that despite the plethora of conferences and institutes in the world, no such international forum, cutting across the boundaries of age, geography and profession seems to exist. And yet it has become one of the most urgent necessities of our time.

When the Constitutional Convention met in 1787 to promulgate the Federal Constitution which has been our guide for almost two centuries, not many believed that the thirteen colonies, some of whom had been at the point of war with one another, could be molded into a united nation. Yet the wise men who constituted that Convention were able to create a document that has not only become the basis for our great Republic, but an inspiration to the rest of mankind.

Let us now consider the possibility of a new federalism, such as our times call for, in which people, young and old, would participate regularly, meeting with one another, thinking with one another, hoping with one another, and striving together instead of against one another. Let us see whether we cannot bring back the hearts of fathers to their sons, and the hearts of sons to their fathers, for the benefit of both generations—and for the good of generations yet to come.

Contributors to this Volume

NATHAN W. ACKERMAN, M.D., Director of Professional Program, The Family Institute, New York City.

LOUIS FINKELSTEIN, Chancellor, The Jewish Theological Seminary of America.

ESTHER M. JACKSON, Professor of Speech and Theatre, University of Wisconsin.

WALTER KAUFMANN, Professor of Philosophy, Princeton University.

MILTON R. KONVITZ, Professor of Law and Professor of Industrial Relations, Cornell University; sometime Visiting Professor, The Hebrew University, Jerusalem.

CHARLES MERRILL, Headmaster, The Commonwealth School, Boston, Massachusetts.

REINHOLD NIEBUHR, Professor Emeritus of Applied Christianity, Union Theological Seminary.

PHILIP SPORN, retired president, consultant, American Electric Power Company.

EARL WARREN, former Chief Justice of the United States.

DANIEL DAY WILLIAMS, Roosevelt Professor of Systematic Theology, Union Theological Seminary.

www.ingramcontent.com/pod-product-compliance
Lightning Source LLC
Chambersburg PA
CBHW020448100426
42813CB00026B/3003